Map of Cuckney and Welbeck and at the top the edge of Worksop Manor Park in the 1820s, showing how little some of the Sherwood villages had developed. (Nottinghamshire County Council)

Sherwood Forest
and the
Dukeries

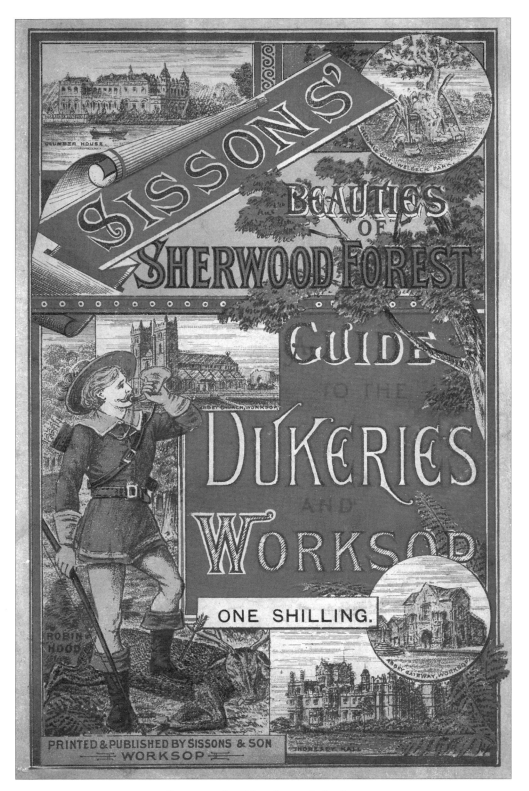

SISSONS'

BEAUTIES OF SHERWOOD FOREST

GUIDE TO THE

DUKERIES AND WORKSOP

ONE SHILLING.

ROBIN HOOD

CLUMBER HOUSE.

WELBECK PARK

ABBEY CHURCH WORKSOP

ABBEY GATEWAY WORKSOP

THORESBY HALL

PRINTED & PUBLISHED BY SISSONS & SON
WORKSOP

Front cover of an Edwardian tourist brochure.

Sherwood Forest
and the
Dukeries

Adrian Gray

Phillimore

2008

Published by
PHILLIMORE & CO. LTD
Chichester, West Sussex, England
www.phillimore.co.uk

ISBN 978-1-86077-482-9

Printed and bound in Great Britain

Contents

List of Illustrations vi

Introduction ix

1. Landscape and Early History 1

2. Barons and Monks 5

3. Sherwood Forest in the Middle Ages 12

4. Dissolution and New Dynasties 20

5. War and Restoration 34

6. The Rise of the Landed Estate 1700-1815 47

7. The Great Days of Land and Industry 1815-1901 74

8. The Decline and Rebirth of the Dukeries 113

Sources and Bibliography 144

Notes 145

Index 147

List of Illustrations

Frontispiece: Front cover of an Edwardian tourist brochure

1   General map of Sherwood Forest and the Dukeries x
2   Birkland forest scene. 2
3   Cave Houses, Mansfield. 3
4   North Road, Nottingham 4
5   Worksop Priory 6
6   Some of the ruins of Worksop Priory 6
7   The principal monastic remains at Newstead. 7
8   An impression of how Nottingham Castle appeared by the 1500s 7
9   Aerial view of Annesley Hall. 8
10 Mansfield Church. 9
11 Grazing sheep in Sherwood Forest 10
12 The Sherwood Forest roll book (extract) 14
13 The Annesley brass, a memorial from 1595 17
14 An artist's impression of a medieval Sherwood Forest ranger. .18
15 The Legend of Robin Hood in a Victorian theatre production, 1860. 19
16 A Victorian reproduction of a map originally printed in 1576 showing enclosed parks. 21
17 Thurland Hall 22
18 John Holles, 1st Earl of Clare 23
19 The great house at Worksop Manor 24
20 Diagrammatic 'family tree' for Bess of Hardwick 27
21 A 1653 view of the stables and other equine facilities built at Welbeck .29
22 Map of Welbeck and Norton in the 1830s 30
23 Aerial view of Haughton Park 31
24 Haughton Park chapel ruin. 32
25 Charles erecting his standard in 1642 35
26 Portrait of William Cavendish, made 1st duke of Newcastle in 1665 36
27 The Holles family home in Lincoln's Inn Fields 41
28 Sherwood mapped in 1776 still showed substantial areas of unenclosed 'forest' 46
29 The famous 'Duke's Walking Stick' in Welbeck Park. 48
30 1776 map showing the annexation of northern Sherwood 49
31 A map of the early 1800s showing the influence of the Thoresby and Clumber estates 50
32 Edward Harley, Earl of Oxford. 54
33 Victorian attempt at the Pelham-Clinton family tree 55
34 A map of London in the early 1830s showing the 'Sherwood' district 56
35 Welbeck in 1726 by Samuel Buck 61
36 Elizabeth Chudleigh with her two 'husbands'. 63
37 The Palladian villa at Nuthall Temple 64
38 Clumber in 1781 showing Stephen Wright's buildings. 66
39 Welbeck and its lake in about 1790 showing the planted woodlands and lake 67
40 Papplewick Hall 68
41 The 'villa in the forest' at Cockglode. 69
42 The Castle Mill at Papplewick 72
43 Map of Nottingham in the 1820s 75
44 The first tractor being used at Black Hills Farm, Edwinstowe 76
45 Clipstone meadows. 76

46 Map of Portland's famous water meadows in a pre-industrial landscape 77
47 The royal visit at Welbeck in 1881 78
48 Nottingham Park in 1901 79
49 The Simon the Foster tree which grew in Sherwood over centuries 80
50 View of the romantic park at Newstead 82
51 The Park at Nottingham 83
52 The Newcastle mausoleum at Markham-Clinton during the interment of the 4th Duke in 1851 84
53 The Prince of Wales' arrival at Clumber in 1861 85
54 The lake at Clumber in 1861 86
55 Clumber Park Church exterior 87
56 Worksop Manor 88
57 Daybrook Laundry 89
58 Henry Savile, shown by *Vanity Fair* in 1880 90
59 Scenes from Thoresby when Lord Newark reached the age of 21 in 1875 90
60 The resurgent splendour of Thoresby in its prime, photographed in 1901 after Salvin's rebuild 91
61 Lord George Bentinck, portrayed at the time of his death 92
62 Welbeck's Lion Gate 93
63 Lord George Bentinck monument in the market place at Mansfield 94
64 Views of Welbeck from 1881, including the tunnels and the 'raising up' of part of the house 95
65 The young 6th Duke of Portland depicted by *Vanity Fair* 96
66 The Winnings at Welbeck 97
67 Bestwood Lodge, 1878 98
68 Map of Arnold and Bestwood in the 1820s 100
69 The art museum in the restored castle at Nottingham 101
70 The Prince of Wales visit to Newcastle's coal mine at Shireaoks 103
71 Map of Newstead and Sutton in Ashfield 104
72 Kirkby or 'Summit' Colliery, closed in 1969 105
73 Mining in the shallow coal field using what may well have been local timber to support the roof 106
74 One of the last surviving stocking frames at work in about 1900 107
75 The mill and millpond at Cuckney 108
76 Windmills at Hucknall 109
77 Advert for the *Midland Hotel* in Mansfield 110
78 The *Dukeries Hotel*, Edwinstowe, part of the late 1800s/early 1900s tourist boom 111
79 Newark from the north in the mid-1800s 112
80 The Grove and Rufford hunts meet at Rufford 114
81 The visit of Edward VII and Queen Alexandra to Rufford in 1904 114
82 Lord Savile depicted in 1908 as every inch the hunting and shooting countryman 115
83 'The Forest' remains an open area on the north side of Nottingham 116
84 A Sherwood Forester from the most famous local regiment 117
85 Part of the huge First World War camp at Clipstone 117
86 The Major Oak 118
87 Thoresby's Beech Avenue 119
88 Edward's Lane, a pleasant corner of Sherwood that existed 100 years ago 120
89 Welbeck at the turn of the century 121
90 Major Seely limbers up for a speech in 1905 125
91 The last great days of Clumber, viewed from across the lake 126
92 Rufford Abbey 129
93 Miners at Rufford Colliery, Rainworth, working on sinking the shaft in 1911-13 131
94 No 2 colliery at Hucknall in the early 1900s 132
95 The colliery at Mansfield Woodhouse, sunk in 1902-3 133
96 Map of the coal mines of Sherwood and its fringes 134
97 Forest Town; one of the earliest, and least inspiring, of the new mining villages 136
98 New Ollerton showing housing and wide streets 137
99 Map of Annesley with parts of Linby 138
100 Bestwood Colliery aerial view 139
101 The famous twin headstocks at Clipstone 141
102 The main sights of the Dukeries crowded into one postcard 142
103 Ollerton Hall in 2007, being prepared for renovation 143

This book is for

Ellie, Hannah and Lydia

Introduction

Sherwood Forest is the one part of Nottinghamshire that is internationally recognised whilst 'the Dukeries' – more properly 'the Dukery' – has more local significance through its history of noble estates.

The forest of Sherwood combines many elements of English history in one place. It was originally dominated by the Norman monarchy with the support of local barons, before doubts over their own immortality resulted in the gifting of land to the monasteries. Thus the monks became the first great owners of Sherwood apart from the king. The dissolution of the monasteries gave space for the rise of acquisitive landowners who through marriage and payment became the new aristocracy. For a brief time these gilded nobles ruled Sherwood and the whole country, building political dynasties on local wealth and influence, with grand houses to match. The discovery of coal seemed to offer an even grander future of limitless wealth, but it all vanished in barely two generations as stiffer taxation combined with excessive gambling, womanising and wasteful living threw away wealth that had taken generations to build up. Today Sherwood and the Dukeries have a different economy, increasingly based on tourism, as visitors come to see a forest that is not really there anymore.

Sherwood is famous for Robin Hood, but the romantic hero's links with the area are tenuous. Nonetheless, the story of Robin Hood has been part of English life through early ballads, stage drama, novels, opera and films. He is a hero who has endured because he combines the love of a 'glorious' past, an English delight in rural living and a traditional fight between good and bad. He is not really a part of Sherwood's history, but certainly figures significantly in it's present. People also come for 'the Dukeries' which consist of two partial ruins, two hotels and a site recently vacated by the military at Welbeck. As an ancient site with monastic and royal associations, but also the subterranean workings of an eccentric Victorian duke, Welbeck somehow encapsulates, through monasticism, monarchy and madness, the real Sherwood of history.

There have been many books about 'the Dukeries', but they have usually concentrated on one family or one house. Given that all the families intermarried at regular intervals and estates were divided by rivalries, this has not always provided the full picture. This book is an attempt to weave together the story of places and people that have made the area special, but not necessarily in the way that tourists imagine.

Adrian Gray
Laneham

1 *General map of Sherwood Forest and the Dukeries, showing the principal religious houses, forest lodges and county estates. (Andrew Nicholson)*

1

Landscape and Early History

Sherwood is the area formed of Bunter or Sherwood sandstone stretching north from the River Trent and bounded on its western side by the valley of the River Erewash. This strip varies between about five and eight miles wide. It was an unattractive area to settlers, with only limited surface water, leaving it free to become a royal hunting forest in medieval times. The physical nature of the forest sandstone area was described by K.C. Edwards:

> The thin, poor soil, so loose in dry weather that strong winds carry it from the fields in dust clouds does not encourage cultivation without special treatment. Vegetation is also somewhat impoverished by the dry conditions, resulting in a large amount of bracken and gorse, interspersed with oak and birch wood …[1]

Rainfall in April and May would have been too little for satisfactory crop growth without artificial watering and so the conflict between settled farming and hunting came very late, although grazing and hunting generally went well together. Sherwood Forest only extended beyond the sandstone belt in two areas: west of Mansfield onto the limestone and north-east of Nottingham on the waterstones and clay.

The main forest consisted of oak woodland with birch and bracken. The birch gave its name to the part of the Forest which became known as Birklands, roughly equating to the area north of Edwinstowe. Birch was more common where gravels occurred beneath thin soils. To the east of the sandstone is the red marl, a clay layer over the sandstone called the waterstones, since water could be extracted by wells. This clay land has a number of streams, often in a shallow ravine, called a 'dumble', and it attracted settlement at a much earlier stage.

To the west is an area of limestone, which forms an impressive scarp in places, most notably at Bolsover. The limestone around Mansfield was much quarried, being used in the construction of the Houses of Parliament and Newark Town Hall. The natural forest of this area was cleared to allow sheep and cattle to graze.

Evidence of early settlement in the Sherwood area is therefore slim. The caves at Cresswell, however, on the north-west edge of the area, have been famous since 1872 as the scene of settlement from the Upper Palaeolithic period. During the Neolithic period, settled farming communities began to develop on the fringes of Sherwood.

By the Iron Age, it is likely that as many as 10 hill forts overlooked the Trent on its west bank and from there across to Mansfield. These population centres were probably connected by trackways, such as Leeming or Leming Lane near Mansfield; an ancient routeway from Nottingham to Bawtry is generally known as Stone Street.

By A.D.47 the Romans had established a border along the Trent and the Humber, close to the Fosse Way. By A.D.49 a network of forts spread across the area, the most important for this region being at Broxtowe[2] although there was another at Farnsfield.

2   *This birkland scene may appear untouched by man, but grazing animals and gathering of ferns helped to give the forest an 'open' feel.*

The Romans built a road connecting the Fosse Way to the lead mines of the Peak District. This passed via Belle Eau and Bilsthorpe, on which alignment there has been some recent excavation.[3] They built a few rural estates, or villas, and known sites include Cromwell and a fairly large centre at Mansfield Woodhouse which would have been close to a conjectured route from Mansfield to Worksop. This site was first excavated by Major Rooke in 1786, who is also associated with the Major Oak. There were two groups of buildings covering a substantial site and a villa at Southwell, but little settlement on the sandstone. Romano-British farmsteads have been located at Broxtowe and Tuxford and claims have been made that there was farming in the Forest during this period[4] with the villa at Mansfield Woodhouse probably having some local supplies. A considerable hoard of Roman silver coins was found at King's Mill during the rebuilding of the Mansfield and Pinxton Railway in 1848. Native settlement continued to develop during the Roman occupation. There was a group of huts at Scratta Wood, west of Worksop, but sites were mainly along the Trent valley.

Anglo-Saxon settlement spread from about the fifth century with the earliest name indicator containing the component *–ingas*, such as Nottingham. The Angles probably came up the river and settled at points along it, rarely venturing to the sandstone interior except along the Leen valley.

In the seventh century, what is now Sherwood was a border zone between the kingdoms of Mercia and, at times, Northumbria or Lindsey. Edwin was King of Northumbria between A.D.617 and A.D.633, having fought and killed Aethelfrith, then the King of Northumbria, on the banks of the River Idle in A.D.616-7. Edwin was helped by Raedwald, King of the East Angles and, according to tradition, the site of Rainworth was where Readwald stayed

3   *An unusual feature of the district was that the soft sandstone could be tunnelled for housing and storage. Cave houses were best known in Nottingham, but these were in Mansfield.*

before his battle against Aethelfrith. In the battle, Readwald's son Regehere was killed, and the site became known as 'Regehere's wath' or ford – being shortened, over the years, to Rainworth.

Edwin was baptised a Christian in A.D.627. It is now accepted that the baptisms occurred in York, not in the Trent. Paulinus allegedly laid the foundation stones of Southwell Minster in the same year, and his attentions may have been necessary for at least one tradition asserts pagan worship took place at various sites, such as at the rocks near Blidworth.[5]

Edwin was killed in a battle on 12 October 633 at *Haethfelth* or 'Hatfield', a clearing in the Forest, possibly Hatfield Chase near Doncaster although the past existence of a chantry chapel dedicated to Edwin at Warsop has been suggested as an alternative.[6]

However, 'Edwinstowe' means 'holy place of Edwin' and there is another Hatfield near Cuckney. In the 1950s between 50 and 200 bodies were found beneath Cuckney church, possibly buried after a battle. Edwin's headless body was supposedly buried in the Forest, and some 70 years later dug up and found to be well preserved.[7]

Danish settlements can be identified through the ending –by. These are often found near rivers penetrating quite far into Sherwood. For example, Bilby and Ranby on the River Ryton, Walesby and Thoresby on the Maun, Linby closer to the Leen. Kirkby and Skegby must have

4   *North of Nottingham lies the higher sandstone ground of Sherwood, along which ran the famous road to the North along whose route a number of armies came.*

been too remote to penetrate at the time. Nottingham was said to have been the site of a British temple, later taken over by the Danes after A.D.868. Swinnerton has claimed that the Danes entered Nottingham by the ancient North Road, from Blyth to Ollerton and Nottingham,[8] and, according to the *Anglo-Saxon Chronicle*,[9] they wintered there in A.D.867-8.

Nottingham was one of the five Danelaw Burghs in 878 and a basic local government began to emerge under the Danish form of a wapentake. The moot or assembly for Broxtow wapentake met in the parish of Bilborough on a site that was later Broxtowe Hall, whilst other parts of the Forest were covered by the wapentakes of Thurgarton and Bassetlaw. Nottingham was captured by King Alfred in A.D.918 after a siege, but was retaken by the Danes in A.D.938 who were then driven out by King Edmund in A.D.942.

Before the Normans, Sherwood was divided into manors that were generally held by Saxons such as Caschin, who held Worksop. Some of these had extensive holdings such as Wulfsi who held estates at Cuckney, Hodsock, Clipstone and Hockerton. The King, Edward 'the Confessor', owned land across much of the area. During this phase Nottingham began to develop a regional role, and the first known reference to Nottinghamshire was in 1016. The town gained its own mint and was declared a royal burgh by King Athelstan.

Sherwood was not an isolated forest. Much of the country was still wooded whilst the area north of Nottingham joined together with Hatfield Chase, another royal hunting ground that had been used by King Edwin and where he had a hunting lodge.

It gained the name of 'Sherwood' by tradition; since its boundaries lay between Nottinghamshire and Derbyshire it was the shire-wood.[10] It has also been suggested that the name derives from *sciryuda*, meaning 'woodland belonging to the shire'. Small clues exist as to how Sherwood was at this time, with Domesday Book referring to the existence of 'waste' or uncultivated land at Ranby, Perlethorpe and Normanton-by-Clumber, although this land would still have been used for extensive grazing.

2

Barons and Monks

The history of Sherwood Forest is closely intertwined with that of Nottingham Castle. In 1068 William I[1] ordered the building of a castle, superintended by William Peverel, who had 49 manors across the county. It remained a royal castle and had numerous important visitors. Not everyone was impressed; Queen Eleanor famously refused to stay there in 1257 because of the smell from coal smoke.[2] Presumably another unhappy visitor was King David of Scotland who was imprisoned there in 1345.

The king held Mansfield, which had been a royal manor before the Conquest. The lands at Worksop and to the north were mostly given by King William to Roger de Busli. De Busli gained 174 manors[3] including Clumber and had 11 houses in Nottingham. He made Blyth his main residence with a castle at Tickhill and he was the dominant figure across much of the region. Blyth subsequently became a Benedictine monastery, gaining great wealth as it was able to levy tolls on the users of roads and the river which was navigable at that time.[4]

Gilbert de Gant was allotted lands which included Roughford or Rugford where his grandson eventually founded the abbey. Ralph de Byron was holder of lands in Nottinghamshire and Derbyshire by 1086.

Walter d'Eincourt and Ralph Fitz-Hubert also became prominent local landholders, though the latter family suffered an ignominious setback when one member was hung from the walls of Devizes Castle during the wars between King Stephen and Empress Matilda.[5] Other families started more obscurely, such as the de Lacy family who were awarded the lordship of Kneesall and who later rose to prominence through military exploits. Sir John de Lacy became the 1st Earl of Lincoln whilst Roger de Lacy achieved fame for his role in the siege of Chateau Gaillard.

Smaller castles were built by the first Norman lords, such as at Bothamsall, which probably arose on the orders of Roger de Busli, whilst later creations intended to preserve a position in troubled times such as that at Cuckney.[6] Laxton was a significant castle and there was another at Egmanton. Legends of a castle at Papplewick are connected with the existence of a castle field.

Through marriage and inheritance the de Busli lands quickly became dominated by the de Lovetot family. De Busli died without heirs and his lands passed to the Crown and then to others. William de Lovetot founded Worksop Priory in 1103 which became Augustinian. Richard, his son, gave the town of Worksop to the priory. He provided other privileges for them, such as allowing the use of two carts to collect fallen timber from his park.

5   *Worksop Priory was founded in 1103 and the church still reflects the romanesque architecture of the period.*

By about 1180 the de Lovetot family had also run out of males to continue the line and young Matilda de Lovetot was left as a ward of King Richard I, who chose Gerard de Furnival to be her husband. De Furnival was the son of one of his own close companions and a veteran of the siege of Acre, who gained estates around Sheffield, York and Nottinghamshire. A descendant of the de Lovetot family sought compensation but King John was bribed to leave the de Furnivals in control. De Furnival was unpopular, and left Worksop for a while to live more safely at Bolsover.[7] He died in 1219 in Palestine. Two of Gerard's sons went to the Holy Land as crusaders where Thomas, the elder son, was killed; his body was brought home by his brother Gerard. He was buried wearing his helmet 'which was richly adorned with gems'.[8] The de Furnivals were granted the right to hold a Wednesday market and an annual fair at Worksop in 1296 and, by 1334, only Newark and Nottingham were more important in the county.

The abbey at Rufford was founded by Gilbert de Gant, Earl of Lincoln, in 1148. It has been claimed that he made the grant of land whilst on his deathbed having evidently played a gambling game between God and mammon![9] The abbey was further endowed by other local landowners: John de Vesci gave the manor of Rotherham to which Christiana, wife of Gerard de Furnival, added other lands.

The monks at Rufford removed the villages of Cratley and Inkersall, so that local people were forced to begin a new settlement at Wellow[10] which was laid out around a triangular green. Wellow was protected by a deep ditch, presumably for defence so that the sheep which normally

6   *Some of the ruins of Worksop Priory.*

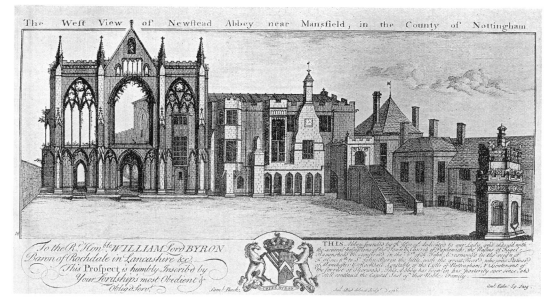

The West View of Newstead Abbey near Mansfield, in the County of Nottingham

To the Rt Honble WILLIAM Lord BYRON Baron of Rochdale in Lancashire &c. This Prospect is humbly Inscrib'd by Your Lordship's most Obedient & Oblig'd Servt

7   *The principal monastic remains were the west front at Newstead.*

grazed in the Forest could be protected from attack. The North Road changed its route several times to avoid Rufford, which prospered from sheep farming in particular and acquired enough land to need 21 granges.

Not all lords sought to expiate their sins by giving land or money. In the reign of Henry II, Hugh de Byron became a monk and held the hermitage at Kersall, an attachment to Lenton Priory.[11] Lenton itself had been founded by William Peverel.

Lands around Cuckney were granted by King William to the de Flammaugh family and one of their first acts was to build a castle.[12] Richard de Flammaugh[13] founded the abbey of Welbeck in 1153 and it was completed by his son Thomas, taking 18 years.[14] Premonstratensian canons arrived from Lincolnshire, installing Berengarius as their first abbot. The abbey was endowed with various lands including mills at Cuckney and Langwith. Welbeck's sheep farming caused conflict with villages such as Carburton, when ancient rights were disputed during Edward II's reign.[15] In 1329, Welbeck was granted additional lands including the manor and 'town' of Cuckney, Norton by Cuckney and Langwith by the Bishop of Ely. Not all the wealth was spent on the comfort of the monks; some money was given to the poor on Good Friday whilst food and alms were distributed at the abbey gates. The abbey also had an important role as the 'father' to another seven Premonstratensian foundations. In 1475 it had 21 clerical staff but seems to have gone into decline by 1482, under the leadership of Abbot Burton who was found

8   *An impression of how Nottingham Castle appeared by the 1500s showing how it had extended, although the park cannot be seen clearly in this view.*

to be guilty of 'incontinence'. Some of the buildings were in a ruinous state and Burton was deposed.

In 1170 Henry II gave Papplewick with its water mill to Newstead Abbey, which was a foundation of the Austin canons, possibly relocated from another site nearby.[16] The abbey was also endowed with a park of 50 acres which was exempt from the control of Sherwood's

9   *Aerial view of Annesley Hall with its mixture of buildings from the medieval period to the 19th century, including the now-ruined church. It is a site with a continuous history dating back to Norman times. (Nottinghamshire County Council)*

verderers. Accommodation was fine enough to attract royal guests and Edward I stayed there in 1280 and 1290, as did his son in 1307 and 1315.

Beauvale, a Carthusian monastery, was founded at the west side of the Forest by Nicholas Cantelupe who also crenellated his house at Greasley[17] in 1346.

In 1152, Ralph de Annesley[18] gave the settlement of Felley for Robert the Hermit and his successors to use. The Austin canons of Felley seem to have had the use of Annesley church which was enlarged by the addition of the Felley chapel in the 14th century. The Austin canons were the most common monastic order in and around Sherwood, with houses at Felley, Newstead, Shelford, Thurgarton and Worksop.

Annesley was inside Sherwood Forest, but nonetheless Reginald de Marc was able to build a fortified house there in the time of Henry III.[19] The Annesley family line itself came to an end in about 1427 when the heiress of Sir John Annesley, Alice, married George Chaworth. Subsequently, Viscount Chaworth created a park named Annesley in Ireland, although the family lived mainly at Wiverton until moving to Annesley in the post-Civil War period.[20]

The struggle between King Stephen and Empress Matilda, as well as the period of uncertainty when John ruled England as prince and king, affected all of these families: to be caught on the wrong side could be disastrous. In 1174 Reginald de Lacy was in control of Nottingham Castle, but was driven out by a force of rebel barons.

Between 1088 and approximately 1350, markets and fairs were widely licensed. The first place to have a market and fair chartered was Blyth, in 1088, long before Mansfield in 1227 and Worksop in 1334. Often charters were granted to lords of the manor, as at 'Cuckney Norton' in 1317 when Henry de Faucumberge secured the rights. Changes in ownership affected the right to hold a market as is evident at Market Warsop. A charter for a Tuesday market was granted to 'John de Lessinteyn'[21] in 1239, along with a fair for 29 June. Presumably the same John de Lexington also gained a charter for a Tuxford market in 1218. In 1329 John Nunes, a Londoner who had bought the manor, had to reapply for the market charter which had been taken into the king's hands, although John de Roos seems to have held a Monday market in the same period. In 1410, William de Roos gained a charter for a Saturday market as well.

Some markets were conspicuous failures; Wellow had one from 1268 but it never grew. Yet Edwinstowe, initially unimportant, later grew in status. Henry and Robert of Edwinstowe granted the manor of North Muskham to the Abbey of Newstead during the reign of Edward III on the condition that it provided two chaplains to say divine service at Edwinstowe.[22] Its two-day annual fair also increased revenues.

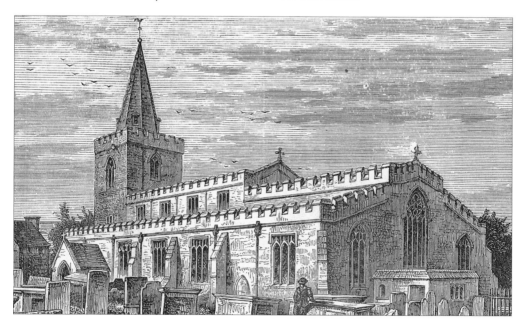

10 *Mansfield developed a substantial medieval church in keeping with its role as the principal town on the Forest's northern flank.*

Bevercotes' fame increased in 1306 when William de Bevercotes was made Chancellor of Scotland by Edward I. The Markham family, who lived at the eastern edge of Sherwood in villages that still bear their names, also rose from humble origins. William de Marcham, whose mother was one of the Lexington family, became Bishop of Wells and was appointed

Lord Treasurer in 1290. Sir John Markham of East Markham became Lord Chief Justice. The family seat was at West Markham but, typically, much of his new wealth and that of his sons was invested in land. In 1455 Sir Robert Markham acquired the manors of Maplebeck, Boughton and parts of Caunton. Markham built a large house at Maplebeck. Sir John Markham, who fought at Stoke in 1488, was 'an unruly spirited man' who apparently killed some people near Long Bennington in an argument over land and had to go into hiding.

11   *Grazing sheep in Sherwood Forest – a scene unchanged from medieval times, making clear the fact that the Forest was not a deserted hunting ground but an active part of the rural economy.*

The Pierrepont family were also landowners in Nottinghamshire. In the late 1200s Henry de Pierrepont married Annora de Manvers and gained the estate at Holme which was to become known as Holme Pierrepont. The manor of Holme had been one of the many granted to Sir Roger de Busli but by 1201 it had been taken over by the Manvers family. Sir William de Pierrepont was also involved in the Battle of Stoke.

We have already noted the name of Lexington, which derives from the village of Laxton. One theory asserts the family descended from Robert de Caux, the father of the illegitimate Richard of Lexington,[23] who was awarded the manor of Laxton by King John and who continued to own property there until at least 1229. He had several famous sons and his daughters married into the Sutton and Markham families. Robert of Lexington was a well-known judge and a justice in eyre under Henry III. Robert, with help from his brother John, who held high legal office as steward to Henry III, was given the lordship of Averham.[24] After his death in 1250, the manor of Averham passed to Lexington's nephew Robert de Sutton and another Nottinghamshire dynasty began to develop, although it was to be 400 years before they attained titled status. More land was left to John who is infamous for his role in the trial and execution of 19 Jews in Lincoln after the alleged murder of a boy named Hugh. The trial and execution was overseen by his brother Henry, the Bishop. Another brother, Stephen, became abbot of Clairvaux.

Towards the end of the medieval period, England was repeatedly riven by the dynastic struggle of the Wars of the Roses. Like the battles between King Stephen and Empress Matilda, this often forced the nobles to take sides. Sir Henry Pierrepont was a firm supporter of Edward IV and was rewarded for 'good and laudable services at his great cost and charges, and with manifold bodily dangers against the king's rebels levying war against him'. He died in 1499 and was buried in a tomb appropriate to his warlike reputation. Another Yorkist was Sir Robert Markham.

The only significant action to occur within or around the area before 1485 was a skirmish, which took place near Worksop in 1460.[25] The fortifications at Nottingham were extended by Edward IV and by Richard of York, who became Richard III in 1483. He was in Nottingham on his way to the royal hunting lodge of Bestwood on 22 June 1485, and was still there on 11 August when he learnt that Henry Tudor had landed in Wales. He left Nottingham on 16 August, but it was Henry who triumphed at Bosworth.

After Bosworth, Henry VII made Sir John Byron Constable of Nottingham Castle in 1485 and Warden or Master of Sherwood, yielding a salary of £40. At the final great battle at Stoke in 1487, the Earl of Lincoln led an army intent on ousting Henry VII and imposing the 'puppet' Lambert Simnel in his stead. It is possible that Henry stayed at Pierrepont's house in Holme at this time and one of the Byron daughters married a Pierrepont son a few years later. Lincoln's army is supposed to have travelled across Sherwood and then crossed the Trent at Fiskerton. Sir John Markham, grandson of the Chief Justice, was a commander on Henry's side. Lincoln lost, and 7,000 died.

A coal trade existed by the 13th century and records refer to the lease of a mine at Cossall, just to the west of Sherwood, in 1282[26] or 1316. In 1397 the prior of Beauvale granted a lease for the extraction of coal at Cossall to William Monyash,[27] whose name indicates origins in the Derbyshire lead mining districts. Coal was dug from the surface outcrops in the west of the county, although mining below the surface followed. A mine opened at Wollaton by the 15th century which 'commanded an extensive and expanding market'.[28] There was also a trade across the Forest in salt, mainly from the Lincolnshire coast, and a number of 'Saltergates' and a Salterford Lane near Sherwood Lodge still exists.

Another principal industry was milling, initially by water power. A number of places like Linby had mills by the time of Domesday Book. Haughton had a mill and so did Ollerton. The towns, notably Newark, also benefited from the wool trade; some of this was linked to Sherwood where grazing was commonplace, for there was a 'sheep walk' for 700 sheep in Cuckney in 1299.

3

Sherwood Forest in the Middle Ages

Simon Schama has written that the medieval Forest of the poetic imagination was 'dense, impenetrable and deserted' but in reality 'there were people in the woods: settled, active, making a livelihood out of its resources …'.[1]

Thoroton relates that the 'ancient forest' was known as Thorneywood, near to Nottingham, and High Forest further north. Sherwood Forest was first mentioned in the mid-12th century, its name implying it to be a wood used by the many shirefolk, rather than the royal forest it became.[2] In 1086 there were extensive areas of waste or wood in many of the parishes, most notably Clipstone which had 1,440 acres of woodland pasture. This idea of woodland pasture is important as grazing animals among the oaks kept down the growth of new saplings of beech or birch and created the 'open' woodland that was ideal for hunting on horseback. The Normans saw hunting as preparation for battle but also an elaborate social ritual and its capacity to provide hunting would certainly have been known to the likes of Peverel and de Busli.

The Forest had its dangers. Sir Ralph Plumpton held land at Mansfield Woodhouse in medieval times that was called 'Wolf Hunt Land'; it was reputedly given to him for his services in driving wolves out of Sherwood.[3] Wild animals shared the Forest with domestic ones, especially pigs, which gorged themselves on acorns from Michaelmas to Martinmas. This made late autumn a busy time in the Forest, for then the pigs were slaughtered, wood gathered for fuel, and the meat turned into smoked sausages for the winter.

King Canute's forest laws of 1016 created structures later adapted by Henry III in the Charter of 1217. Canute defined how the animals were to be treated; for example, a 'Hart Royal' was a royal deer that, if it escaped into non-hunting land, had to be captured and returned. He created the 'lespegend', who conducted triennial inspections of the forests to check for trespass, reporting any offences to a forest court. The 'paegend' were appointed to care for the venison and the 'vert' or woodland.

To the English, the forest was another form of rural economy but the Normans arrived with very different ideas.[4] The Normans saw it as land set aside for the King's use which required a different legal system. Within 100 years of the Conquest, almost a quarter of England had been designated 'forest' with Henry I and Henry II especially keen to afforest new lands. Stricter laws were introduced to protect the venison and the 'vert', and 'A sovereign's paternal care was understood less to apply to Anglo-Saxon men than to red fallow deer …

the lives of the latter were esteemed the most valuable'.[5] The *Anglo-Saxon Chronicle* informs us that in the New Forest, William I:

> … made many deer-parks, and he established laws therewith; so that whosoever slew a hart, or a hind, should be deprived of his eyesight. As he forbad men to kill the harts, so also the boars; and he loved the tall deer as if he were their father. Likewise he decreed respecting the hares that they should go free. His rich men bemoaned it, and the poor men shuddered at it.

Then his son William II introduced penalties of death and mutilation:

> … *William Rufus* is recorded in History for the Severity of his Proceedings against all that hunted in his Forests; inflicting the Punishment of Death upon such as killed a Stag or Buck in his Forests, without any other Law than that of his own Will.[6]

Not all land within royal Sherwood belonged to the king, some was owned by the noble landowners, such as Roger de Busli's wooden castle at Bothamsall. These landowners resented royally imposed restrictions which eventually led to the Magna Carta.

The Norman kings installed lord wardens, to be assisted by the foresters, for each royal forest. Officials included the woodward, the verderer, the ranger and the agister who collected money due from the king's property. From the early 12th century the hereditary wardenship of the Forest was conferred on the de Caux family who ran forest courts at their castle in Laxton until 1287 and entertained passing kings.[7] The last of the male line was Robert de Caux, who died in about 1168. Maud de Caux was left as a young orphan and Henry II arranged her marriage to Ralph fitzStephen, formerly his Chamberlain. King John granted some rights in the Forest to Maud de Caux and her husband including the right to hunt hare, wildcat, fox and squirrel as well as to collect windfall wood. They could also tax passing wagons of salt by taking one 'skep' from each passing load.[8] When her husband died in 1202, John deprived Maud of her hereditary duty, seized the castle and conferred them on Richard de Lexington in 1204; it has been suggested that he was 'possibly a bastard member of the same family'.[9] Richard had custody of the manor of Laxton and the Forest, except for the royal enclosures which were the responsibility of the sheriff.

Richard de Lexington fell out with King John, possibly for abuse of forest rights, and was sacked in 1207, with the result that the village of Laxton had to pay a heavy bribe to avoid being burnt down. Brian de Lisle took over as deputy to the Chief Forest Justice, Hugh de Neville. When John died in 1217, Maud de Caux regained her rights after an 18-year struggle. She died in 1224 but the keeper's role remained in her family line until 1287. John of Lexington was appointed Chief Justice of the forests north of the Trent from 1252 to 1257. The de Everingham family became lords of Laxton and keepers of the royal Forest from the 1230s, although Robert de Everingham was imprisoned in Nottingham Castle in 1286 and sacked from his post for stealing royal venison. The next year the de Everinghams abandoned Laxton altogether. This brought an end to the glory days of Laxton Castle, but its significance in Sherwood had been irretrievably altered by Henry III's reduction of the Forest's size in 1227-32 which already had substantial areas of field by 1189.[10] The post of warden continued for centuries, generally being a political appointment such as that conferred upon Sir John Byron in 1485.

12   *An extract from the Sherwood Forest roll book, which gives a clear indication that the Forest was run as part of government business.*

In 1160 the Bishop of Durham presided over the first court of justices for offences committed in Sherwood Forest.[11] Further courts were held under Henry III and Edward I, the latter meeting at Blidworth. These were the ultimate rule for an area of about 100 square miles. Minor offences were dealt with through verderers' courts that met every 40 days at Calverton, Edwinstowe, Linby and Mansfield on successive days.

'Eyre' courts with their own justices, or courts of forest pleas, heard serious cases and the 'swanimote' courts the less serious. The courts were attended by the verderers, who were generally owners of land within the Forest. The Forest was divided into Bilhagh, Birkland, Rumwood, Ouseland and Fulwood. In 1251 it was being run in three 'keepings' or wards, each with their own verderers and also with 'agisters' who regulated pasturage and pannage for pigs.[12]

Henry II codified the laws of the royal forests, making them applicable to clergymen also, with his 'Assize of the Forest', which was passed at Woodstock in 1184. It was lenient in the treatment of the first two offences, but the third offence could only be resolved on 'the body of the misdoer'.[13] No tanning or bleaching was allowed in a forest and dogs were to be 'lawed'.

Given that Henry II was one of the 'expanders' of the Forest, the story associated with his visit to Sutton is especially ironic. King Henry lost his way when passing through

Sherwood and sought shelter for the night at Sutton Mill. The miller, identified as 'the Miller of Mansfield', provided him with an excellent meal of a succulent venison pasty which was made from venison poached from the King's own forest.

Much of royal Sherwood derived from lands associated with the king's manor, Mansfield.[14] Mansfield Manor covered a wide area, including Budby, Carburton and Clipstone. Under Henry II and King John the Forest was extended to include some of the clay districts of north-east Nottinghamshire and areas to the north of Worksop, but this expansion did not endure. Henry III reduced its size from 1227 and by 1232 the Forest was bounded by Nottingham, Mansfield and Worksop, amounting to about 100,000 acres. Within the Forest were the 'Hays', which were enclosures for deer surrounded by hedges such as those at Clipstone, Linby and Bestwood, which contained mainly fallow deer. Deer parks were surrounded with a wooden fence or paling; hence the phrase 'beyond the pale'.

Nottingham Castle was regularly used by nobles and royalty and thus needed a deer park of its own. The expansion of the Forest under Henry II therefore included the enclosure of 10 'forest acres' (equivalent to about 500 actual acres) of land near the castle to form an 'orchard'.[15] Though small compared with other deer parks, it was convenient since Nottingham remained the main royal castle in the Midlands until 1485.

New land was being cultivated in Sherwood under licences awarded to many of the religious bodies including Newstead, Lenton, Welbeck, Rufford and Southwell. These were called 'assarts' and were given improved legal status by Edward I.[16] In 1304 King Edward granted 30 acres in the 'Haye of Lyndeby' for the use of Thomas de la Hay and his heirs for cattle or cultivation; this was an early enclosure, with a ditch and a hedge.[17] Along with new land came new settlements such as Felley and Nether Langwith which emerged in the 12th and 13th centuries.[18] Lambley, a village in the south-eastern corner of the Forest held by the Cromwell family, was regularly granted licence to assart, so that by 1436 about a quarter of its 2,092 acres had been enclosed.[19]

As population increased in the 13th century, there was pressure to assart without permission. In 1287 the town of Nottingham was fined 40s. for raising banks and hedges contrary to the Assize of the Forest.[20]

The Forest's royal visitors were supported by several hunting lodges, some of which were also used by forest officials. There is evidence that the king had a 'chamber' in Mansfield by 1130. One claim for the origins of Bestwood Lodge was that it housed the mistresses of Henry I between 1100 and 1135.[21] The earliest reference to a royal hunting lodge at Clipstone is from 1164, but it was probably more greatly developed between 1176 and 1180.[22] It became the most significant hunting lodge and influenced the whole area; Edwinstowe was seen as an outlying settlement or 'berne',[23] its inhabitants surviving by having the right to pasture animals in the king's 'hays' of Bilhagh and Birkland, thus helping to maintain the open forest for hunting. A hunting lodge was built at Rainworth in 1190, where one of King John's hunting colleagues, Rufus Clarke, was living in 1212; Cockglode was also suggested.[24] The lodge at Kingshaugh was rebuilt in about 1210 but within a few years the forest boundary moved and it was left isolated, except for its own deer park.

Lodges seem to have come in and out of use. It has been argued that a lodge at Langton Arbour near Blidworth, although not marked on a map in 1407, was clearly in use by 1474 when forester John Gleve was paid 4d. a day to keep deer there.[25] In 1580 the ranger of Blidworth Forest, Thomas Leek, lived there and made improvements to the house so that it became known as 'Leek's Folly'; he was killed in an alehouse fight in 1598 and buried at Blidworth church. By 1633, however, the ranger at Langton had moved to Bestwood and, by 1669, Langton was in a 'ruinous' state.

Richard I visited Clipstone for the first time in 1193. A legend assocciated with the Forest relates that on 2 April 1194, a newly-freed King Richard met William 'the Lion' of Scotland at a spot known as 'King's Trist', where the Scot congratulated the Lionheart on his release from captivity. This would have been a rare meeting between two Lions in Sherwood. [26]

King John enjoyed hunting and extended the royal forests. He visited Nottingham in 1199 and then went to Clipstone. Sherwood saw some of its greatest moments during his time, as well as some of its most infamous such as that in 1212 when John, who was enjoying life at Clipstone, received news of a Welsh revolt. He summoned a council of barons, meeting by legend at the 'Parliament Oak' near Clipstone. John ordered and watched the execution of young Welsh hostages at Nottingham, returning to Clipstone for food and hunting. His misuse of the forests was one cause of the trouble with the barons, and Magna Carta of 1215 contained five clauses relating to royal forests. King John died at Newark in 1216, whilst actually en route back to Clipstone. According to Thoroton, the lodge at Clipstone had been burnt down and rebuilt by 1220. In 1290 Edward I met many of the country's leaders at Clipstone and on 14 October swore to 'take the cross' and go on a crusade. The 'palace' was in ruins again by 1525. Edward II has been claimed as the most frequent user of 'King John's Palace'. [27]

Royal use of the Forest was commemorated at 'King's Stand', on the edge of Mansfield. This was reputedly a place where the monarch could stand and survey the course of the hunt. There is also a King's Stand just west of Rufford.

John was succeeded by Henry III, who issued the Charter of the Forest on 6 November 1217. This was the forest equivalent of Magna Carta, defining the law and returning to previous usage many areas only recently enforested. It reflected the ideas of Canute, with the 'regarders' reporting forest offences to courts called swanimotes or eyres, and verderers taking care of the 'vert' and the venison. A chief justice in eyre reported directly to the Privy Council, one for both north and south of the Trent. Some of the most punitive of the old forest laws were abandoned. Details included rules on lawing of dogs: 'three toes shall be cut off a forefoot without [injuring] the ball [of the foot]'. [28] Following this, between 1219 and 1227, some areas of forest land, including those on the eastern clays, were disafforested, [29] releasing some local people from the control of the foresters. [30]

Edward I introduced sworn juries in the forest courts and took other steps to control corruption amongst the forest officials in his 'Ordinance of the Forest'. A vast area of royal land was Thorneywood Chase, which included land in Basford, Gedling, Lambley, Woodborough and Calverton. Sir John Stanhope, an ancestor of the earls of Chesterfield, was appointed its keeper, and his heirs in perpetuity and, in return, he had the right to kill the royal beasts.

In 1232 the first official 'perambulation' surveyed legal forest boundaries. When the eyre met in 1287, one case involved three men hunting with servants, bows, arrows and hunting dogs. It is not clear why the courts then lapsed until the eyre of 1334 which tried a succession of cases involving people who should have known better; the rector of Annesley and the vicar of Edwinstowe were both in trouble and Lord John Grey was found to have chased a herd of deer at Bestwood with six greyhounds, killing two of the hinds. A man from Breadsall was fined for killing a deer at Clipstone.

Records show that one of the biggest problems was the abuse of the 'vert'. The eyre of 1287 had three times as many offences against the vert as the venison and in 1334 there were 809 vert offences. Among the worst were those committed by the abbot of Rufford's men who felled 483 oaks for building, but the abbot argued his way out of the situation by reference to his charter. In the early 13th century the Grey Friars of Nottingham were permitted some oak for building purposes.[31] In the 1240s, four Sherwood oaks were made available to repair the Trent bridge and the castle, and in 1268 three oaks were granted for the repair of the west gate at Nottingham.

Also in 1268 the monks of Worksop were granted access to the Forest after their trees in Grave Wood were cut down by the king's son to make weapons for attacking the Isle of Axholme.[32] In 1323-4 Sherwood oak was used to build nine catapults for the war in Aquitaine.

Oak bark was also stripped off to use in the tanning of leather, which was a noted industry in Nottingham. The felling of timber by those who lived within the Forest could result in imprisonment in Nottingham, whilst outsiders who stole the 'vert' were liable to execution. It was acceptable to collect the brushwood and other ground materials for fuel. Not all of the Forest belonged to the king. Some woodland at Blidworth was held by the Archbishopric of York, although when the See was vacant between archbishops, the king had the rights to the land; Edward II took his opportunity to fell timber for charcoal and fuel.

In 1278 one of the irregular forest inquisitions was held at Blidworth. This ruled that dogs could be 'expediated' – have their feet cut so that they could not be used in hunting. The Inquisition also dealt with a dispute over the Manor of Arnold, which was within the Forest. Rulings also allowed parcels of land to be removed from the Forest altogether; thus, in 1298, 80 acres of land at Bulwell Rise was

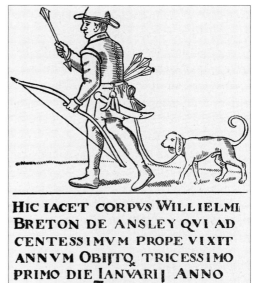

HIC IACET CORPVS WILLIELMI BRETON DE ANSLEY QVI AD CENTESSIMVM PROPE VIXIT ANNVM OBIJTQ TRICESSIMO PRIMO DIE IANVARIJ ANNO DNI 1595.

13   *The Annesley brass, a memorial from 1595, depicts a scene that might have been typical over the previous several hundred years – except a man hunting in the royal forest with a dog might have got into considerable trouble!*

'demised' to Philip Willoughby in return for 26s. 8d. a year, to be enclosed with a hedge and ditch; the land was later given to the monks of Newstead and eventually formed the estate of the Byron family. At the time, Sir William Trussebutts was keeper of the Forest, so he had to visit Bulwell with the verderers to measure out the land. On both occasions payments were made to the royal exchequer.[33] An exact definition of measurements was required to measure the land, such as the 'forest foot' which was 18 inches, and scales were inscribed into the walls of Edwinstowe church, St Mary's Nottingham and Newstead Priory for this very purpose.

The monastic houses were among the most active agents of change in the Forest. Though they could benefit from grazing sheep among the trees on the 'wastes', they also exploited land grants to clear the Forest altogether. In 1304, Newstead was given 180 acres of waste at Linby with permission to enclose and cultivate.[34]

The king's deer were free to roam the Forest, but the various noble estates also had their own deer which had to be fenced. The first deer parks were at Clipstone and Nottingham, with the former certainly in existence by 1176-80 and Nottingham Park by 1178.[35] Maud de Caux was granted the right to keep a deer park at Laxton by King John; there were two in the village by the 1190s. The Furnival estate at Worksop Manor had its own deer park, although it suffered the attentions of some poachers, such as the abbot of Welbeck's staff, who stole deer from it in 1334. There were occasional problems with monks hunting in the Forest and in 1478 the monks of Welbeck were banned by their own Order from hunting or shooting in the woods, although one was found guilty of the offence in 1488. Illegal hunting, however, was not the only threat to the deer. Diseases such as murrain could take a heavy toll and 350 red deer died in 1285.

During the period of the Forest's greatest extent, around 1200, there were parks at Colwick, Boughton and South Muskham while a park at Kingshaugh was added in 1220. The Rufford monks held the Boughton deer park in about 1203 and there was possibly another held by Gilbert de Gant near Eakring.[36] With the deforestation that took place after 1227, more parks were created both in Kneesall, by about 1226, and Grimston in 1229. Laxton also gained a third park after 1227 and there was one near Tuxford in 1259. The royal deer park at Bestwood came later. It seems to have been a 'hay', surrounded by hedge in 1251[37] and with a lodge by 1284 for the use of the foresters. The Close Rolls refer to Robert de Maule being ordered to fell and sell timber in Linby Hay in order to pay for the emparking of 'Beskwode' in 1349-57.[38] It was referred to as being enclosed within a fence or pale, and in the keeping of Sir Richard de la Vache when Edward visited in 1357. Parks like this had their own foresters, there being three at Bestwood in 1251. The park was stocked with red deer but these were often leased out. It was host to Richard III on 16 August 1485, shortly before he was killed in the Battle of Bosworth.[39]

14 *An artist's impression of a medieval Sherwood Forest ranger.*

Bestwood was one of the fewer parks in the west, where the Forest was less affected by the reduction of 1227. There was a park at Bilborough by 1302 and one at Kirkby in 1310. The more famous Wollaton Park is not known before 1325, when it was developed by Chief Justice, Sir Richard de Willoughby before he was disgraced in 1341 with accusations of abusing the forest laws.

The Forest was not 'impenetrable' because it was crossed by several roads, although these had a bad reputation. The principal road through the area was originally that from Nottingham to Blyth, known as the North Road. It was certainly in existence by Norman times as many parishes adopted it as a boundary line and in 1218 part of it was being used as a boundary for the Forest. Since there was no bridge across the Trent at Newark until about 1200 its importance must have been considerable, but its use gradually declined in favour of the more westerly route through Mansfield and Worksop. The original land grants for Welbeck Abbey in the 12th century referred to a 'wheel road' nearby, which may well have been this more westerly route. Nonetheless crossing the Forest still presented problems

15   *The enduring 'medieval myth' of Robin Hood was especially popular in Victorian times and occasionally surfaced as an 'opera', musical or patomime - this effort is from 1860.*

as can be seen from an incident in 1393 when important legal documents known as the court rolls were being taken from York to Nottingham by court officials. Heavy rain had made the going particularly arduous and extra horses were needed to handle the work. The officials took two horses from John Turnour of Norton on the main road south from Worksop. Despite their intention to pay for the horses at a later date, they were attacked by an angry crowd led by the vicar of Cuckney and some of the Welbeck Abbey servants who sought revenge, in the course of which the court rolls were damaged!

By the 14th century, the form of Sherwood was well-established. Within it the king's wild deer roamed the open forest between sections that were fenced or hedged off for private or royal use. The forest pastures were well-used by the people of local villages for their animals and to collect fern and leaves whilst various nobles had the right to take rabbits and foxes, but never venison unless they held special rights. Furthermore, aside from the obvious trades, its sandstone was soft and easy to work which made it excellent for interior stonework; in 1338 the king granted a licence for its stone to be quarried, probably from near Mansfield, for the choir of Southwell Minster. Thus the Forest was not a wasteland, but a thriving sub-economy in its own right.

4

Dissolution and New Dynasties

Sherwood Forest was still a recognised legal entity in 1500, but its days of glory had passed. No monarch is known to have visited Nottinghamshire at all from the Battle of Stoke in 1487 to James I in 1603. Female monarchs had little interest in stag-hunting. The endless acres were being broken up by the enclosed deer parks and the Enclosure Inquisition of 1517 found that enclosure for 'sport' was greater in Nottinghamshire than anywhere else.

The enclosure of Wollaton Park under Henry VII set the pace. By the time of Henry VIII 'private' deer parks included Thorneywood, Nottingham Park, Bestwood and Blidworth, which was 'fenced and gated against the deer' to separate its deer from the king's animals in the Forest. Bestwood and Clipstone were royal parks, though Thomas Markham had been appointed their keeper (the Markham family were aggrieved when they lost control to the Earl of Rutland under James I). Edward Stanhope enclosed a park of 240 acres at Haughton in 1509 'for the purpose of rearing wild animals'. Worksop Park was a private deer park with its own hunting lodge. Although Nottingham Park was only 120 acres and Bulwell 326, some of these parks were immense : in 1609 Bestwood was recorded as having 3,672 acres and Clipstone 1,583.[1] In 1514 Nicholas Strelley 'emparked' 50 acres of waste at Linby with 'paling' to rear 'wild animals',[2] presumably deer.

A commission of Henry VIII in 1531 found 4,280 red deer and 1,131 fallow in the Forest. The red deer were allowed free rein across the Forest except for the 200 confined within the deer park at Bestwood. In 1538 there were 1,000 red deer in Sherwood; out of 840 deer at Bestwood, 140 were red; 80 were at Clipstone, with a quarter of them red. In 1616, 1,263 deer were recorded.

The 'wastes' were used for grazing sheep and cattle. Papplewick was an important centre for the wool trade, with an annual sheep fair. Butler says that much illegal enclosing took place here and that Seven Mile House was built on a site to stop sheep straying out to Arnold – perhaps after human encouragement.

In the time of Elizabeth I it was still the case that the 'gentry' held the offices such as that of Verderer. Henry, Earl of Rutland, was made Chief Justice from 1549 until his death in 1563 and George Talbot was appointed Chief Justice in Eyre in 1590. Richard Poe of Papplewick was Chief Forester under James I and was buried under the church porch there. Legal protection was required because pressure on the trees continued: in 1506 John Halley of Linby was in trouble for cutting down three of the king's oaks. The last regular court of eyre met in 1538. Some improvement to the official structure was intended with the creation in

16 *A Victorian reproduction of a map originally printed in 1576. Enclosed parks can be identified, such as Worksop Manor and Welbeck, with Bestwood in the south.*

1607 of a surveyor general of woods, forests, parks and chases. Honorary posts also continued with John Deverell being ranger and also official bowbearer in 1606.

A 1609 survey of Sherwood showed that much of it had been filtered into private control by emparking. The Forest was divided into three 'walks': the north, middle and south. It was reported to include 'ancient enclosures' of 44,839 acres and 'ancient woods' of 9,486 acres. Ancient 'wastes and moors' accounted for another 35,080 acres, so roughly half was relatively unspoilt. Within its bounds were four deer parks: Clipstone (1,583a), Bestwood

(3,672a), Bulwell (326a) and Nottingham (129a). The whole Forest covered 95,115 acres but almost half of it had been 'enclosed' for some time. Royal forests were depleted by cash-strapped monarchs selling off lands; Charles I dispensed with 1,500 acres of Birkland and Bilhagh, which later passed to Newcastle and then to the Duke of Portland.

The Forest had enjoyed few days of royal patronage, but one great occasion was the arrival of James I on his journey down from Scotland to England after gaining the throne, following the death of Elizabeth I. James arrived at Shrewsbury's house at Worksop in April 1603 and was 'accosted by kneeling huntsmen in Lincoln coats, who offered to show him some game thereabouts, a very welcome offer'.[3] James spent a day with the huntsmen, being 'very much delighted'. He enjoyed 'excellent soul-ravishing musique' in the evening, and a lavish breakfast the following morning. James then continued via Rufford to Newark, where his views on the summary execution of criminals nearly sparked a major legal crisis when he ordered the execution of a 'cutpurse' who had followed him from Berwick, not realising that the English insisted on a judge and jury. Soon afterwards, the future Charles I also stopped at Worksop on his way to London, where he was looked after by the 12-year-old William Cavendish. In 1636 John Harrison described it as 'a very stately house' with 800 fallow deer and much timber.

James I hunted regularly. In 1614 he visited Rufford and Newstead, enjoying much hunting through August. He stayed at Sir John Holles' house in Nottingham, Thurland Hall. He stayed again in 1616, and later created Holles Baron Haughton, Earl of Clare. James I returned in 1619, 1621 and 1624, in which year a forest fire caused by charcoal destroyed six square miles, with only a change in the wind and the digging of a large trench stopping it from spreading further. He stayed at Rufford in 1624 and famously lost his temper after losing a stag in the chase and being surprised by a clown. James's successor, Charles I, stayed at Welbeck on his way to being crowned King of Scotland; the dramatist Ben Jonson wrote a masque for him, *Love's Welcome at Welbeck*, which was performed by local gentry.[4]

In 1634 the king and queen stayed at Thurland Hall, entertained by the Earl of Newcastle, as Holles, Earl of Clare, had become. The days of Nottingham Castle as a venue for grand occasions had gone; it had been in ruins in 1540 and, although Elizabeth I authorised repairs, they had not been completed by 1603. James I gave up the

17   *Thurland Hall was built in Nottingham some time before 1474, bought by Thomas Markham and then sold to the Holles family and demolished in 1831.*

royal interest and granted the castle to the Earl of Rutland in 1622-3.[5] It passed to George Villiers, 2nd Duke of Buckingham, and was leased to William Cavendish in 1641, for 21 years at £8 a year. The insignificance of the castle was confirmed at perhaps the most crucial moment in Nottingham's history: when Charles I raised his standard there in 1642, he stayed at Thurland Hall.

The forest economy was increasingly influenced by grazing sheep among the trees. Sir William de Pierrepont was active in enclosing the fields at Holme for sheep, with the result that farm labourers lost their jobs and houses fell into ruin.[6] Landowners also argued that the Forest posed a threat to neighbouring farmland; Sir William Savile tried to get permission to plough up parts of the Forest to destroy rabbits. Others just wanted to enrich themselves at the expense of lesser people's rights since any pressure to enclose forest and wasteland tended to be at the expense of commoners and others who had rights over its use; in 1601, when Sir John Byron tried to enclose Bulwell Moor, copyholders and tenants got up a petition to the Privy Council. On this occasion they won, but the tide of history favoured those who tried to enclose. Villagers wanted to clear the land for crops, and this had generally relied on the tradition of asking for permission to create 'brecks'.[7] Forest villages often had these, and by the early 1600s they were commonly extensive, Carburton having 518 acres in 1615. By the early 17th century, modern root crops were becoming more common and provided a good opportunity to use the poorer sandstone soils, thereby hastening the eradication of the forest.

18 *John Holles, 1st Earl of Clare, derived his wealth from London property of which Clare Market was to remain in the family for generations.*

Several families dominated the district at the start of the Tudor period, but among the best established were the Shrewsburys[8] at Worksop Manor. The main house there had really been a hunting lodge until after Shrewsbury's marriage to Bess of Hardwick in 1567.[9] Worksop Manor was built, possibly with the architect Robert Smythson having a hand in its design, in 1580-5. It gained some brief notoriety when Mary Queen of Scots was kept prisoner there while in Shrewsbury's care from 1569-84. In 1583 he allowed her to visit Worksop but denied claims that she was allowed to wander in Sherwood Forest. When his second wife, Bess of Hardwick, alleged an affair between Shrewsbury and Mary, their marriage was fatally flawed.

Worksop Manor Lodge was built around 1596 and also showed Smythson's influence;[10] it has been suggested that it was a hunting lodge or a lodge for a keeper, but in size and aspect is similar to a building at Bolsover Castle.

Worksop Manor was built from scratch to be a house but other significant stately homes began as monasteries. During the period 1536-9 Thomas Cromwell, acting at the behest of Henry VIII, began the closure of the monasteries known as the Dissolution. This released land to gentry and nobles, thereby creating a power base for future growth. For the most part the local religious houses closed with barely a whimper, only Lenton Priory offering enough opposition for several of its denizens to be executed and the Prior of Beauvale was also executed in London.

Cromwell moved against some of the smaller houses first. In 1536 Blyth, Felley, Rufford and Strelley were dissolved. Felley amounted to 40 acres of arable and 356 acres of pasture.

Worksop Priory's lands at Osberton were given to the Bolles family. Welbeck, Lenton and Worksop were dissolved in 1538 with Beauvale, Newstead and Wallingwells following in 1539. Shelford Priory was also surrendered in 1538, its lands passing to the Stanhopes who gained land in a further 20 villages. Opposition developed in 1536 in Lincolnshire, but Nottinghamshire sided with the King and George Talbot, 4th Earl of Shrewsbury, earned favour through his spirited attack on the rebels. During the same era the manor of Clipstone was given to the Duke of Norfolk by Henry VIII.[11] Some of the monks found useful employment, Christopher Matterson and Henry Tinker becoming the parish priests of Walesby and Edwinstowe.

This was not an era of executions and public burnings, as it was further south. Religious rebellion was most commonly by priests with puritan inclinations not wearing a surplice, such as the vicar of Greasley in 1574 and the vicar of Edwinstowe in 1587. The men who were to become the Pilgrim Fathers lived further north and east. Within the region, Thomas Helwys of Broxtowe was a noted Puritan by 1595 although his friend, Richard Bernard, vicar of Worksop, counselled moderation. He left for Holland in 1607 but returned in 1612-13 to set up at Spitalfields the first Baptist church in England.

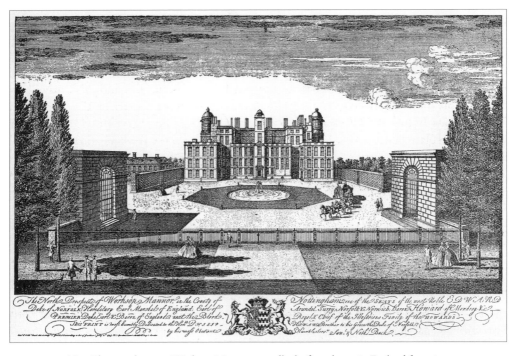

19   *The great house at Worksop Manor, reputedly the finest house in England for a time.*

The leading religious radical was George Fox, the founder of the Quakers. Born in Leicestershire, he was living in Mansfield as a shoemaker in 1646-7 when he began his ministry. He was imprisoned for causing a disturbance in a Nottingham church in 1648 but succeeded in converting his gaoler, and then moved to Mansfield Woodhouse where he spent time in the stocks. When he attempted to preach after a church service in Mansfield Woodhouse, he was soundly beaten. Elizabeth Hooton of Skegby was one of his first converts and became the first female preacher for the Society of Friends.

Rufford Abbey was assessed in 1536 as having 344 acres of arable land and 640 acres of pasture as well as further meadows, three water mills and fisheries. It had lands and granges in the immediate area, such as at Walesby and Ollerton, but also further afield. At first the abbey was granted to Sir John Markham for 21 years at £22 8s. a year, but in 1537 it was granted to the Earl of Shrewsbury instead, perhaps because of the help he had given Henry VIII in quelling the rebellion. Shrewsbury gained additional lands in 25 villages altogether[12] including Bilsthorpe, Warsop and Wellow. When he died in 1538, the lands passed, through the marriage of his daughter, to Sir George Savile (c.1549-1622) of Barrowby near Grantham.

The Rufford buildings were adapted into a house, where Bess of Hardwick married off her daughter Elizabeth Cavendish to Charles Stuart, the Earl of Lennox, in 1574. According to tradition, Bess had heard that the Countess of Lennox had an eligible son, and persuaded her to stop at Rufford on her way to Scotland. She then kept the countess occupied so that the young couple could spend time together, getting them married before the journey could continue. The daughter of this marriage was Arabella, who died in the Tower of London after being involved in a plot to replace King James I; Sir Griffin Markham of Ollerton was also involved.

The Cottam branch of the Markham family bought land at Ollerton in the later 1500s. Reportedly a favourite of Queen Elizabeth, Thomas Markham was High Steward of Mansfield, keeper of Bestwood and Clipstone parks (on behalf of the monarch) and a ranger of Sherwood. His sons, however, supported the Catholic faith and this caused him considerable difficulty; his oldest, Sir Griffin, was banished from court by Elizabeth until her dying day. In July 1603 Sir Griffin was arrested for being part of a plot with Sir Walter Raleigh to replace James I with Arabella Stuart. He was led out to be beheaded but refused a covering over his eyes saying, 'I am still able to look death in the face without blushing'. Just as the axe was about to swing a gentleman stepped forward with a stay of execution, and Sir Griffin was banished from the country instead. His local lands were given to Sir John Harington, a writer who was his cousin,[13] whilst his wife, Anne Roos of Laxton, married her servant bigamously and was forced to do public penance. Another branch of the family settled at Worksop Lodge in 1670.

The family that was to have a lasting connection with Rufford was that of Savile. The founding personality was Sir Henry Savile of Lupset (c.1518-68) who married Joan Vernon, an heiress from Lincolnshire, from whom he acquired Barrowby. He was living in the Yorkshire branch of the family's Thornhill Hall by 1564. His son, Sir George, married Shrewsbury's daughter Lady Mary Talbot and through this route the Rufford estates came into the Savile family. This was partly engineered by George Talbot, 6th Earl of Shrewsbury, who had been guardian of one of the Savile heirs,[14] and is an example of two families from the fringes of Sherwood coming together to form a powerful new oligarchy. Lady Mary had died by about 1599. Savile remarried, causing a family dispute when he sought to give precedence to the children of his second marriage over George, his son from the first.

In 1604 the Saviles also inherited extensive lands from the branch of the family based at Thornhill in Yorkshire. Sir George purchased a baronetcy from James I in 1611. The son from the first marriage to Lady Mary Talbot died before his father, although he left two sons in his own right. These boys fought their grandfather through the courts with the support of Sir Thomas Wentworth and in 1617 old Sir George and his second wife were both committed to prison for contempt. A key issue was the Rufford estate, as, although Lady Mary Talbot had left it to her children, Wentworth had to fight to ensure that this happened. Ironically, the Talbot variant of the Savile line petered out with the death of Henry Savile, 2nd Marquess of Halifax, in 1700, and the estates reverted to the descendants of Sir George by his second wife – as he had wanted.

The 2nd Baronet, also Sir George, inherited in 1622 nearly 40,000 acres from the Yorkshire side of the family and, in 1625, nearly 25,000 acres from the Shrewsbury side which included 16,800 acres of Nottinghamshire. It did him little good, for he died from smallpox in 1626. The 3rd Baronet was his younger brother, Sir William, who was elected to Parliament in 1641 and briefly imprisoned in the Tower when his uncle Wentworth, the Earl of Strafford, was executed. He died in 1644.

Land belonging to the monks of Newstead passed to Sir John Byron[15] of Colwick in 1540 for £810. Byron gained Papplewick, Linby, and Bulwell Wood, where he built Bulwell Wood Hall. Byron was 'Lieutenant' of Sherwood Forest and enjoyed royal favour; he was appointed steward of Manchester and Rochdale, having lands in Lancashire.[16] As one of the four foresters he was given a wage of 4d. a day.[17] Newstead's abbey church was unroofed and then dismantled in part so that it could be rebuilt as a house. Byron did not lead an entirely blameless existence and had to be pardoned by Edward VI in 1547. His offences included hunting and fishing without permission, wrongly sowing hemp, shooting with guns and crossbows and adding machicolations without authority! In the 17th century Sir John Byron became the 1st Lord Byron, and also Lieutenant of the Tower in 1641. He died in Paris in 1652. In 1636 the Byrons were reported to be living by preference at Bulwell Park, although by the end of the century they seem to have left Bulwell for others to inhabit.

The Byrons gained from the growing coal trade in the south-west corner of the region. In 1603 they leased mines at Strelley and Bilborough to Huntingdon Beaumont, who constructed in 1604 what was possibly the first railway in Britain from Strelley to Wollaton lane end,[18] using wooden rails. The Byrons, therefore, enjoyed a fixed rental income whilst others took the risk of developing the mines. Beaumont did not make the profits he had hoped for, however, and he moved to the North East where he continued a range of technical innovations. He was unsuccessful and died in Nottingham Gaol in 1624. In 1651 there was a legal dispute after 24 oak trees in Strelley Park had been cut down, apparently for mining materials, for which Lord Byron was blamed.[19]

William Byron married the daughter of Lord Chaworth in 1660 in a typical local alliance. His son William married the daughter of William Bentinck, Earl of Portland, and so connected the Byrons with a family that was to have great significance in Sherwood.

Welbeck Abbey surrendered to the king in 1538. In January 1539 Richard Whalley of Screveton paid £500 for the abbey's properties. The estates were gradually broken up in succeeding generations. Just after Elizabeth's accession, Whalley sold much of it to Edward Osborne, a London merchant,[20] including the site of the abbey itself, two granges including Gledthorpe and Hardwick, and the manor of Norton. Osborne's descendants settled at Kiveton Park and became dukes of Leeds. In 1540 the granges of Osberton and Hardwick were granted to Robert Deighton and in 1541 several other Welbeck granges, including Langwith and Woodhouse, were granted to George Pierrepont, providing further foundation for another emerging dynasty. In 1584 Welbeck's lease was assigned to Gilbert Talbot, Earl of Shrewsbury,[21] who allowed his stepbrother, Charles Cavendish, to live there; this gave rise to the tradition that Welbeck was bought by Bess of Hardwick, whose fourth marriage was to Talbot's father, for the son of her second marriage, Charles Cavendish. The purchase, for Charles 'through intermediaries', was completed in 1607.

'Bess of Hardwick' was first married at 14 and widowed not long after. She inherited the Hardwick land when her brother died. The key event in the formation of the dynasty was the marriage of William Cavendish to Elizabeth Barley[22] née Hardwick, who was aged 27. William Cavendish had made a fortune as a financial expert and auditor moving in government circles, personally profiting from the dissolution of the monasteries. He was knighted in 1546. After marrying Bess, he restructured his estates; Derbyshire became especially important and he began to build Chatsworth. He died in 1557 and Bess married again; their children, however, are of great importance to the story, because William Cavendish became the 1st Earl of Devonshire, Charles Cavendish was the father of the 1st Duke of Newcastle and Frances married Sir Henry Pierrepont and was the mother of the 1st Earl of Kingston. Thus William Cavendish and his wife played a pivotal dynastic role in Sherwood.

Bess's third husband, St Loe, was a substantial landowner, but Bess persuaded him to alter his will in her favour, excluding his daughters by a previous marriage. He duly passed away and she married the Earl of Shrewsbury in 1568. This union was cemented by the marriage of Bess's youngest daughter to the earl's second son, and the earl's daughter, Grace, to the oldest of Bess's Cavendish progeny, Henry, in February 1568. Bess's energetic approach to construction was shown in the completion of Worksop Manor.

Charles Cavendish seems to have gained Welbeck from his half-brother Gilbert Talbot, the 7th Earl, in 1607;[23] to confuse the story even further, Gilbert was married to Mary

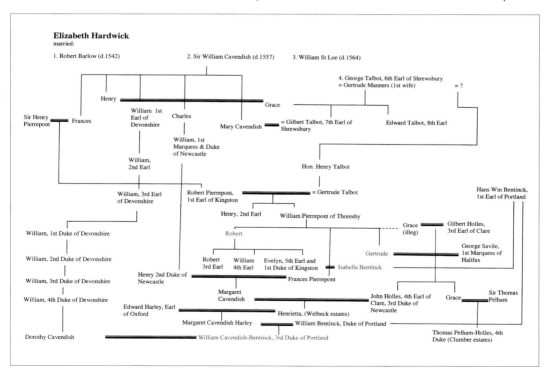

20   *Diagrammatic 'family' tree for Bess of Hardwick, showing her connections with the principal Sherwood families. Heavy black lines indicate 'dynastic' marriages between the families.*

Cavendish. Another version recounts that Gilbert Talbot 'passed over the lease' to Charles, who was his step-brother and his brother-in-law.[24] The 7th Earl had no real need of Welbeck – he had many other houses to choose from.

Sir Charles Cavendish gained notoriety from a dispute with Sir John Stanhope in 1599. Stanhope, along with 20 horsemen, attacked Cavendish and two pages near his new house at Annesley Woodhouse. Although Cavendish's horse was shot from under him and he himself received a bullet in the thigh, his side managed to kill two of the Stanhope gang and unhorse another six. A third person died in the Forest and a fourth was severely injured. Queen Elizabeth ordered that both men should give sureties for good behaviour. Thoroton implied that Cavendish then stopped work on Annesley, perhaps explaining his interest in Welbeck. Cavendish also bought the manor and castle of Bolsover from Talbot in 1608.

Charles Cavendish's son, William, was born in 1592 and became the 1st Duke of Newcastle on Tyne in 1665. As a young nobleman he entertained a young Prince Charles at Worksop Manor in 1604 and was made a Knight of the Bath in 1610. In 1617 he succeeded to the estates of his father, Sir Charles, who was buried at Bolsover. After a European tour he pleased his mother by marrying a rich widow who brought him about £3,000 a year. Robert Smythson and his son John worked at Bolsover on the 'Little Castle' in 1621 as well as the riding school at Welbeck. Cavendish developed both sites for great occasions, his social position being helped by King James' visits to Welbeck and Worksop Manor, such as that in 1619 when the entertainment was reportedly magnificent. It was no coincidence that he was made Viscount Mansfield a year later, and his younger brother Charles knighted. James I stopped at Welbeck on his final trip to Sherwood in 1624. Pleasing his majesty cost Cavendish over £4,000. This was favour-seeking on a grand scale and the reward, for Cavendish, was to be made Earl of Newcastle in 1628.

When King Charles visited in 1633 there was 'such an excess of feasting, as had never before been known in England'. On another occasion the Prince Elector Palatine and Prince Rupert stayed at great expense. In 1634 King Charles came back bringing the queen with him. A small glade in Welback Park became known as the 'Banqueting Dale' after it provided an entertainment for Charles I during his visit. The cost to Cavendish was estimated at over £14,000. Cavendish's approach to the king's visit makes clear that his view of his houses was changing. Welbeck became the 'lodging' of the royal party, and Bolsover was used to provide the entertainment. Not everyone was overwhelmed, and Cavendish's wife referred to Welbeck as 'not so magnificent as useful'.[25] Cavendish lavished much to keep the royals happy:

> (He) endeavoured for it with all possible care and industry, sparing nothing that might add splendour to that feast, which both their Majesties were pleased to honour with their presence. Ben Jonson he employed in fitting such scenes and speeches as he could best devise; and sent for all the gentry of the country, to come and wait upon their Majesties; and, in short, did all that ever he could imagine, to render it great, and worthy of their royal acceptance.

William Cavendish also looked further south and in 1641 took out a lease on Nottingham Castle and the adjacent park, completing the purchase from the Duke of Buckingham in

21   *A 1653 view of the stables and other equine facilities at Welbeck.*

1662. His rise to power and influence was then interrupted during the Civil War and he spent years in exile. In Paris he met Lady Margaret Lucas, sister of the 'martyred' Royalist hero Sir Charles Lucas who was executed at Colchester in 1648, and she became his second wife, his first having died in 1643. His loyalty to the Crown won him the dukedom in 1665.

The Duke of Newcastle is renowned for his system for training horses, having influenced the Viennese riding schools for generations, and his riding schools at Welbeck and Bolsover have both survived; he laid down the rules for ménage and produced a book on the subject, *Methode Nouvelle*, in 1657-8 which became enormously influential. His title passed to his son Henry but became extinct – for the time being – in 1691.

A rising star of Tudor England was Sir William Holles, a mercer of the City of London, who acquired wealth and influence which laid the foundations of a family for centuries to come. Claims have been made that he was a baker,[26] although he actually became master of the Mercers' Company in 1529. Sir William was Sheriff of London from 1527-8 and was knighted in 1533, when he attended the baptism of Princess Elizabeth; he was Lord Mayor in 1539-40[27] when he showed himself to be an ardent prosecutor of Protestants. In 1531 he bought St Clement's Inn, one of the inns of Chancery, which remained in the family until 1677.

Whereas most previous lords of Sherwood had won lands through battle and political influence, the Holles family were merchants. Sir William speculated on land from the dissolved religious houses, presumably not seeing any compromise with his erstwhile religious views. The London land that he acquired was to remain significant for the family for generations.

Holles was 'known for his sharp business practices';[28] one technique was to make short-term loans to landowners on the security of their estates, then to foreclose quickly and grab the land. He also bought land and manors on the open market. He encouraged his sons to do the same and his second son William bought the Haughton estate from John Babington[29] in 1537.[30] The large duck decoy on the Haughton estate has been claimed repeatedly as being 'of considerable antiquity' and possibly the oldest in the country; its use survived into the 20th century.

Sir William Holles left an income of £10,000 per year and has been rated as the second wealthiest man in the City of London. At Haughton his second son, Sir William, became

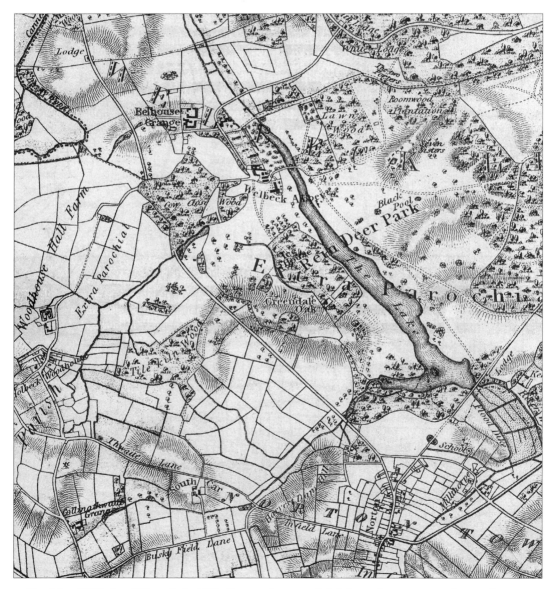

22   *Map of Welbeck and Norton in the 1830s. Features of interest include Belhouse Grange, a name indicative of monastic lands, and the interestingly named 'Rein Deer' Park. Note also the Greendale Oak. (Nottinghamshire County Council)*

a sheriff of Nottinghamshire for a time. Sir William married Anne Denzel of Cornwall, something of an heiress in her own right, and the name Denzil became a family tradition. His oldest brother 'wasted it all in riotous living, and died a prisoner for debt, leaving his family in utter destitution'.[31] The younger William, however, was of a different character: '12 days at Christmas he served up a fat ox every day, sheep and other articles for the table in proportion. During the whole time from All Hallows Tide until Candlemas any man was permitted to share the hospitality of his table without being asked whence he came, or who, or what he was'. Haughton had a moat and a 'lofty tower' to which William added a Great Hall in 1545. On the opposite bank of the river stood a small chapel which Sir William attended twice a day and to which he left money for its maintenance 'forever'. Rogers tells the story that William once bought 'The Lownd'[32] off a neighbour, but the neighbour's wife was so distressed about moving that William allowed them to remain, leading to later legal disputes.

John Holles (1564-1637) was the second of Sir William's sons. He earned his knighthood through his work against rebels in Ireland.[33] He married Anne Stanhope and spent some of his time at Thurland Hall in Nottingham when on official duties. This marriage seems to have incurred the wrath of the Earl of Shrewsbury, Rodgers alleging that this was because Sir William had arranged for his son to marry a Shrewsbury, and therefore Talbot, relative instead.

In 1598, whilst Sir John was riding back to Shelford with his mother-in-law Lady Stanhope, after the christening of his son Denzil at Haughton,[34] he met Gervase Markham, an ally of the Earl of Shrewsbury. The two men had been on bad terms since 1593 and after a few sharp words Sir John ran his sword into Markham 'between the privities and the bottom

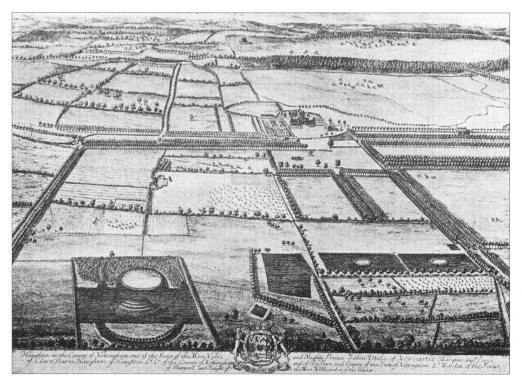

23 *A famous aerial view of Haughton Park showing the main house at right of centre with the chapel beside the river on the extreme right. The centre is dominated by the famous duck decoy.*

of the gutts up to the hilt and out behinde'. Expecting Markham to die, Shrewsbury gathered 120 men for an attack on Haughton, where Holles had returned. Holles asked Lord Sheffield to send him 60 men to help, but the dispute cooled when Markham began to recover. [35]

Holles was briefly imprisoned by James I, largely due to his having conversations with condemned Jesuits. A friendship with Sir Walter Raleigh cannot have helped, and Holles was present at Raleigh's execution in 1618. He was the first of the Holles family to be ennobled as Baron Haughton and Earl of Clare through the patronage of James I, though it reputedly cost him £10,000 in 1615 for the baronetcy and a further £5,000 for the earldom in 1624. [36] He hitched his career to King James' oldest son, Prince Henry, and was appointed Comptroller of his Household. The Prince visited Haughton for a 'great entertainment' but his death left Holles politically weakened. His attempts to win influence were doomed to failure and 'he became a bitter, sour old man.'[37]

24   *Haughton Park had its own small chapel, but neither house nor chapel survived the later rise of Clumber. Nowadays the chapel is a romantic ruin.*

He died in 1637 having already shown his opposition to Charles I and been reprimanded in 1629; he lost his role as a Nottinghamshire justice. His son and the 2nd Earl, John, was born at Haughton in 1595 and lived until 1665 though it was the second son, Denzil, who was to achieve lasting fame. The 2nd Earl set up Clare Market near his home in London in about 1657, which became an enduring source of income.

Holme was still the main seat of the Pierrepont family and King James's wife, Queen Anne, stayed there in 1603. Sir Henry Pierrepont strengthened his position by marrying Lady Frances Cavendish of Chatsworth. Their son Robert became an MP at the age of 17, having been found a seat by his uncle, the 7th Earl of Shrewsbury. In 1627 he became Baron Pierrepont and Viscount Newark, assiduously exploiting the king's lack of money in order to buy himself rank and title. He became the 1st Earl of Kingston upon Hull in 1628, a title which he purchased in similar manner to the Earl of Newcastle.

Robert succeeded to the estates in 1616 and bought the old manor of Thoresby in 1634. He died in the Civil War and was buried at Cuckney. The 2nd Earl, Henry, was more interested in Holme Pierrepont, and later enjoyed an interest in scientific matters, becoming a member of the Royal Society. He spent much of his time in London, took up medicine and is said to have killed a daughter, a coachman and five other patients with his medicines![38] In 1638 he got into trouble for assaulting a man at Westminster Abbey during divine service and in 1660 challenged Lord Roos to a duel. In 1667 he had a fight with the Duke of Buckingham which resulted in both of them being sent to the Tower for a few days. After the war, two of his houses were too ruined to inhabit so he lived for a time in Worksop Manor, although his brother William lived at Thoresby, which was known to be an unhealthy site, too close to the water. William Pierrepont's daughter Gertrude became the second wife of Viscount Halifax of Rufford, thus connecting the Pierrepont and Savile families. The 2nd Earl had no son, so the title passed to Robert Pierrepont, the 3rd Earl of Kingston from 1680, who was from the Thoresby branch.

The Annesley family left the district, taking their name to Ireland. Sir Frances Annesley was heavily involved in the plantation of Munster, for which he became a baronet in 1620 and was made a peer in 1621. The Chaworth family eventually ran out of male heirs. Mary Chaworth then married a member of the Musters family, who had lands at Colwick and Wiverton, and Sir John Musters eventually took the name of Chaworth.[39]

Another family that did well was the Hewet family. Sir William Hewet was Lord Mayor of London from 1559-60 and made a fortune from cloth, although the family had its origins in local villages such as Wales and Killamarsh.[40] Thomas Hewet became wealthy in the same way and was able to buy the Shireoaks estate from the Thornhill family who had acquired it from Henry VIII, it having previously been a grange of Worksop Priory. Sir William only had a daughter, but through her his line was linked to the dukes of Leeds.

In 1589 William Lee of Calverton invented a stocking frame that could do a row of stitches in one, rather than stitching each individually. Although Queen Elizabeth accepted a pair of silk stockings knitted with Lee's frame, he failed to profit from the invention and died in poverty in France in 1610. His brother James came home and set up a partnership in the county. The idea was taken up slowly so that by 1664 there were 200 workmen in Nottinghamshire using 100 lace knitting frames.[41] From 1597 a similar trade in weaving lace began to develop in Nottingham.

There was also an iron industry. George Sitwell had iron forges at Cuckney and Clipstone and the Duke of Newcastle leased land at Carburton and Norton to a man who built an iron forge and dam; in 1696 he wanted compensation after the dam caused a flood. There was a water-powered forge at Papplewick in 1675, 'with weighty hammers bigger than man can handle, they knock or beat out long bars of iron when they are made red-hot in the great forge or fire'.[42]

5

War and Restoration

As crisis loomed, some local notables were clear in their opinions, others less committed. It was assumed that the Holles family, earls of Clare, were opponents of the king, perhaps because of their roots in London mercantile society. The House of Commons put Clare in charge of the Nottinghamshire militia, a move opposed by Charles. The Byrons, however, supported the king. In 1641, as sides were drawn up, Sir John Byron was removed from his post as Lieutenant of the Tower by King Charles in a move that was seen as an attempt to appease his opponents. Most uncertain was Robert Pierrepont, who eventually took the king's side.[1] Sutton, later the first Lord Lexington, and Sir Gervase Clifton emerged as prominent royalists. William Cavendish, later the Duke of Newcastle, was a keen royalist, enduring years of exile as a result. In one account, he lost about £700,000 through his support of the King.[2]

Denzil Holles was one of the MPs accused of high treason by King Charles, and whom the king tried to arrest in the Commons on 4 January 1642. Nottinghamshire's lord lieutenants, Lord Newark (Henry Pierrepont) and John Digby of Mansfield Woodhouse, were royalists, so Parliament attempted to replace them in March 1642 with the Earl of Clare who promptly went to join the the king at York.[3] In early August, Lord Newark and the newly knighted Sir John Digby attempted to seize the county magazine for the king's service but they were resisted without bloodshed by John Hutchinson who was destined to play a significant role. In July, King Charles visited Nottingham and Newark, and then in August travelled from Lincoln to Nottingham again. Digby made a renewed and successful attempt to capture the magazine.

Charles I unfurled his royal standard at Nottingham on 22 August 1642, largely for strategic reasons, with some local dignitaries in attendance, including Sir William Savile of Rufford, Sir John Byron and Sir Gervase Clifton. Nottingham was not a main centre of royalist support, but it was closer to London than some of the places that were.

As war began, the Sherwood families were fairly unified in support of the king, but it could be costly; the Earl of Chesterfield was to lose all his property and three of his sons. All seven Byron brothers were royalists and three of them died for the cause.[4] Sir John Byron fought for the royalists at the Battle of Newbury and was made Lord Rochdale as a reward. His brother Richard, who became the 2nd Lord Byron, fought for the king at Edgehill in October 1642. Gervase and William Holles also fought for the king. The Earl of Chesterfield, Sir Thomas Blackwell of Mansfield Woodhouse[5] and Lord Chaworth were royalists, as was Thomas Markham, a natural supporter of the king because he was a Catholic and had a small enclave of fellow believers at Ollerton. There were other Catholic enclaves surviving at Cuckney, West Markham, Mansfield and Edwinstowe. There were few prominent men on the parliamentary side but the parson of Gedling, Laurence Palmer, must have been one of the most unusual when he combined his clerical duties with leading a troop of men. John Hill, rector of Nuthall, fought for the king. Newark became a royalist garrison, firstly under the command of Sir John Digby in December 1642, and then Sir John Henderson followed by William Cavendish, the Marquess of Newcastle from 1643. Nottingham was a parliamentary garrison with Hutchinson in control.

The Earl of Kingston and his oldest son, Henry, Lord Lincoln, chose to side with the king but his sons, William and Francis, were among the few gentry who supported Parliament, the latter actively trying to raise a regiment. Kingston's delay in declaring his hand and the family 'division' have been seen as tactics for making sure they survived the war without loss of their estates.[6] It took until July 1643 for Kingston to decide: 'When I take arms with the King against parliament, or with the parliament against the King, let a cannon-ball divide me between them,' he said, and at the time judged the royalists to be winning.

Newcastle was already active around York and on 6 December 1642 won a battle at Tadcaster, sending on reinforcements to Newark. Over the winter, Newcastle and Sir William Savile fought to control West Yorkshire for the king.

The small royalist force in Newark was exposed but parliamentary attacks in February 1643 had only limited success. By March, Newcastle was confident enough of his position to pay a visit to Welbeck, which is probably the occasion when he ordered that it should be

25 *Charles erecting his standard in Nottingham in 1642, an event signalling the start of hostilities. The artist's attention to detail includes the spade used to put up the flagpole!*

fortified.[7] The parliamentarians in Nottingham were also weak, but help arrived by May – one of the helpers being a certain Colonel Oliver Cromwell. In June, Queen Henrietta Maria arrived in England with over 4,000 troops specially imported via Bridlington and joined Newcastle at York. She then travelled to Oxford to join the king, spending several days in Newark on the way.

Kingston was appointed to a senior royalist command. His men were soon involved in a disastrous raid on Gainsborough when a bridge of boats was not ready in time. Kingston was captured from a burning house and accidentally killed by royalist fire while being taken by boat to Hull on 25 July 1643. When the pinnace in which he was travelling was shot at from the banks by Newcastle's army, Kingston had decided to go up on deck 'to show himself, and to prevail with them to forbear shooting, but as soon as he appeared a cannon bullet flew from the King's army and divided him in the middle …'.[8] This was seen as a reflection of his words from a few weeks before.

On 28 July, royalists from Nottinghamshire were caught by Cromwell as they advanced on Gainsborough with the Trent on their left. Sir Charles Cavendish was killed and Colonel Thomas Markham was probably drowned whilst the Marquess of Newcastle watched helplessly from the other bank. Rodgers[9] states, however, that Markham was wounded and came back to Ollerton to die on 22 July 1643. Newcastle was quickly able to force Cromwell out and retake Gainsborough. He was poised, as Nottinghamshire's leading landowner, to retake control of the county.

Sir William Savile had joined the king's army at York in June 1642. In January 1643 he lost command of Leeds and had to escape by swimming the river to safety. He left Lady Savile at Rufford, but this was hardly safe so she took up a variety of refuges across the country until Sir William was appointed governor of Sheffield Castle and then of York. Sir William died in January 1644 and Lady Savile endured a siege at York before returning to Rufford in August 1644.

Sir Richard Byron was appointed as the royalist governor of Newark and launched raids against Nottingham, where Colonel Hutchinson was in charge of its tumbledown castle from June 1643. On 18 September 1643 the town of Nottingham was briefly taken by royalists following treachery and again attacked in January 1644 on a snowy night. Parliament responded with an attack on Newark in February 1644, which also failed.

Meanwhile Newcastle had been made a marquess by his grateful monarch in October 1643. He moved south that autumn, establishing a base at Welbeck. His men fanned out over the region, seizing valuables from the homes of opponents. Newcastle enjoyed Christmas at home before leaving to face an army of Scots in the first weeks of 1644.

Hutchinson acted immediately. He sent a raiding party north, looting Newstead and gathering supplies from Mansfield. These supplies were nearly lost to a raiding party from royalist Wingfield in a lane near Bestwood Park.[10]

26 *Portrait of William Cavendish, made 1st Duke of Newcastle in 1665. The portrait includes many references to his achievements in war and learning.*

Sir Richard Byron was left isolated as defender of the royalist position at Newark. He was rescued in March 1644 by Prince Rupert, with much fighting in the area of Muskham Bridge. Rupert, like Newcastle before him, chose not to press home this advantage by attacking Nottingham Castle. Instead Rupert and Newcastle tasted bitter defeat at Marston Moor outside York on 2 July 1644 and the Marquess fled abroad.

In August 1644, the Earl of Manchester marched from York to Lincoln via Blyth and Welbeck, taking the opportunity to wreck the house and hold it captive, although it was later retaken. Welbeck was garrisoned by 200 foot-soldiers, some horsemen and several pieces of ordinance, but quickly surrendered. Newcastle's daughters were allowed to remain there.

Colonel Thornhagh marched to Thurgarton where Sir Roger Cooper had fortified his house against Parliament. Parlimentary forces captured the house, arresting Sir Roger only to be surprised by Newark royalists and defeated at Upton. All this was overshadowed by Parliament's victory at Naseby in June 1645, after which Charles I struggled to survive at all. Meanwhile, the Scottish army passed by Sherwood and Nottingham in June.

Newark royalists were quite capable of raiding across Sherwood. On 16 July they managed to retake control of Welbeck after hiding out and waiting for the drawbridge to be lowered to re-admit some roundhead scouts.[11]

King Charles now planned to journey to Scotland to join his supporter, Montrose. Charles arrived at Welbeck on 15 August 1645 but his advance north got no further than Doncaster. On 21 August he went to Newark, considering it as a winter base, but retreated southwards. On 4 October 1645 an increasingly desperate Charles returned to Newark, hoping that the Scots under Montrose were coming to his aid. He quartered his men thereabouts; Sir William Blakiston encamped with a number of men at Welbeck.[12] The king set off to find Montrose, going first to Tuxford on 12 October and then to Welbeck the next day. The King stayed two days, but with no good news of the Scots, he returned to Newark via Southwell. He sent some of his Welbeck forces north to help Montrose but they never arrived. For a brief period the two key figures of royalism, King Charles and his nephew Prince Rupert, were both in Newark, but the relationship between them had become strained.

Colonel Poyntz, commanding the Northern Association, advanced southwards hoping to trap the king in Newark. He reached Warsop on 18 October but had only got as far as Southwell four days later – perhaps he enjoyed the Sherwood scenery. He left Welbeck alone for the time being, firstly attacking Philip Stanhope, Lord Chesterfield's son, who was holed up in Shelford on the south side of the Trent; the battle ended in one of the most unnecessary slaughters of the war. Charles fled from Newark in the middle of the night on 3 November. After this Colonel Frescheville at Welbeck offered to 'slight' the garrison there if the parliamentarians did the same for Bolsover and Tickhill; this was agreed, and Bolsover ceased to be a royalist garrison.

The siege of Newark dragged out over the winter of 1644-5 with fighting at Stoke and Muskham Bridge. Both sets of men sought to get plunder and supplies from the area, with raiding parties going far out into Sherwood. The Earl of Clare, now a supporter of Parliament, complained that roundheads had been to a village near Haughton and taken goods from his servants worth £4.[13] To add insult to injury, the roundheads were thrown into prison for not producing enough goods, having previously been raided by the royalists. The impact of 7,000 Scots on the villages north of the Trent can be imagined.

Charles I hoped to get better terms by surrendering to the Scottish army at Newark. He arrived in Southwell at 7am on 5 May 1646, disguised as a priest, riding into the yard of what is now the *Saracen's Head*. He was taken as a virtual prisoner of the Scots to Kelham and told Newark to surrender. Newark's men marched out on 8 May, including Lord Lexington who had previously been plain Robert Sutton. Colonel Hutchinson then marched in and the plague followed soon after.

Parliament exacted a financial revenge on its opponents and by June 1646 it had taken control of the lands of Kingston, Newcastle, Chesterfield and Sir Richard Byron. The system of 'compounding' was introduced, whereby landowners effectively paid a type of forfeit. The Pierreponts did well for the fine on the father, Kingston, and the first son, Lord Newark, reverted to the two sons who had supported Parliament! Thomas Lindley of Skegby and Robert Brunts of Mansfield were appointed commissioners in this process in 1652. Their duties included managing the estates of Newcastle and Byron, both considered too wicked to forgive.

There was renewed fighting in 1648. Lord Byron had worked to revive the royalist interest with the help of his brother, Colonel Gilbert. At Willoughby in Nottinghamshire in July, Colonel Gilbert Byron was captured and Colonel Stanhope killed. Another local landowner, Lord Capel, who owned estates at Hucknall was captured and beheaded after fighting for the royalist cause in the lengthy siege of Colchester. When peace returned, Colonel Hutchinson demolished much of Nottingham Castle in 1651.

The King's lands were confiscated, including Bestwood Park which was placed in the care of Jonathan Grove on behalf of Colonel Whalley's regiment.[14] Attempts were made to sell it in 1650.[15] In the ensuing turbulence of the Protectorate period, William Pierrepont won a reputation for 'wisdom and soundness of judgment'.[16] He was one of the county's representatives in the Parliament of 1654.

A royalist rebellion was planned in 1655 for Rufford. Lord Richard Byron, its supposed leader, stayed in London. The sons of Sir Roger Cooper of Thurgarton certainly played a part, with John Cooper's house providing a convenient base for activity. Sir George Savile of Rufford allowed his men and horses to be involved, but he himself kept out of the way in London. On the night of 8 March 300 men wound their way through darkened Sherwood assembling at the *New Inn* at Rufford. While the Cooper brothers were in the inn, news arrived that a planned revolt in Yorkshire had collapsed and so they dispersed. Parliamentary soldiers soon arrived and found a cache of arms in a barn at Farnsfield; John Cooper fled abroad but was back home by 1662. Savile and Byron escaped without punishment. One other local victim was the royalist Rev. Dr John Hewet of the Shireoaks family, who was beheaded in 1659 on Tower Hill. Cromwell then placed the area under the control of Edward Whalley. His committee included Philip Lacock, who lived at Woodborough.

Byron conceived a plan to seize Newark back and, on 12 August 1659, he made another attempt, mustering men at Sansom Wood, six miles north of Nottingham, but without success. The set of commissioners appointed in February 1660 showed a new spirit of compromise; the Earl of Clare sat with William Pierrepont, Viscount Chaworth and others of royalist inclinations. The parliament of April saw the return of William Pierrepont and the Earl of Clare's son, Lord Gilbert and, within a month, Charles II had been proclaimed.

Recriminations continued well into the Restoration period. Robert Sutton of Averham, Lord Lexington, brought a law case against Colonel Hutchinson, the former commander of the Nottingham garrison, for damages. Hutchinson had managed to retain his estate at Owthorpe, but on 11 October 1663 he was arrested there and taken to Newark, before being taken to Kent; he died in 1664 at Sandown Castle and was buried at Owthorpe. His escape from serious punishment has been credited to Lord Byron.[17] Chief among those singled out for vengeance were the 'regicides', those who had approved the execution of Charles I; one of these, Millington, was from the family who had acquired monastic lands at Felley from James I, but his death sentence was commuted to life imprisonment. Denzil Holles also survived, dying in 1679. Several other local gentry such as Colonel Hacker suffered excruciating deaths. Lord Lexington died in 1668 and was buried at Averham, his inscription stating that he was 'a loyall subject, a lover of his country, a good Husband, Father, Friend, Landlord, Master, and Neighbour'.

War and the Forest

The years of fighting had a serious impact on Sherwood. The trees suffered severely; under the Commonwealth one man, a Mr Clark, had gained the rights to fell 28,000 trees. The animals were seriously reduced, and in 1661 red and fallow deer had to be imported from Germany to restock the forest glades. Numbers had fallen from about 1,700 in 1616 to only 248 in 1648. Charles protected his imported animals from 1662 with a new law banning their slaughter except in the royal presence. In 1662 there was a new perambulation of the forest boundaries, obviously intended to help the king re-assert some control. Twelve jurymen inspected the bounds of Sherwood as far north as 'the High Street of Blith' and to Trent Bridge in the south.

Charles II attempted to revive the forest traditions. The Marquess of Newcastle and his son Henry, Lord Mansfield (1663-80), later acted as lord chief justices in a revived eyre. The eyre, and the '40 day courts' held at Edwinstowe, Linby, Mansfield and Calverton, were seen as a means of raising money. William Willoughby held Bestwood Park for the king; 3,000 acres now included 100 of arable and 16 acres enclosed by the keepers themselves.[18] Lengthy hearings at Mansfield heard old claims. Edwinstowe blacksmith Thomas Cotton rode to court through the Forest and shot a hart on the way, for which he was fined 40s. Later, William III appointed Newcastle, John Holles, as Lord Warden of Sherwood Forest; 'an office which the duke transformed into virtual ownership, in return for keeping for the King some hundreds of red deer'.[19] The exploitation of this office formed a sound financial platform for further Holles aggrandisement.

Although the enclosure of forest land for 'sport' was affected by the Civil War, it continued afterwards, and in 1661 Sir Patrick Chaworth got permission from the Crown to enclose 1,200 acres at Annesley. Charles II had understood that the main profit from Sherwood would be in selling privileges within it to the highest bidder. This situation encouraged local landowners to accelerate the enclosure process, so that in 1663 the verderer John Trueman complained that 'thousands' of acres were being ploughed illegally. He objected that the Duke of Newcastle had gained control of Lindhurst and Norman's Woods from the Crown by a process of abuse. In 1675 the timber of Thorneywood Chase was wrested from the control of forest officials by John Musters, intent on enclosing land and also creating Colwick Park,[20] but at least his claim shows that there were still forest officers to reckon with.

The 4th Earl of Kingston paid £7,100 in 1683 to empark 442 acres of the Forest and 828 acres of Perlethorpe to form what became Thoresby Park,[21] where he built a house designed by William Talman who found greater fame as the architect of Chatsworth. From this point Thoresby supplanted Holme Pierrepont as their main residence.[22]

The importance of the Forest for royal hunting declined but it remained a significant source of timber. Flemish merchants had established trade links with monastic estates such as Rufford and Newstead. Under Charles II there was a phase of 'extravagant' felling of timber for the Navy, and the wharf at Blyth was reportedly 'clogged' with the timber traffic in 1664. It took 3,800 trees to build a 'ship of the line' at this time. One story reports that the Countess of Newcastle obtained royal permission to fell timber for the repair of Newark Castle, but in fact sold the timber for her own profit.[23] By 1670 it was said that there was 'not any timber left in the woods'.[24] This led wild deer to move out into farmland to seek food, thus hastening the final enclosures of the deer into semi-domesticated parkland. Charcoal burning was widespread: Thomas Baskerville saw '… many old decayed oaks, of which abundance were cut down by the Duke of Newcastle's order, to make charcoal'.[25] In 1680 the villagers of Edwinstowe were permitted to fell 200 oaks to repair their fallen church spire, whilst in about 1695, oak from Sherwood was used to provide beams in the building of the new St Paul's Cathedral after Wren wrote, asking for oak from the Welbeck estate.[26] Some huge trees did survive and in 1727 the Greendale Oak was supposedly big enough for a coach and six to be driven through it.

Author John Evelyn encouraged landowners to plant more timber on their estates for the benefit of the Navy. Evelyn referred to Worksop Manor as a 'sweet and delectable country seat' in his book *Silva, or Discourse on Forest Trees* in 1664, adding a detailed commentary on the size of oak trees at Worksop, including one on its side that had a 'boal' of over 29ft wide. Another tree was known to have been 180ft from the tip of one bough to another.[27] Evelyn described the 'Grindal Oak' in Welbeck Lane and the Shire Oak, which stood on the former Hewet lands close to the boundary of the three counties. Evelyn claimed a Worksop oak could shelter 942 horses, and a beech tree blown down in 1865 apparently covered an area of 1,000 square yards, producing 40 tons of good timber.[28]

The Survival of the Nobles

As has been seen, Newcastle was involved in the disastrous battle of Marston Moor, following which he abandoned the struggle and fled from Scarborough on a boat to Hamburg with two sons and his brother Sir Charles – and only £90. Parliament confiscated his estates, allowing no ransoming of them back. When Charles II was invited to return to England, Newcastle could barely contain his enthusiasm and hired a vessel to get back as quickly as possible.

Newcastle's losses were estimated at £941,000.[29] Welbeck and Bolsover were in bad repair and, of the eight parks he owned before the war, only Welbeck was 'not an utter ruin'. Clipstone was mentioned as being in an especially poor state, with its wood, fence and deer all gone. One source said that the Civil War led to 'the destruction of all the trees in Clipstone Park'.[30] Newcastle began to restore his deer parks and restocked them with animals given by friends. He was able to complete the purchase of estates in Nottingham in 1662-3, but he only finally secured the ruined castle itself from the Duke of Buckingham in 1674. Meanwhile, Charles II made him a duke in 1665. He decided to make the castle his 'town house' and began a lavish rebuilding as an Italianate palace that was not finished until 1679, although he died in 1676. He was able to re-enclose and re-stock Nottingham deer park. His second wife, Margaret, was known as the 'Learned Lady' who wrote poems and plays as well as a biography of her husband; of her Pepys wrote 'all that she does is romantic'. The Duke of Newcastle was described by Clarendon, a royalist, as 'a very fine gentleman, active, full of courage, and most accomplished in all the qualities of horsemanship, dancing and fencing, which accompany a good breeding, and in which his delight was … he loved monarchy, as it was the foundation of his own greatness'. After his death, the duke's titles passed to his son Henry Cavendish who was married to Frances Pierrepont of Thoresby.

During all the trouble, the Holles' maintained their business interests. John Holles, the 2nd Earl of Clare, built a house at the end of Clare Street close to their property of St Clement's Inn in London and and gained an Act of Parliament permitting Clare Market to operate three days a week, from which they collected rental. This provided a lucrative income until the 1800s; by 1853 it was merely a meat market and had declined to a few street stalls by the 1880s. Nonetheless, it demonstrated a pattern for the future in which the country life in Nottinghamshire was paid for by London property.

It was through a process of well-chosen marriages that the Holles family grew from interlopers into being the premier family of Sherwood. Gilbert Holles, the 3rd Earl of Clare, married Grace, one of the Pierreponts of Thoresby. In 1670 he added to their estates by finally buying Bothamsall, Lound and West Drayton from Sir Thomas Williamson. He died in Holborn in 1689. Their son John, Lord Haughton and later the 4th Earl of Clare, married his cousin Margaret Cavendish, heiress and daughter of the 2nd Duke of Newcastle, in 1690. Lord Haughton had only been a member of the House of Commons for two days when his father died so, becoming Earl of Clare, he moved to the Lords. Gilbert's second son, William, was killed in the siege of Luxembourg and was interred at Haughton. The chapel there was largely in ruins in 1658; Gervase Holles[31] blamed this on the puritanical zeal of the Countess of Clare, although some repairs seem to have been conducted later.

27 *The Holles family home in Lincoln's Inn Fields, adjacent to Clare Market, still stands today though in a heavily restored state.*

When Henry Cavendish, the 2nd Duke of Newcastle died, Margaret Cavendish inherited his estates, which were found to carry debts of £80,000, although the Earl of Clare seems to have been able to pay this off without difficulty.[32] This consolidated much of Sherwood into one estate. The will stipulated that the estates had to remain undivided in the Cavendish line and that Margaret's descendants had to take the Cavendish name. Disputes arose over the inheritance and Clare had to fight a duel with his wife's father-in-law, the Earl of Thanet, in 1692 in which both were wounded. [33] Although the inheritance did not include all the Cavendish properties in Derbyshire and Nottinghamshire, it did include the park and castle in Nottingham and also Welbeck.[34] From this point on Haughton gradually lost favour and it was at Welbeck that the Earl of Clare entertained the king in 1695.

Rodgers views Clare in a poor light: 'one cannot help thinking that he owed his elevation in the world to his practice of pushing his own interests to the detriment of others'.[35] To support this, Rodgers quotes a letter from the Earl of Clare, written from Haughton in 1691, begging to be made a duke. On being rebuffed, he surrendered his royal household duties and retired to Haughton 'taking his favourite diversion in hunting, and minding the improvement of his estates'. In fact, Clare was an efficient landowner amd has been described as 'an informed and careful steward'. [36] The titles of 3rd Duke of Newcastle upon Tyne and Marquess of Clare were eventually conferred upon him in May 1694. This success was attributed by Rodgers to his gaining the estates of Denzil, Lord Holles of Ifield, thereby making him an even greater landowner. His pre-eminence was confirmed by becoming Lord Lieutenant of Nottinghamshire in June 1694. Newcastle was able to show his gratitude when King William came to Nottinghamshire in 1695; Newcastle met him at Dunham Ferry and took him to Welbeck where the king stayed for two days, apparently at a cost of £5,042, before going to Holme-Pierrepont. From then on he enjoyed a form of a political career, nurturing his own parliamentary seats by the control of elections in East Retford and elsewhere, and holding office as Lord Privy Seal.

The Duke of Newcastle's daughter, Henrietta, stood to inherit all the lands of her parents and also those of her grandfather on the Cavendish side. In 1706 Newcastle came close to linking her with royalty by proposing a marriage to the son of the Elector of Hanover. Only the duke himself, his attorney Peter Walter, and a servant knew the full details of the will that was drawn up and signed at Welbeck in 1707.

The will remained a secret until the duke fell from his horse while stag hunting between Thoresby and Welbeck in July 1711. The *Nottingham Post* recorded:

> Tis said his grace being a stag hunter, his horse fell under him in the chase, and he fell on his shoulders, yet for the present felt no great harm. When the stag was killed, finding himself worse, getting into a coach he ordered to be driven home, fell into convulsions and died.

His will caused problems. The duke's sister, Grace, was married to Sir Thomas Pelham of Sussex, whilst his aunt had married Lord Clinton and both marriages were significant. After Newcastle's death, his will revealed that most of his landed property had not been left to his daughter Henrietta but to his nephew, Thomas Pelham, born in 1693, who was required to take the name of Holles, thus becoming Thomas Pelham-Holles. Former Cavendish estates at Welbeck and Worksop derived to Henrietta's side of the family when they were inherited from Margaret, Duchess of Newcastle in 1716, but Clumber and Haughton passed to the Pelham-Holles side. Grace Holles's son, Thomas Pelham-Holles, was the main beneficiary: he succeeded to the Holles lands as well as those acquired through marriage into the Cavendishes. Soon he was also to be the last Duke of Newcastle upon Tyne; he later became First Lord of the Treasury and Prime Minister as his brother Henry Pelham had been before him. The tangled web was completed by Henry Pelham-Clinton: his mother was Lucy Pelham, Sir Thomas's sister, and he married his second cousin Catherine Pelham, the daughter of Henry Pelham.

Within a generation, therefore, the Holles family had married into Pierrepont, Cavendish, Harley, Clinton and Pelham families. Then, in the 18th century, they produced two successive prime ministers. It had been a fantastic rise to the top of society.

The Saviles also suffered during the Civil War and Sir George Savile, aged only 13 when he inherited a huge estate on the death of his father, took refuge in France in 1647 although he had returned to England by 1652. He lost his principal family home when Thornhill Hall was accidentally blown up when being surrendered after a siege in 1648.

Sir George Savile was a royalist, as his father had been. In early March 1655 his uncle William Coventry and one of his mother's circle, Charles Davison, were involved in a revolt against the government; Coventry rode from London to meet the plotters at Rufford. Savile wisely stayed in London and escaped arrest. His financial position was equally precarious because his father had left him huge debts as well as estates, and these were only partly balanced by his marriage to Lady Dorothy Spencer in December 1656 who brought him £10,000.

Savile sought royal favour to help cover his debts, but his initial progress was slow. He was elected MP for Pontefract in 1660. He made a good impression on James, Duke of York, when he entertained him at Rufford in 1665 and the duke recommended him for a peerage, although this was blocked by the Earl of Clarendon who disliked Savile's liberal religious views. Savile was an associate of the Duke of Buckingham and prospered after Clarendon's downfall in 1667. In January 1668 he became Baron Savile of Eland and Viscount Halifax but moved to a position of championing the king against the influence of any mere nobleman, such as the Duke of Buckingham. In 1672 he married again to Gertrude Pierrepont of Thoresby, a granddaughter of the Earl of Kingston. Thus another part of the interconnecting web of Nottinghamshire families was in place.

In 1669 Savile chose Rev. William Mompesson as priest of Eakring. Mompesson had been a vicar of the Derbyshire village of Eyam during the plague in 1665-6, achieving lasting fame for his bravery. Legend relates that the villagers of Eakring were worried that Mompesson would bring the plague with him and refused to let him into the village; instead he had to live in a small house, possibly only a hut, in the park at Rufford until they were sure he was safe. He apparently preached beneath a tree that became known as the Pulpit Ash, and which Lord Savile replaced with a cross in 1893 after it was blown down. Some suggestions have been made that Mompesson preached outside becasue his church was in such a bad state of repair! He died in 1709.

The 1670s were challenging for Halifax. In the crisis of 1678 he exploited fears of Popery and the French to improve his position, but made himself very unpopular with King Charles and his brother. He returned to the Privy Council despite the king's bitter opposition, although in later years his restoration was attributed to his ability to impress the king by his 'lively and libertine conversation';[37] he was renowned for his brilliant intellect. His management of the crisis over the royal succession earned him the earldom of Halifax in 1679 but within a few months he appeared ill and disillusioned, possibly due to depression, and retired briefly to Rufford. As royal spokesman, Halifax was condemned by Parliament as an enemy of king and kingdom for having given Charles poor advice. By January 1681 he was back at Rufford, preparing for further pressures. He was outwitted by his enemies again in 1682 and palmed off with being made Marquess of Halifax as well as Lord Privy Seal – a title which carried a hefty income. His daughter Anne married Lord Vaughan, 24 years her elder, and took a portion of £10,000; Vaughan was one of those who had voted to condemn his father-in-law as an enemy of king and country! Halifax became known as 'The Trimmer' because he believed in trimming 'between extremes' in politics, and also as the 'Black Marquis' becasue of his dark complexion and even his ugliness; he also had remarkable wit. When James II took power, Halifax was dismissed from office but later dragged back into direct action when William of Orange stood against James II. Sent as an envoy to William, Halifax returned to find that James II had fled and promptly declared for the Orange cause. As Speaker, he formally offered the crowns to William and Mary.

Between 1651 and 1695 he increased land rentals at Rufford from £6,550 to £14,704 and his estates were worth around £300,000.[38] He was able to improve the old monastic ruins into a credible country residence and in 1680 described his work to his brother: 'I have still left some decayed front of old building, yet there are none of the rags of Rome remaining … I have at least so much reverence for it now as I had when it was encumbered with those sanctified ruins'. Many old buildings were demolished in 1677 and he doubled the size of the house to 123 rooms. The inevitable fire occurred in 1692 and cost £2,000 for the damage to be restored.

Halifax spent heavily on a London house which he even fitted with piped water to a bath. He died there in 1695 from a combination of undercooked chicken, violent vomiting, constipated intestines, old ruptures and gangrene, three days before the wedding of his son, Lord Eland, was due. Whether he died anticipating salvation is a moot point; accused of atheism, he complained that 'he believed as much as he could' but 'could not digest iron'.

Halifax's younger brother, Henry (1642-87), was born at Rufford. Since his father and brother had established strong credentials with the royal family, Henry found quick employment as a courtier. His main reputation, however, was for licentious behaviour: 'Savile and the others consumed drink and were entertained by prostitutes on a scale that caused comment even at the Caroline court; there were also rumours of nefarious activities involving young boys'.[39] He was romantically involved with the Duke of York's wife, who briefly became Queen of England. In 1669 he was imprisoned for challenging his uncle to a duel and subsequently banished. He dabbled in politics and even seems to have begun a fine Dukeries tradition, by being a younger son of one of the Sherwood families who fought a corrupt election at Newark. This occurred in 1677 when the campaign involved 'four days swallowing more good ale and ill sack than one would have thought a country town could have held'. Perhaps his greatest time came when sent to France on diplomatic duties, where he drew attention to the harrowing plight of the Huguenots. He died in Paris in 1687.

The 2nd Marquess of Halifax, William Savile, was probably born at Rufford in about 1664-5. In 1687 he became Lord Eland in place of his brother. He died in 1700; with no direct heir, the peerage became extinct. Three daughters survived, two of whom became countesses of Thanet and Burlington. This ended the Talbot side of the Savile family, and Rufford reverted to the Yorkshire branch of Saviles of Thornhill who were descended from a second wife rather than a first.

Charles II granted Bestwood Park to Henry Beauclerk, the Duke of St Albans and master falconer of England, in about 1683. This was not a recognition of Beauclerk's talents, but his origins as illegitimate son of Nell Gwynne and the king himself. A number of legends are told about his childhood; in one version Charles greeted him with the words, 'Come here, you little bastard,' and elevated him to the peerage. In an alternative version it was Nell Gwynne who, spying the king nearby, said to the little boy, 'Come here you little bastard and greet your father'. When Charles expressed disapproval, his mother said, 'Your majesty has given me no other name to call him'. In yet another version, his mother threatened to drop him out of the window unless he was given a peerage, and Charles obliged by making him Earl of Burford in 1670. A year after being granted Bestwood he was made Duke of St Albans.

The accession of William of Orange in 1688 resulted in the rise of another family to prominence: the Bentincks. Hans William Bentinck introduced this name to Sherwood, being a firm favourite of the Prince of Orange since childhood due to a bizarre belief about smallpox. When the prince had become ill with the disease, Bentinck suggested that it could be helped by putting a 'healthy body' into the bed with him, almost as if to share the burden; in this case it worked, and Bentinck's fortune was made.

As an emissary for William of Orange to the court of Charles II, he even went to England to convince James II that William had played no part in the Monmouth rebellion; James' daughter Mary was William's wife. There was considerable support in England for a change of monarch, including that from William Cavendish, Earl of Devonshire, and Charles Talbot, Earl of Shrewsbury. Bentinck played a leading role in the 'invasion' that followed. When William and Mary accepted the crown in February 1689, Bentinck's reward was to be created 1st Earl of Portland and he became an ambassador in Paris.[40] There he appeared 'with amazing personal brilliance, polish, an air of a man of the world and of the court, gallantry and graceful manners ...' reported Saint Simon. Bentinck gained vast lands in Ireland following the Battle of the Boyne and in 1698 he was granted lands in Soho by the king.

He embarked on a considerable acquisition of estates. One estate was at Bulstrode in Buckinghamshire, which he bought in 1707 and where he died in 1709; he also bought Theobalds on the Essex and Hertfordshire border. He divided his estates between his two surviving sons leaving the English estates to one son and those in Holland to the other. The family's connections with Sherwood were slim at this stage: Bentinck's third daughter married William, the 4th Lord Byron, in 1706 but died in 1712 and another daughter married Evelyn Pierrepont, future Duke of Kingston. Bentinck was succeeded by his son Henry, who became the 1st Duke of Portland in 1716.

In the first years of the 18th century, Sherwood was poised for a prosperous new age and its key families were positioned for unbridled self-aggrandisement.

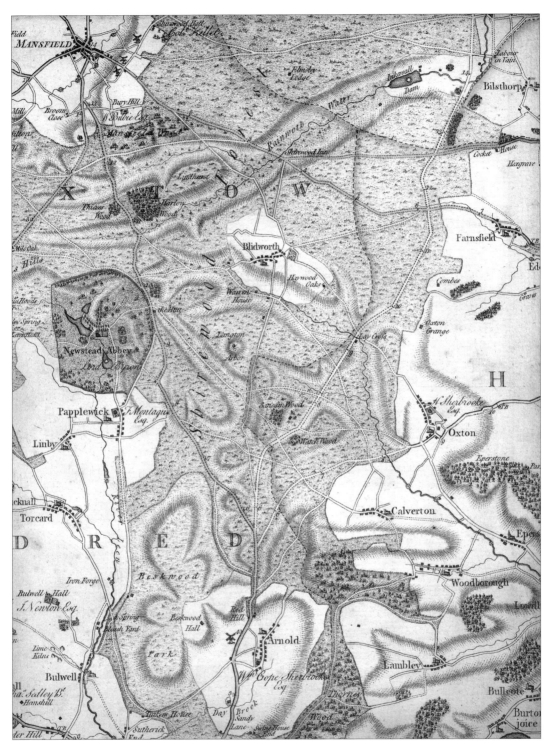

28   *Sherwood, mapped in 1776, still showed substantial areas of unenclosed 'forest' with the park at Newstead clearly separate – though Bestwood is no longer so distinct. Note that Rainworth barely grazes the reader's attention, and also the old hunting lodge of Langton Arbour.*

6

The Rise of the Landed Estate 1700-1815

The idea I gave Lord Rockingham of this county was four Dukes[1], two Lords and three rabbit warrens.

Sir George Savile (1769)

The great landed estates of the Dukeries included those that had old monastic foundations and others created anew from the landscape of Sherwood, generally from deer parks. The traditional Sherwood wild deer declined and by 1815 there were few, if any, remaining. Old traditions passed away and William, Lord Byron was the last ever official 'bow bearer' of Sherwood Forest when he was appointed by the Duke of Norfolk in 1702. Some forest officials did continue, however, lacking only a forest to regulate.

During Queen Anne's reign, royal finances were reorganised. The ancient land revenues due to the Crown from territory such as Sherwood became part of national revenues under the Queen Anne Civil List Act, and the Queen was paid an allowance of £700,000 a year instead.

The Forest shrank. By 1790 there were only 10,117 oak trees left; there had been 49,909 in 1609.[2] Some old character was retained including its important trees, such as the Greendale or 'Grindall' Oak in Welbeck Park; in 1724 this was said to include a gap in the trunk big enough for 'a carriage and six with a cocked hat coachman on the box'.[3] The opening was supposedly cut in 1724 after the Earl of Oxford had made an after-dinner bet that he had a tree on his estate through which a coach and six would fit. The Countess of Oxford had a cabinet made from the oak that was cut from it; this had inlaid representations of the tree with the carriage and horses driving though it.[4] Other noted oaks at the time included the Major,[5] Parliament and Shambles oaks. The old Pilgrim Oak outside the gates of Newstead, which was used as a site for local festivals, survived a scare when Lord Byron decided to chop it down but was prevented by a campaign of local people who 'hastened to ransom it from destruction'.[6]

Oak avenues were also part of the scenery in the early 18th century, with some of the grandest oaks growing between Welbeck and Worksop Manor. Another avenue led up to Welbeck from the south-east, along which was Charles I's 'Banqueting Dale'.

The emerging class of great landowners formed a powerful voice against some of the legal traditions of the Forest, which were in decline by 1700; 'with the accession of Queen Anne the courts began to doze and drift down the stream ... [the] reign saw a genial laxity in forest government'.[7] Isaac Knight of Langold complained that royal deer 'break into barns to get hay, and they eat and destroy all poor people's cabbages and carrots that live near the forest'.[8] In 1708 the lords met at Rufford[9] and complained to Queen Anne that there were too many red deer because the animals were protected, so that numbers increased from 300 to 900 just as farmland was nibbling away at the genuine forest. Landowners complained that the animals were eating crops as far north as Hatfield, causing 'infinite oppression, injury and loss'.[10] They wanted an Act of Parliament 'to get forest boundaries correctly indicated', arguing that the Crown really had no territory since 'all those woods which belonged to your said forest being, by your predecessors, given or granted away'. A punishment of up to 12 months' imprisonment for anyone killing a deer within the Forest had been introduced in the previous reign, but no-one actually knew where the Forest began and ended. The landowners claimed that the situation had been made worse by the deputy warden whose new keepers 'terrified' the farm people. They complained, 'Unless we have the limits of the Forest ascertained we shall have such a clog and burden upon our estates that our posterity will never be able to shake off'.[11]

29   *The famous 'Duke's Walking Stick' in Welbeck Park. (Nottinghamshire County Council)*

According to Bailey, the petition 'does not appear to have been well received by Her Majesty's ministers' because the landowners had acquired their property with full knowledge of the forest rights. The House of Commons rejected the petition and the Crown employed four forest keepers and four deputies to protect the animals on which it undoubtedly lost money – winter hay had to be bought in at a cost of £100. One of the suggested solutions was to create a restricted park for them. From 1708, however, landowners on the northern edge, or 'purlieus', of the Forest were permitted to kill deer in 'fair chase'.

Bailey, writing over 150 years later, was scathing about these protests. He drew a parallel between what was happening in 1708 and what happened in the early 19th century under the game laws; these allowed the game birds of a landowner to eat the crops of a tenant. Bailey pointed out that those who enjoyed the game privilege in the 1800s were the descendants of those who complained so bitterly about royal deer in the 1700s!

The deer were also attractive to poachers. After a spate of poaching in Hampshire, the so-called 'Black Act' was passed in 1723 which threatened savage punishment on anyone caught poaching deer in 'a forest, chase, park or enclosed ground'. There seem to have been few cases in Nottinghamshire and no executions. Although the ancient traditions of justices in eyre and swanimote courts still existed, they rarely, if ever, functioned properly and had been discredited by the abuses of Charles I. In 1795, Portland was Lord Lieutenant, Steward,

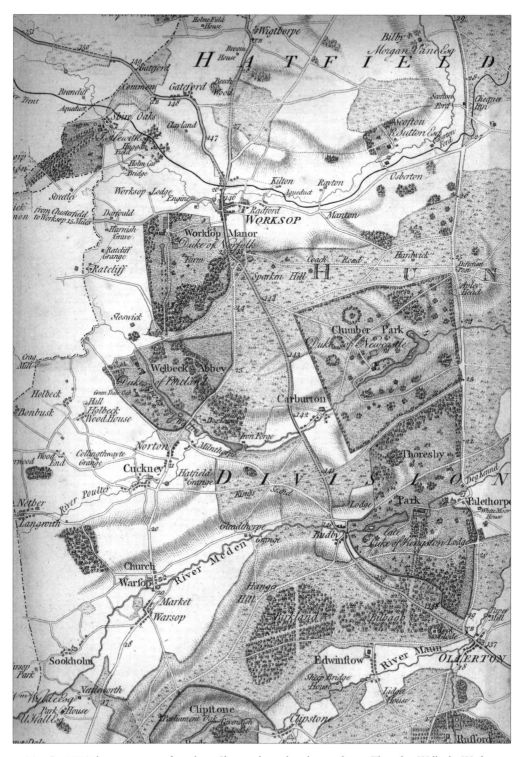

30   *By 1776 the annexation of northern Sherwood was largely complete – Thoresby, Welbeck, Worksop Manor and Clumber were barely separated by any open land. Note the iron forge at Carburton and the house at Cockglode.*

Keeper and Guardian of Sherwood and the park of Folewood. In 1809, parliamentary commissioners found the swanimote to be largely ineffective despite the parallel laws – statute and forest – that still existed.

Newcastle decided that keeping Nottingham Park stocked was uneconomic. In 1717 the remaining deer were sold off and for later hunts they were bought in for the occasion.[12] The stripping of this unusual part of Sherwood Forest included the sale of the old fishponds for use as a reservoir by a water company in about 1720, though they were later filled in. The Company of Proprietors of Nottingham Waterworks, formed in 1696, pumped water from the River Leen to a site on the ancient postern near to what became the General Hospital.[13] Rodgers reports that the old fishpond site was parcelled out for gardens in 1792.

31   *This map of the early 1800s clearly shows how the Thoresby and Clumber estates carved up much of Sherwood, leaving only fragments unclaimed by this time. (Nottinghamshire County Council)*

By 1770 the wild deer were confined to parts of Bilhagh and Birkland, but by 1793 there were none except in Thorneywood. According to the Rev. J Cox, the deer were killed off by local people with the connivance of Newcastle and Kingston – whose farmland increased in value as a result. Crops no longer needed guarding from hungry animals with horns and fires. Deer were still considered an ornament to a gentleman's estate and there were deer parks at Thoresby, Welbeck, Rufford, Annesley and Wollaton. Even these declined and when Robert Thoroton visited Bestwood before publishing his history in 1797, he found 'much of it ploughed so there is scarce any wood or venison, which is also likely to be the fate of the whole Forest of Sherwood'.[14] Farmers and landowners took significant portions. Newcastle, as 'Justice in eyre', was asked by the people of Market Warsop to allow a 400-acre breck for a period of seven years.[15]

The leading families were being paid to protect Sherwood but they were also the Forests clearest enemy. When challenged by the forest laws, the big landowner could 'afford without difficulty to find his recognisances and could then continue his offence with impunity'.[16] They were encouraged by John Musters' success in grabbing control of much of Thorneywood Chase in 1675. Newcastle, as Lord Warden, claimed considerable amounts in 1703 to cover costs such as the deer, wardens, keepers and fodder; the surveyor general of woods and forests paid him £366 a year from 1703 to 1707. Additionally, he had the rights to ten brace a year of royal deer, but asked for an increase and was allowed 15 brace from 1708. His successors continued to claim these for years to come.

The problem was made worse by the lower officials. Verderers were usually substantial farmers who were unlikely to prosecute each other. Attempts to revive the swanimote courts in 1717 were doomed and the new officials by the end of the 1700s were the gamekeepers and estate workers who displayed markedly different attitudes to visitors and travellers, as John Throsby discovered:

> I cannot help remarking here that, in [Clumber] park, the stranger is accommodated at every crossroad with an excellent direction-post; in Thoresby park such posts appear, but for some reason they have lately had boards nailed over the inscriptions, they therefore are as intelligent as a dumb man; in Welbec park you may get into a road, which a man might expect would lead him out of the park, but at the end of which one of these unfriendly gentlemen presents you with his broad face and angerly says, *No road this way*.[17]

This privatisation of Sherwood was the result of what Bailey described as 'infamous abuses allowed by a profligate government to be perpetrated on this branch of the national revenue'. E.P. Thompson agreed, referring to Newcastle as a 'great predator' and reporting his activities as much worse than those of a poacher. The trailblazer in northern Sherwood was the Earl of Kingston, who in 1706 decided that it would be nice to have a 'ride' through the woods of Bilhagh to his mansion at Thoresby. This involved Crown property, on which some trees rather inconveniently stood. Having got the land off the Crown, Kingston then charged the Crown for removing its own timber, worth £385. Instead of making a profit, the Crown found itself paying various sums including £183 for keepers to supervise the tree cutting, with the Treasury finally paying Kingston £23.

This was a great ruse, taken to a higher level by Newcastle. In 1707 the duke applied for a licence to make a deer park of 3,000 acres at his mansion of Clumber, and in 1709 followed this with an 80-yard 'broad riding way' through the Birkland woods that became known as 'the Duke's Ride'; both used some land previously belonging to the Crown estates. He took land back off tenants, enclosed ancient commons and levelled rabbit warrens. Creating the ride involved chopping down trees which then provided the timber for fencing the deer park – saving the duke an estimated £1,500. The duke, however, charged the nation £118 for the privilege of giving its own timber to him! He presented the deer park as a way of looking after the queen's deer for her, securing permits to enclose land both in and out of the Forest which he justified by saying that the deer park would be the queen's for her lifetime, and then revert to his own family in perpetuity.

He charged the nation £1,000 a year for employing keepers, largely for his own purposes, on land which had not been entirely his previously. Some was his own land, some was from the Forest but he also gained a considerable amount from that which had been common land used by local people.[18] In Bailey's view,

> The Duke thus contrived not only to obtain a park comprising 3000 acres of land, immediately contiguous to his own mansion, exonerated from all compensation due to the crown for the loss of its territorial rights over that large tract of land – not only procured it to be fenced in through its whole extent with valuable timber, the property of the nation, but, then, actually made these circumstances the main ground of a claim for a salary of *a thousand pounds a year*.[19]

Joseph Rodgers was far more obsequious in interpreting Newcastle's behaviour in creating Clumber Park. Using a memorial from John Holles, Duke of Newcastle, to Queen Anne as evidence, Rodgers argues that the making of Clumber Park was beneficial to the monarch. Written in 1707, the memorial asserts that the new park was 'for the enjoyment of her majesty during the whole course of her life, the improvement and ornament of the royal forest of Sherwood, also for the use of the proprietors and tenants of the adjacent land'. Rodgers believed that this was the reasoning for the duke's decision 'to enclose not less than three thousand acres of the duke's own land of inheritance'.[20] Another article, which leans rather heavily towards suggesting that the duke was acting for the good of his monarch (who was not known as a hunting woman) grudgingly suggests that 'Queen Anne's deer effectively became Newcastle's deer'. There was some exchange of stock between Clumber Park and Sherwood Forest:[21] in 1715 there were 1,069 red deer in the Forest, but by 1723 there were barely 400 left yet over 1,000 in Clumber Park.

Rodgers' view of the 'ride' was that it was cut through the queen's 'decayed wood' to provide the timber for the park's pale (or fence) and its buildings, but, as this would not be enough, 'his grace agreed to supply the deficiency from his own woods'. Newcastle also claimed £1,000 in expenses for constructing the park, to be paid quarterly from Michaelmas 1708, and appointed himself ranger of the park.

Bailey gives another example of the felling of trees which took place on the lordship of Edwinstowe. This manor had been held by the crown until the seventh year of Charles I, when it had been sold and then resold, ending up in the hands of the Newcastle family but without them having the right to the 'great trees' that stood on it. In 1707 the Treasury began a scheme to cut down trees worth £1,827 in order to bring in revenue, but the duke, as Lord Warden, raised various costs, including £1,089 to pay for six keepers and hay for the deer during the upheaval. The result for the Treasury was only £200 profit but, one suspects, rather more for the duke.

Newcastle's successor, Lord Harley, was still claiming a 1642 Cavendish right to cut timber in 1721, when he was accused of having royal deer in his park at Clumber. Deer were finally removed from Clumber after about 1760 and in 1793 the Commissioners of Land Revenue blamed the landowners for the loss of the deer, singling out Byron, Kingston and Portland by name. Newcastle used Haughton as his deer park and kept sheep at Clumber instead.

The 'tempestuous hurricane' of 1719 brought down hundreds of oaks, worth about £2,473 in timber. Many claims were then made to the chief justice in eyre in respect of rights to bark, tree tops and other parts leaving only £850 to the Treasury. Another £530 was deducted for various costs and then a fee to cover two deputies for a period of 800 days was levied at 4s. a day leaving precisely nil to the Treasury. A windfall indeed, but not for the owner of the trees!

It was not all destruction. Sir George Savile was commended by Daniel Defoe for planting 'a whole country' to allow Sherwood the future dignity of being 'cloathed in wood'. Savile planted 1,100 acres of land around Rufford, but he also enclosed and cultivated about 2,000 acres of forest land, which he divided into farms.[22]

When the Crown interests were wound up in 1786 it was found that the nation was rather surprisingly in debt to the tune of £10,500.[23] More recent writers have seen a clear link between the rise of the landed estates and the fall of the Royal Forest: 'local domination of these estates was greatly enhanced by the collapse of royal forest administration in the 18th century'.[24] When the parliamentary commission investigating the Crown lands visited Mansfield in 1792 they found much evidence of abuse and that 'the rights of the Crown had long been lost sight of'.[25] By this time the herds of royal deer had dwindled to a few fallow deer in Thorneywood.

Of the main houses, Rufford Abbey passed into the hands of the Saviles soon after dissolution. The Saviles were created earls of Halifax in 1682. When the 2nd Marquess of Halifax died in 1700 the peerage became extinct but the baronetcy continued and with it a tangle of financial liabilities. Legal battles continued for over 20 years and were not fully resolved until 1743.

George Savile was born in 1678. His father, the rector of Thornhill, was in the role commonly reserved for poor relatives of a landed family. The 2nd Marquess of Halifax's death in 1700 brought an end to the line of the family descended from Sir George Savile, the 1st Baronet, and his first wife; George Savile was descended from the second wife. The baronetcy initially went to a bachelor, John Savile, until 1704, but the bulk of the money, about £6,000 a year, went to George. The only catch to this was that money had to be found to support the weddings of the 2nd Marquess's four daughters.[26]

Savile took up his country residence at Rufford. In 1722 he married Mary Pratt, an Irish girl reputedly the illegitimate daughter of the Earl of Shelburne; she was 16 and he was 44. Not all went well, however, as his father-in-law was meant to confer £10,000 on him as the marriage settlement but cheated him out of half of it and was arrested for embezzlement in 1725. His wife had an affair with William Levinz, a Nottinghamshire MP from Grove. By 1737 she was living with her mother and Lord Shelburne, her supposed father.

32   *Edward Harley, Earl of Oxford, contracted one of the key marriages in Sherwood history.*

Sir George died in 1743 and was buried back at Thornhill; one suspects that his great inheritance had never entirely brought him happiness. The Rufford estates were expanded in 1743 when the last of the Markhams of Ollerton died and their estates were bought.[27]

His son, also George, died in 1784 without male children. He was a defender of the rights of Catholics as a result of which he had a house burned down in the Gordon Riots. The line was therefore retraced through the 7th Baronet's daughter Barbara,[28] who had married Richard Lumley, 4th Earl of Scarbrough, in 1752. Richard and John Lumley assumed the surname of Savile in 1782, in accordance with the wishes of their uncle Sir George Savile (1726-84) of Rufford.

Sir Richard, the first of the Lumley-Saviles, inherited most of the estates in Nottinghamshire and Yorkshire, but some were left to the 8th Baronet's niece, Mrs Foljambe. In 1807 Sir Richard became Earl of Scarbrough and, because of a clause in the 8th Baronet's will, Rufford passed to the Rev. Sir John Lumley-Savile who in turn became 7th Earl of Scarbrough in 1832.

The Holles family were also on the ascendant. They were already well equipped with titles; John, Duke of Newcastle upon Tyne in 1702, was also Marquess and 3rd Earl of Clare, Baron Haughton of Haughton, Lord Lieutenant of Nottinghamshire and Lord Warden of Sherwood Forest. He was Lord of Edwinstowe, Clipstone, Mansfield, Mansfield Woodhouse, Sutton and Kirkby. His sister, Grace Holles, became the second wife of Baron Pelham of Laughton in Sussex, but John had no sons to maintain the family name despite being 'one of the richest men in the kingdom.'[29] Holles acquired property in Lincoln's Inn Fields as his London home in 1705; originally known as Powis House, this became Newcastle House and was conveniently close to the property at Clare Market. The house was inherited by Pelham, the Prime Minister, but later split into two houses after a fire. It was restored by Lutyens in 1930.[30]

As noted in the last chapter, John Holles decided not to leave the bulk of his estates to his daughter Henrietta, but to his nephew, Thomas Pelham. One of the conditions was that any subsequent generation inheriting the lands had to have, or assume, the name of Holles. Almost immediately, Thomas Pelham's own father began writing to him as 'Mr Holles'.

The Duchess of Newcastle, mother of the disinherited Henrietta, challenged the will because the lands she had brought into the marriage were now to go to others. Lord Pelham organised a defence on his son's behalf but the duchess refused to produce the documents proving that her husband had taken over the title to her lands until the court ordered the sequestering of her remaining estates. Her case was dismissed by the Lords in 1713; 'her cause … was so bad that not one Lord, Whig or Tory, opened his lips for her …', the Earl of Oxford wrote.[31] There remained some confusion, however, over which land came within the scope of the will through the marriage settlement, and which had remained the duchess' individual property. Pelham-Holles wanted a residence in the North and so demanded both Welbeck and Bolsover. On being refused, because these were old Cavendish properties, he demanded Nottingham Castle.

In the midst of the arguing, Henrietta married, against her mother's will, Lord Edward Harley at Wimpole in 1713, bringing with her a sizeable fortune[32] of £20,000 a year under the 1714 settlement as well as some of the scattered Cavendish estates, not including the Holles' land. The financial settlement was verified by a private Act of Parliament in 1719. Henrietta and the Harleys gained what had been Cavendish lands at the time of her grandfather, including Welbeck, while Pelham-Holles got timber off the Welbeck estate worth £10,000 and all the Holles' land.

The late duke had bought the manor of Tybourn, later St Marylebone, for £17,500 in 1710. Harley began the development of Cavendish Square and the streets around it in about 1715-8, previously part of Newcastle's Marylebone estate which subsequently passed to the Portlands through marriage. Many new streets were built to the north of Tybourn Road, which was renamed Oxford Street. Harley became Earl of Oxford in 1724. Further development took place in the 1780s in particular. If you seek a memorial to the Sherwood aristocracy, seek it here.[33]

The Cavendish-Harley side retained Welbeck and Bolsover and, through due process of marriages, eventually merged into the Portland dynasty. The Pelham-Holles faction retained the former Haughton estate, Nottingham Castle and a visible presence in Nottinghamshire that was eventually to flower at Clumber. The Pelham-Holles also controlled the parliamentary

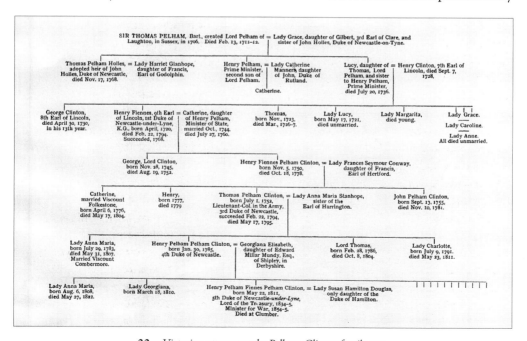

33   *Victorian attempt at the Pelham-Clinton family tree.*

boroughs in Yorkshire that underpinned their political ambitions. The two families retained some mutual distrust for at least a generation;[34] a siege at Haughton, a fight at Annesley, a number of duels and family feuds bear witness that the lords of Sherwood retained their traditional rivalries whilst marrying in and out of each other's families.

Thomas Pelham-Holles became Viscount Pelham and Earl of Clare in October 1714, and then Duke and Marquess of Newcastle upon Tyne[35] in November 1715 when the

34　*A map of London in the early 1830s showing the 'Sherwood' district. Working from west to east, the following associations can be identified: Stanhope Square, Bentinck Chapel, Oxford Street, Devonshire Street, Nottingham Street and Place, Henrietta Street, Bentinck Street, Bulstrode Street, Welbeck Street, Wigmore Street, Chesterfield Street, Devonshire Place, Wimpole Street, Harley Street, Mansfield Street, Titchfield Street, Cavendish Square (with Harcourt House), Portland Place, Great Portland Street, Clipstone Street and possibly others!*

ducal title was re-created. This was a reward for his support for King George I during his succession to the throne and during the 1715 Jacobite unrest. In 1717 he was appointed Lord Chamberlain of the Royal Household, a post he held for seven years. He was also steward, warden and keeper of Sherwood Forest and of the park, Fulwood. In 1718 he married Henrietta or 'Harriot' Godolphin, who brought him £20,000 but never an heir. Newcastle had land in 11 counties, a lucrative market rental in London, and an annual income of about

£27,000 of which £7,000 came from Nottinghamshire. His favourite home was Halland in Sussex, where he had a deer park, and his favourite hunting lodge was in the same county. In the North he only had Nottingham Castle, which did not fit the bill of a gentleman's country home.[36] In about 1716 he bought Claremont, which was near Esher and gave him a country seat near to 'town'; his brother bought Esher Place nearby.

Newcastle sent Sir John Vanbrugh up to Nottingham to see what could be done with the castle. Vanbrugh reported that it was 'much better than it had been represented to him ... Upon the whole I think I may reasonably congratulate your Grace upon being Master of this Noble Dwelling'. Newcastle then decided to visit it at Christmas in 1718. His view was that it was 'in the main very Noble and pretty convenient'. Apart from at election times, however, he used it little, despite promising his wife that she would have the 'Snuggest Bed Chamber ever'.

Newcastle was 'a paragon of economic irrationality'.[37] He was in severe financial trouble by 1737 and remained there for most of his life. His sins, however, were less conspicuous than many of the other Dukeries nobility:

> He avoided the sins of the flesh, he gambled only socially, he drank moderately except at election entertainments or great celebrations and he consciously sought to avoid viciousness in his relationships with his fellow men ... He was surely the strangest man in public life in 18th-century England, and his eccentricities may well have helped him escape the added charge of dullness.[38]

He impressed others with his oddness. One contemporary noted his 'notorious insincerity ... and servility', which others interpreted as a desire to be liked; everyone agreed he did a lot of grinning, hugging and embracing.

The duke spent energetically on his homes and politics. In 1718 he was refurbishing Nottingham Castle and in 1721 he was down on the election trail in Sussex, spending and drinking copiously. As a political man, he liked

London; he was certainly not at home in Sherwood. In a way, his main home was Newcastle House in Lincoln's Inn Fields, which was also the centre for his business interests. He spent regularly to nurse the political interest in 'his' boroughs, having some in Sussex, Yorkshire and Nottinghamshire. Voters in Nottingham were offered 1s. each to vote for his candidates in 1715. In this election there was the galling defeat of one of his nominees by a member from the dowager duchess's faction.

The election of 1722 was especially costly for the duke who started to make soundings about appointments to lucrative government posts under Walpole. His appointment to be Secretary of State for the Southern Department in 1724, with a salary of £5,680, was at least a partial reward for his financial sacrifice in the Whig cause.

By 1725 Newcastle was a distinguished man both politically and as a landowner but he was not a businessman. He employed John Bristowe as keeper of Clumber Park, but by 1746 the Nottinghamshire estate was a financial drain and Bristowe owed it £2,600 himself. It was necessary by 1738 to set up a trust to protect the estate from creditors. He began selling off large chunks of the Lincolnshire estate, and in 1752 he borrowed £20,000 on the security of his Nottinghamshire estates. At the time he had colossal debts of about £66,000 with an annual income of about £11,000 which put a strain on his relationship with his brother Henry who was much more careful.

His brother Henry Pelham became an MP for Seaford in Sussex in 1717, and sat for Sussex from 1722 to his death in 1754. He became first secretary for war in 1724 and then paymaster-general in 1730, which conferred a higher salary; Pelham was in many ways a 'professional' politician but he generally avoided charges of open corruption and history has judged him well. He succeeded Wilmington as Prime Minister in 1743. Pelham gained peace with France, reformed national finances and moved the country to the Gregorian calendar so that new years henceforth started on 1 January instead of 25 March.

The relationship between Pelham and Newcastle was not always smooth, but they promoted the Marriage Act of 1753 together whereby banns of marriage had to be read publicly before a couple could marry, and an age of consent for marriage was established. Supposedly this arose from the 'public breakfast balls' which were notorious for encouraging promiscuity: at one of these, Pelham's sister had become involved with the highwayman Maclane. Henry Pelham married Lady Catherine Manners, the daughter of the Duke of Rutland, in 1726. It was a marriage of affection and the couple had apparently been living on intimate terms. Through her wealth he was able to acquire significant estates in Lincolnshire.

Pelham died suddenly in 1754 whilst still Prime Minister, having 'eaten too much and exercised too little'. He was succeeded by his brother, the Duke of Newcastle, though he was considered 'greatly inferior as a statesman'.[39] Newcastle had enjoyed a prominent role in foreign affairs in the 1740s and in 1749, and had been elected Chancellor of Cambridge University.[40] He resigned office in 1756 but returned as First Lord of the Treasury in 1757 in partnership with Pitt, until dismissed by George III in 1762. In consequence of his opposition to the government, he lost his two lord lieutenant titles in 1762-3 but regained the Nottinghamshire title in 1765. He regained office as Lord Privy Seal from 1765 to 1766, but was becoming ill and retired from office.

The duke financed his extravagances by mortgages on Claremont and Newcastle House, both of which were 'called in' by his bankers in 1759; only the support of Lord Clive saved him from embarrassment. As 'Prime Minister' his salary dropped and he had to spend heavily to celebrate his own armed forces' military triumphs. The coronation of a new king, young George III, in 1761, followed by his marriage, cost him dearly. He died in 1768 without any male descendants; Horace Walpole wrote that, 'There was no expense to which he was not addicted, but generosity. His houses, gardens, table, and equipage, swallowed immense treasures: the sums he owed were only exceeded by those he wasted'.[41]

To prevent the 'Newcastle' title dying out again after his death, Thomas had been made 1st Duke of Newcastle under Lyne in 1756 as this title could be conferred upon a nephew. Thus for three years until his death, Thomas was the Duke of Newcastle twice over! The Newcastle under Lyne title passed to Henry Clinton, the son-in-law of his brother Henry. Henry's daughter, Catherine, had married her cousin Henry Clinton, who was Earl of Lincoln and also a Holles nephew, in 1744. This was a 'dynastic marriage' to perpetuate the family names and consolidate their estates, and according to historian Ray Kelch,[42] it is unlikely Catherine had a free choice in the matter, even though Clinton was reputedly 'the most handsome man in England.' He already had a child by a mistress, and was said by some to have been a lover of Horace Walpole. Henry Clinton's own father, the 7th Earl of Lincoln, had died when he was about 18 and Newcastle had become his guardian. His older brother, the 8th Earl, died in 1730. The marriage to Newcastle's niece, the daughter of another uncle, kept the lands of both Pelham brothers and the titles within the Holles-Pelham family. The subsequent name of Holles-Pelham-Clinton accurately reflected the nature of the family as a sort of corporate amalgamation of dynastic enterprise. Henry Pelham-Clinton also benefited from the patronage of his uncles with some lucrative appointments, including that of Master of the Jewel Office and Controller of Customs at the port of London.

The new Earl of Lincoln initially followed the political influence of his uncles. The relationship was not always good, however, and in 1757 he had become estranged from Newcastle and William Pitt, clinging to offices which he owed to his erstwhile allies. Later he became a supporter of Pitt against Newcastle's wishes.[43] Catherine, the Countess of Lincoln, died in 1760. She had been a favourite of the old Duke of Newcastle and, without her, there was little emotional bond between the future duke and the existing one. Clinton had won the titles and the lands, and now he was free of any remaining dependence on his benefactor. In the election of 1768, the last for which the old duke was alive, he manipulated the properties he had been given at Newark by Newcastle against him. No doubt the old duke died soon afterwards with some regrets about the marriage into which he had persuaded his niece.

The death of the 1st Duke in 1768 re-orientated the Holles-Pelham-Clinton estates. Claremont, beloved of the 1st Duke, was promptly sold to one of his creditors. Thomas, Lord Pelham, bought another part of the Sussex estate. The 2nd Duke of Newcastle under Lyne took a much greater Nottinghamshire role than his predecessor. This was partly due to his property dealings. The Clintons brought their own properties into what was becoming almost an empire. The 7th Earl had inherited Oatlands Park in Surrey in 1716, together with much of the Bedford Levels in the Fens. Oatlands Park became the 9th Earl's favourite house, but he transferred his affections to Clumber after 1770. He sold Oatlands in 1788 and Clumber became the main family seat for 150 years. They still held Nottingham Castle and the Park, as well as Thurland Hall. In 1780 one acre of Nottingham Park was given for use as a new General Hospital.

Henry became a steward of Sherwood Forest and Lord Lieutenant of Nottinghamshire in 1768. He preferred sport and rural pursuits to political life; although he used the MPs under his control to support Pitt in forming a ministry, he was happier creating the Clumber spaniel by crossing a Basset hound with an Alpine spaniel.[44]

The 2nd Duke of Newcastle under Lyne died in 1794; Thomas, the 3rd Duke, died in 1795 after a brief parliamentary and military career, mainly in America. The 2nd Duke left most of his wealth to his grandson, Henry, the 4th Duke, who inherited the title in 1795 while still a minor and, because of this, the role of lord lieutenant passed to the 3rd Duke of Portland.

Henry Bentinck, the son of Hans William Bentinck, had been made the 1st Duke of Portland and Marquess of Titchfield in 1716 by George I, partly as a reward for his father's support.[45] Appointed as Governor of Jamaica in 1722, the climate killed him by 1726. The 2nd Duke of Portland, another William Bentinck, married Margaret Cavendish Harley in 1734 who was, most crucially, a Cavendish and Holles grandchild. She brought him to Welbeck, which became their favourite residence. It is also one of the ironies of the Dukeries history that the entire Bentinck-Harley-Holles group was involved in the development of London at this time. The Bentinck line had been granted a large area of Soho Fields in 1698 which was developed during the 1720s and 1730s, at the same time as the Cavendish descendants were developing Cavendish Square.

Portland's father-in-law was the 2nd Earl of Oxford, Edward Harley, who had married into the Cavendish line with Henrietta Holles, gaining some of the former Cavendish estates including Worksop and Welbeck. Despite great wealth Oxford incurred debts and had to sell off the Harley estate of Wimpole in 1740. A proportion of Harley's library had been inherited from the Duchess of Newcastle's collection at Welbeck,[46] but he spent prodigiously and cared little for financial management. Oxford left an enormous collection of books and manuscripts, some of which were sold by his widow to the British Museum in 1753 perhaps to finance the improvements she made at Welbeck after his death, on which she spent £40,000.[47]

Lady Margaret Cavendish Bentinck, née Harley, was the one surviving child of the 2nd Earl of Oxford and Henrietta Holles, and a key person in the Dukeries aristocracy. Here was a woman whose blood was almost a perfect combination: she was Cavendish, Harley and Holles, she married one of the rising Bentincks; she was connected to both Newcastle and Portland dynasties. In marriage she took the former Newcastle estates around Cavendish Square into the Portland line, so that the streets with the Cavendish name ended up with Bentinck owners. Being an only child, she was a great prize for marriage but her parents reportedly chose William Bentinck as a man unlikely to stray into vice.

The 2nd Duke of Portland and his wife lived at Bulstrode in Buckinghamshire as Welbeck remained the home of Henrietta, Lady Margaret's mother. At Bulstrode, where she stayed after her husband's death in 1762, Lady Margaret created a huge natural history and art collection. The herbarium she created formed part of the Kew collection. In 1784 she bought the Barberini Vase from Sir William Hamilton, a fabulous piece of Roman art made up of layers of deep blue and white glass decorated with classical scenes. This vase, later known as the 'Portland Vase', was sold after Lady Margaret died but later bought back by her son the 3rd Duke and loaned to the British Museum in 1810, where it was smashed in February 1845. William Lloyd, an Irish theatrical scene painter, admitted committing the crime when in a state of 'nervous excitement'. He was fined £3, although the vase was worth £1,600: it was painstakingly pieced back together. Lady Margaret died in 1785 and most of her art collection was sold, with the sale taking 38 days.

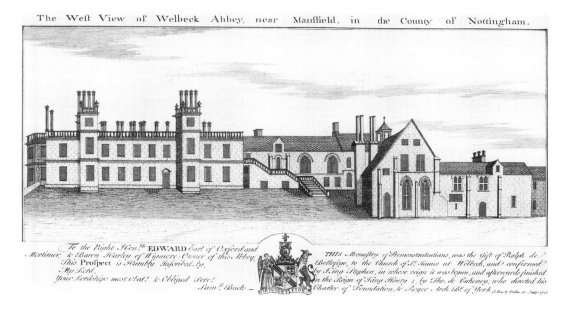

The Weſt View of Welbeck Abbey, near Manſfield, in the County of Nottingham.

To the Right Honble EDWARD Earl of Oxford and Mortimer, & Baron Harley of Wigmore Owner of this Abbey. This Proſpect is Humbly Inſcribed, by My Lord, Your Lordſhips moſt Obedt. & Obliged Servt. Saml. Buck.

THIS Monaſtry of Premonstratenſians, was the Gift of Ralph de Belleſiær, to the Church of St. James at Welbeck, and confirmed by King Stephen, in whoſe reign it was begun, and afterwards finished in the Reign of King Henry 2, by Tho. de Cukeney, who directed his Charter of Foundation, to Roger Arch Bp. of York.

35   *A view of Welbeck in 1726 by Samuel Buck. (Nottinghamshire County Council)*

Lady Henrietta's development of Welbeck created a family seat fit for a leading statesman. Her grandson, the 3rd Duke of Portland, William Cavendish-Bentinck, born in 1738, became Prime Minister and also married a Cavendish – Lady Dorothy, the daughter of the 4th Duke of Devonshire, who had also been Prime Minister. In 1801 he obtained royal permission to add the Cavendish name to his own. His grandmother, however, did not leave him with the wealth necessary for a political career – 'his estate, considering his rank, was not large, being encumbered with an immense jointure to his mother, the dowager'[48] – which kept him tightly restricted until her death.

William Cavendish-Bentinck opposed increased royal power and become a Whig. This damaged his relationship with his mother, who had an interest in much of the family estates, and he subsequently chose Welbeck as his main seat largely because it was the place where his mother was not. His London base was Burlington House. In politics he was aligned with his neighbour the Duke of Newcastle and with his Devonshire in-laws. He poured large amounts of money into elections, but rarely spoke in public, preferring to be seen as an organiser. His role in politics saw him dragged into a legal battle with Sir James Lowther over lands in the North West, which resulted in a bitter defeat. It took him ten costly years to win the lands back, but the struggle left his finances in tatters and much of the land in the North West had to be sold anyway. In 1772 he raised £80,000 by mortgaging some of the Soho estate. In 1783 he became Prime Minister as the head of an uneasy coalition before falling from power when the king engineered opposition in the Lords to his India Bill.

The death of his mother eased his financial worries and allowed a return to Burlington House. He sold parts of the Soho estate to fund Carr's improvements to Welbeck in 1792. In July 1794 the duke became Home Secretary under Pitt. The same year he replaced Newcastle as Recorder of Nottingham, holding a 'sumptuous entertainment' at Thurland Hall to celebrate. One of his efforts was to secure the Act of Union with Ireland. He left the Home Office in 1801 to be replaced by Thomas Pelham. He remained in the cabinet until 1806 when he became Prime Minister in 'the ministry of all the talents'. By this time he was old and ill, and found that the combined tasks of running the Treasury and keeping a group of misfit politicians together was too much for him. On 11 August 1809 he was taken seriously ill in his carriage. His ministry ended with the unprecedented disgrace of two of its leading ministers, Canning and Castlereagh, fighting a duel on Putney Heath. He died a few weeks later with debts of £500,000, totally overshadowing an income of about £17,000 a year. Rodgers sourly condemned him as 'not one of those ministers to be classed among the illustrious'. After his death, the family sold Bulstrode in 1810.

The third family of Sherwood, the Pierreponts, developed at Thoresby from 1633. Robert Pierrepont married Elizabeth Evelyn who brought him an estate in Wiltshire at West Dean. Evelyn Pierrepont was born at West Dean in about 1665, the second son; he became MP for East Retford in 1689 and 5th Earl of Kingston upon Hull in 1690. After this he accumulated titles and jobs which included being a Commissioner for the Union with Scotland in 1706. He held various roles in Nottinghamshire and Wiltshire, including that of Chief Justice in Eyre for north of the Trent. He later married Isabella, the daughter of the Earl of Portland. He became Marquess of Dorchester in 1706 and in 1715 was created 1st Duke of Kingston upon Hull. He died at Holme Pierrepont in 1726. One of the earl's daughters was Lady Mary, who became Lady Mary Wortley Montagu and a noted political hostess, poet and intellectual of her day; born in 1690, she died in 1765.

The 2nd Duke of Kingston went to Eton, after which he enjoyed the highs and lows of continental life by gambling and womanising. He acquired a French mistress, Marie-Therese de Fontaine de la Touche, whom he brought back to England in 1736 though he never married her and they separated in 1750. 1745 was a remarkable year for the duke, who gained some prestige by raising a regiment called Kingston's Light Horse to fight Bonnie Prince Charlie. He became a general in 1772.

Fire struck Thoresby Old Hall in 1745[49] and everything was lost except deeds, plate and some furniture, but the duke continued to live there in a 'makeshift residence'.[50] He employed John Carr to build a new house on the same 'rather low' site, which was finished by 1772 at a cost of £17,000. Thoresby was rebuilt during the time of the infamous Chudleigh marriage, and the ersatz duchess referred to it as an 'inchanted castle'. She has been credited with an influence in the construction of gardens 'in a German style'. The house at Thoresby received an unusual addition after Nelson's victory in the Battle of the Nile, when a pyramid was built in the grounds.[51] Holme Pierrepont was eventually relegated to the status of a dower house and then rented out.

In 1763 the Duke of Kingston was appointed Lord Lieutenant of Nottinghamshire. He was buried at Holme Pierrepont in 1773. As he had no male child, the Kingston title became extinct.

Kingston's marriage in 1769 to Elizabeth Chudleigh, who was 48, turned out to be one of the great scandals of a fairly scandalous age. In 1744, when she was about 18 years old, she had met and fallen in love with the Honourable Augustus Hervey of the renowned Bristol family, who was of a similar age. Hervey eventually became Earl of Bristol in 1775. Though neither possessed the customary fortune, they were encouraged into a secret midnight marriage by Miss Chudleigh's aunt. Virtually no-one knew of the marriage and they met only a few more times before Hervey's naval career took him far away. In 1769 the supposedly unmarried Miss Chudleigh married Kingston after a long relationship dating back to 1753 and the two seem to have enjoyed a good relationship, though it was openly discussed as bigamous.[52] The childless duke intended that his wife should be comfortable after his death until her own, and then the estates should pass to the second son of his sister Frances, who had married Philip Medows. The son was Charles, but his older brother Evelyn clearly felt spited by the will and challenged it amidst which the truth about Miss Chudleigh and Augustus Hervey emerged. Meanwhile The 2nd Duke's 'widow' was tried for bigamy by the House of Lords in April 1776. The only peer to pronounce her 'guilty erroneously, but not intentionally' was the 2nd Duke of Newcastle, Henry Pelham-Clinton.[53] She was found guilty but claimed a right as a peeress and was able to leave the country, spending the rest of her time in Russia and France. Having been forcibly returned to her earlier state, Miss Chudleigh openly called herself the Countess of Bristol but asked to be buried in the Pierrepont family tomb with her coffin chained to that of her second 'husband'. This was refused, perhaps fittingly as the 'Duchess' had only ever been to Holme Pierrepont once – and did not like it. Charles Medows was left well-positioned for a prosperous future.

36 *The scandal of Elizabeth Chudleigh attracted great press attention for its day. Here she is seen with her two 'husbands'. (National Portrait Gallery)*

A Sherwood estate that is often overlooked in importance is Bestwood, the home of
the dukes of St Albans. One member of the family was Lord Sidney Beauclerk, 'notorious
in his day as a fortune-hunter'.[54] He somehow managed to persuade Richard Topham, MP
for Windsor, to bequeath him all his money, taking his name in respect. Beauclerk showed
his inheritance as the great-grandson of Nell Gwynne and Charles II by being 'aristocratic,
idle and accomplished'. He built up a huge library which required Robert Adam to design
a space in which to keep it. Topham Beauclerk contributed to the family annals of scandal
through his marriage to Lady Diana Spencer[55] which took place two days after her divorce
from Viscount Bolingbroke. Lady Diana had left her husband in November 1766 and given
birth to a son 11 months later, leading her husband to assume she had committed adultery.
Fearing that the child could claim his estate, Bolingbroke was forced to take legal action
in 1768. The divorce required an Act of Parliament and much discussion by the House of
Lords. Before the divorce had gone through, Lady Diana had lost the first child and given
birth to two others, with another son arriving soon afterwards.

This profligacy was followed by a period of no progeny at all. The 3rd Duke of St
Albans, George, died in 1786 without children; the title passed to another line of the family
in George, the 4th Duke, who died in 1787 aged 28 and unmarried. At least the 5th Duke,
Aubrey, had seven children. Only the father of the 5th Duke, Admiral Vere Beauclerk (1740-
1802) achieved any standing through personal merit.

The Byrons developed renewed taste for adventure in the person of William who was
born in 1722 and who eventually became 5th Lord Byron. He enjoyed a brief naval career
after succeeding to the title in 1736, joining the *Falkland* when sixteen.

The Byron family manor of Bulwell was the cause of a famous dispute. William
Chaworth suggested in 1765 that the manor belonged rightfully to Sir Charles Sedley and not

37   *The impressive Palladian villa at Nuthall Temple, later to be home of a motorway!*

to the Byron family, although Bailey gives evidence that the argument was actually triggered by a quarrel over the preserving of game. Lord Byron challenged Chaworth to a duel as he believed his good name had been slighted. The duel was fought in a dark room within the *Star & Garter Tavern* and Chaworth was fatally wounded. Chaworth was brought home for burial at Annesley. It was alleged that Byron had acted unfairly and so he was tried for murder by his peers in Westminster Hall in April 1765. Byron was found guilty of manslaughter, but was let off under a legal technicality known as claiming 'the benefit of statute of Edward IV'. He went back to Newstead where 'he grew gloomy, morose and indulged in fits of passion that made him the theme of rural wonder'.[56] He reputedly once threw Lady Byron into the lake in a fit of anger. His profligate and licentious lifestyle incurred severe debts and, in a pattern that was to emerge more frequently by the end of the 19th century, the Byron family's hold on its estates was mortally wounded by overspending.

Lord Byron's children and his only grandson died before he did in 1798, so the succession depended on the line of his brother, Admiral John Byron. The Admiral's oldest son became 'Mad Jack' Byron. John Byron, to give him his proper name, led a colourful life; his first marriage was to the Marchioness of Carnarvon, who had been divorced from the Duke of Leeds. Their daughter, Augusta, married Colonel Leigh in 1807. The death of his first wife deprived Byron of £4,000 a year but he soon met and married Catherine Gordon, who had a fortune of £23,000. After spending much of the money in France, the couple returned to England where their son, George Gordon, the future poet, was born in Holles Street, London.

With a financial crisis ensuing, Mrs Byron returned to Scotland and lived frugally in Aberdeen with her son. John Byron visited to get some money before fleeing to France where he died. George Gordon became the next Lord Byron, inheriting perhaps the greatest financial muddle of any of the Dukeries estates. He was never able to repair the damage.

Another family worth mentioning is that of Sedley. William Sedley began the Sedleina Lectures at Oxford and was the first to be created a baronet. The most noteworthy member of the famiy was Sir Charles Sedley, who was responsible for the building of Nuthall Temple in 1754-7 on the renowned villa pattern developed by Palladio.

Much the most interesting denizen of the relatively modest Shireoaks Hall was Sir Thomas Hewet, who died in 1726. He became Surveyor General of Woods to William III and of Works to George I. These posts enabled him to make significant improvements to Shireoaks which included adding a costly banqueting hall and setting up a deer park. According to tradition he disinherited his only child, a girl, when she ran off with a fortune teller and the estate passed first to the Thornhaughs of Osberton and then to the Rev. John Hewet of Harthill. Shireoaks later became part of the Newcastle estates.

The Houses and Estates

These powerful and increasingly wealthy families set about developing the landscape and houses of the Sherwood area, creating the Dukeries as a result. Clumber had been acquired firstly by John Holles, the Duke of Newcastle upon Tyne. In 1708 the duke obtained 4,000 acres of Sherwood and this became a major project for the dynasty.

In 1770, after the park at Clumber was completed, work began on the construction of a suitable house under the direction of Stephen Wright for Henry Pelham-Clinton, the Duke of Newcastle.[57] Wright was well known to the Newcastles, who had employed him to build the 'Old Schools' at Cambridge University in 1754-8 and he had earlier worked at Oatlands in Surrey for the Earl of Lincoln. The sale of Oatlands probably helped cover the costs of developing Clumber, where the house cost £43,000. Work included the outbuildings and the great walled garden. The hothouses were the best that money could buy and varieties of grapes were brought from Welbeck to be grown there alongside the fashionable pineapple. Much investment was also made in replanting and landscaping the park of 4,000 acres between 1774 and 1789, with many water features and a large lake. The resulting house was felt by Throsby, in 1796, to be 'truly magnificent, although the building is neither lofty nor very extensive'.

The rebuilding of Welbeck was largely due to Henrietta, Countess of Oxford, who wanted to create a family estate for the Holles-Cavendish line. Works included a new south wing, the Oxford wing, the building of a new entrance hall and rebuilding of the west front. Also the creation of ersatz-medieval masterpieces such as the 'Gothic Hall', whose impressive ceiling still survives. Marble fireplaces were copied from her great-grandfather's Jacobean models at Bolsover Castle. She assembled an enormous collection of pictures reflecting her passion for ancestors and horses. Extensive planting and landscaping of the areas around the house took place and some of the 'waste' on the estate was converted into enclosed lands presumably in the hope of yielding a higher income.[58] Work continued at other times in the century, with some contributions from Humphry Repton in 1790 and John Carr in 1792 under the 3rd Duke of Portland. One of Repton's dislikes was a house that appeared to 'sit low' in its landscape and he solved this problem at Welbeck by burying the ground floor so that the house appeared to rest higher than it did in reality! At this time Welbeck acted as the

38   *A view of Clumber in 1781 showing Stephen Wright's buildings. (Nottinghamshire County Council)*

39   *Welbeck and its lake in about 1790 showing the substantial planted woodlands and lake, which was being extended at this time by the 3rd Duke of Portland. (Nottinghamshire County Council)*

family's 'summer house' but Bulstrode in Buckinghamshire was more convenient for shorter breaks[59] whilst Burlington House was the London home. The family's wealth depended on its estates in Marylebone, the value of which were boosted considerably in 1785 when local magistrates acted to close down houses of ill fame which were depressing rentals.

In 1722 the Duke of Kingston applied for permission to enclose 1,217 acres to enlarge Thoresby Park, which involved depriving villagers of their common rights. The park had been set up by the purchases of 1683 and already contained about 1,200 acres. Thoresby came to be the main house of the Kingston family and, by 1754, work on rebuilding after the 1745 fire was commencing; it was commented that the old house had been built in a bad site low down in the park and that the new one should be built somewhere better.[60] The new house was of brick and formed a 'bulky square'. Close up, a visitor would be impressed by 'the richness of the window frames over laid with gold, glittering in the sunshine'.[61] Charles Medows Pierrepont, later 1st Earl Manvers, employed Humphry Repton to landscape the grounds between 1788 and 1803 at a cost of £22,500.

Worksop Manor remained a significant house, with supposedly 500 rooms, and the 8th Duke of Norfolk lived there much of the time from about 1710. Its last great years were perhaps as the home of Edward Howard, 9th Duke of Norfolk, who preferred Worksop to Arundel. He and his wife spent two decades restoring the house. Ambitious landscaping work, including a 'canal', was in hand from 1720-2. North-west of the house there was a wood called the Menagerie where one of the duchesses had kept a collection of birds. The first menagerie was built in 1731 and a second added later. A new house had nearly been completed when fire broke out in 26 October 1761,[62] causing losses of up to £100,000. According to one report, the fire had been burning for two days before anyone noticed, destroying all except the chapel and part of the east wing. James Paine was commissioned, under the supervision of the Duchess of Norfolk, to build the replacement at a cost of £32,000 but only one wing was constructed and building was abandoned in 1767; the wing was later demolished in the 1840s when the Duke of Newcastle bought it for £375,000. The original plan had been a square block of four 300-foot frontages but the Duchess ordered work to stop when the duke's nephew and heir died of measles in 1767. Their house passed with the title to a distant relative, who became the 10th Duke.

Papplewick Hall was the domain of the Montagu family. In 1756 it was described as 'much improved' and overlooked the River Leen, 'a very pretty brook that runs briskly and forms two or three cascades'.[63] One of these, Rt Hon. Frederick Montagu, built the house in 1787 and created a series of plantations which he named after naval heroes – Vincent, Warren, Duncan, Howe and Nelson – between 1794 and 1798. He built a monument to George III near Papplewick Forest Farm and others to his poet friends Mason and Gray. He also built a new church in 1795. The hall was designed by the Adams brothers on the same site as the previous building.

William Mellish of Blyth (*c.*1710-91) married young widow Catherine Villareal in 1735, whose much older husband had been Joseph Villareal of Edwinstowe.[64] Both Catherine and Joseph were Jews of Portuguese origin, although she converted to Christianity after marrying Mellish, promting her cousin, Philip da Costa, to sue for breach of promise.[65] Mellish himself enjoyed a modest political career due to Newcastle's patronage, becoming MP for East Retford in 1741. William had seemed to cement the family fortunes by marrying a Jewish heiress, but he could only inherit on condition that he became an MP. In a story

40   *Papplewick Hall.*

that echoes Tristan and Isolde, Mellish is reputed to have bought two horses: a grey one to send back to his wife if he were elected, and a bay one if he were not. He was elected and so sent back a messenger on the grey horse, and apparently his wife was so overcome with excitement that she collapsed and died three days later.[66] Catherine's son William Villareal built the Edwinstowe farmhouse that still bears the name.

Cockglode was built in 1774 by Dr George Aldrich, who lived there until 1797, passing into the Foljambe line.

Sherwood continued to be reduced in size by the enclosure of its lands into private fields. This practice did not always involve unspoilt land; parts of Welbeck Park were turned into ploughland in the 1740s. Generally the land involved was 'waste' – rough grazing land, much used by villagers for their animals. Enclosure inevitably resulted in the major landowners taking a large share of this into their control, often through claiming rights as lord of the manor. Sir George Savile enclosed about 2,000 acres of 'forest' in the mid-1770s.

41   *The 'villa in the forest' at Cockglode eventually lost out to the Thoresby colliery slagheaps.*

Thorneywood Chase stretched across several parishes north of Nottingham. This had been royal land, but the Earl of Chesterfield claimed rights through ancestral links to the keepership of the Chase. In 1780 Chesterfield gained 500 acres of the Chase in the enclosure of Calverton and 750 more when Arnold was enclosed in 1790. Altogether he laid claim to 4,710 acres.[67] With the enclosure of the Chase, the Crown was to be compensated with one-fortieth of the land, but Chesterfield claimed twice as much in 1792.

Between 1789 and 1796 a succession of enclosure acts brought into cultivation former forest lands at Arnold, Basford, Sutton in Ashfield, Kirkby in Ashfield, Lenton and Radford, amounting to over 8,000 acres. The enclosures at Kirkby and Sutton in 1794-5 involved 1,900 acres of 'waste' and common land, most of which became the private property of the Duke of Portland, who promoted the Bills and happened to be Home Secretary at the time. As Lord of the Manor, Portland was awarded a quarter of the 'waste' and common. The Bolsover Enclosure Act of 1796 expressly awarded mineral rights to the Duke of Portland who soon afterwards became Prime Minister; it was later claimed that he had used his political influence for personal enrichment.

Other major enclosures included Gateford and Shireoaks in 1796, Worksop in 1803, and Annesley, Bilborough and Skegby in 1808. At Blidworth, 3,000 acres of 'waste' land was enclosed in 1809 in a move that had a severe impact on many local people. At Lambley only 600 acres remained to be enclosed in 1792, mostly coppices and waste at the edge of the parish.[68] In most cases the effect of this was to consolidate property in the hands of those who already had much, such as the Archbishopric of York at Blidworth. Chambers estimated that about 4,000 acres of Sherwood were enclosed by Acts during the 1700s and nearly another 10,000 during the 1800s – this was mainly done by 1815. Clumber Park became 2,000 acres of arable farmland plus pasture for 3,000 or so sheep, while Newstead was made into three farms in 1794. An agricultural survey in 1798 found there were 7,197 acres of parkland in Sherwood, comprising 23 different parks. Its author, Lowe, found only two open areas left: between Rufford and Mansfield, and between Blidworth and Newstead; both these were 'rabbit warrens'. All this ended Sherwood's life as a 'royal' forest; by 1800 the Crown held only small areas in Bilhagh and Birkland. One enthusiastic advocate of enclosure was Charles Medows Pierrepont, who was active from the 1780s until just before his death in 1816; he and his sons were involved in nearly sixty enclosure acts.

On the fringes of Sherwood there were several villages that were enclosed very late and one of these, Laxton, has never been fully enclosed at all; its claim to be the last 'unenclosed' village is surely limited by the fact that fewer than 500 acres remain unenclosed. Egmanton and Walesby were not enclosed until 1821, Boughton and Wellow followed in 1871 and some parts of Eakring remained 'open' even longer. All of these villages were on the Keuper marl at the Forest's eastern edge.

The enclosures brought to an end the forest tradition of 'brecks'. These temporary enclosures of forest land could be used in common for sheep and cattle but also by the king's deer. A breck might be between 40 and 250 acres and was usually kept as tillage for about five years, after which it reverted to forest land. Permission was needed from the lord of the manor and brecks were inspected by two verderers with reports to the lord chief justice in eyre, though the tradition seems to have died out by about 1798.

Thoroton's history in 1795 recorded the last rites as farming ensnared the remaining forest: 'Population in many instances, and avarice in others, have laid the splendour of nature in the dust; here grandeur and sublimity is prostrate, degraded by culture, and lost … for ever.'[69]

In later years there emerged a view that the Nottinghamshire aristocracy enriched themselves during the 18th century at the expense of others. One of these 'others' was the Crown itself and, in a new attitude of frugal enquiry under the influence of William Huskisson, commissioners investigated the parlous state of the royal estates in 1830. They found that the Crown's Sherwood estate of 95,000 acres managed to lose £9,037 between 1760 and 1786 'owing to mismanagement'. They were concerned that Portland sold the 'perpetual advowson' of the Parish of St Marylebone in London to the Crown in exchange for £40,000 and the Crown rights to lands in Birkland and Bilhagh. The St Marylebone interest ought to have made a profit of £2,000 a year, but turned out to be encumbered with repair costs for various chapels amounting to a further £10,000. This shabby deal was sanctioned by an Act of Parliament, the clear inference being that Portland had used his political powers to his own financial advantage. Huskisson also noted that the Crown's remaining rights in Sherwood depended on the value of deer, 'and there was not a deer in it, so that the right was worth no more than waste paper'. Huskisson responded by organising the enclosure of the remaining lands and appointing a land agent to represent Crown interests.

Charges that the great estates had been built on robbery resurfaced in the early 20th century. In 1909 *The Times* reported allegations that 'the Bentincks even robbed the Crown by seizing the Royal Forest of Sherwood'. Arthur Markham MP was said to be one of the accusers, as was Sir James Yoxall who alleged that the Duke of Portland had got himself appointed ranger so that he could 'filch 60,000 acres from the people of the County'. This stung the trustees of the Portland estate into action, their argument being that the Sherwood lands had actually come to the 2nd Duke in 1755 when they had been inherited by his wife, Lady Margaret Harley. The trustees claimed that the Portlands had only gained 930 acres from the Crown in the early 1800s, paying £35,000. Interestingly, this debate coincided closely with the publication of Joseph Rodgers' *The Scenery of Sherwood Forest* in 1908, and Rodgers wrote a prominent defence of the Newcastle side at least; his reference to Clumber Park that 'it is said now to contain about four thousand acres, but there is little evidence remaining that it once constituted a part of Sherwood Forest'[70] stretches credulity a little too far. He was much more critical of the Portland side, saying that they had taken over Lyndhurst Wood and No Man's Wood without any evidence that they had been granted by the Crown; Portland's defence to the commission in 1792 was that the family had been allowed use of the land for so long that they could claim it under an act of George III.[71] Rodgers states that Portland agreed a compromise of paying the Crown £100 an acre, but that there was no evidence the money was ever paid, although the oaks on the land alone were worth £17,000. Some of this land was later swapped with Manvers.

Arthur Markham replied to the Portland defence, saying that he had not alleged theft from the Crown, but theft from the common people. Markham said that the Portlands had effectively stolen huge areas of common land from the people through the enclosures and were now benefiting from vast mining incomes which were not rightfully theirs.

Many of the landowners played a prominent role in national politics through the House of Lords, but they also depended on a local power base of members elected to the House of Commons. The electoral system included 'boroughs', electing usually one or two MPs, some of which contained very small electorates and could be 'bought', since there was no secret ballot.

The MPs for Newark usually reflected the interests of the Newcastle family from Clumber or the dukes of Rutland, the Manners, from Belvoir. The Kelham interest also held sway there; Thomas Manners Sutton stood in 1796 while Lord William Bentinck and Evelyn Pierrepont were elected as MPs for the county.

The Newcastles spent heavily in 1776 and 1778 to ensure the election of their candidates in Nottinghamshire, Newark, East Retford and Nottingham itself. Charles Medows Pierrepont became MP for Nottinghamshire in 1778 with the support of Newcastle. In 1796 one of the duke's candidates lost at East Retford, 'outbid in price for the sweet voices of the freemen'.[72] The Corporation, knowing which side the bread was buttered, voted in an extra 38 freemen who could be relied on to vote for the duke – even if he was a child. As a result, a London banker named Bowles brought a case to have the appointing of freemen made illegal, for it was said that a man could sell his two votes for 150 guineas. So the election of 1802 was bitterly contested by two of the duke's candidates and two independents, including Bowles, but the duke's men still won. Thomas Highams was elected in 1806, reputedly after the highest ever expenditure, but then lost his seat only eight months later.

Many of the Sherwood settlements were very poor but only glimpses of the conditions can be gained. For example, a workman making a tomb in Blidworth church in September 1736 undermined a pillar, causing the collapse of part of the building because the church was 'in a very ruinous condition' at the time, thus suggesting the poverty of its parishioners.[73] The poorer classes mattered most when they were angry, for then they threatened the security of the gentry. One such occasion was the attempt in 1757 to put the new Militia Act into practice, which would have meant unpopular military service for many. The Nottinghamshire deputy lieutenants met at Mansfield, only to be greeted by a baying mob of 500 or so who destroyed the rooms in which they were assembled. Some of the gentry, including Sir George

42   *The Castle Mill at Papplewick was built in about 1782 and was involved in a costly legal battle with Lord Byron over access to water. (Nottinghamshire County Council)*

Savile, were 'shamefully maltreated'. Rather than endure this treatment again in 1759, the gentry opted to pay a fine, so the county had no militia until 1775.

The 18th century also saw the rapid growth of the hosiery industry. This was partly due to the success of William Lee's knitting frame, with 8,000 frames active in the region by 1714; the principle was taken up and developed by Strutt, Hargreaves and Arkwright, three great inventors of the era. By the end of the 1700s the banks of the Leen, Meden and Dover Beck were 'dotted with the new cotton and worsted factories' and there were at least 700 hand-frames in Mansfield alone.[74] Robinson's mill at Papplewick was the first to adopt a Watt rotary steam engine in 1785[75] to power Arkwright frames, although it probably still depended primarily on water power. Another engine was installed at Linby Mill in 1791. Both mills seem to have depended on a supply of pauper children from London and a lodging house was built for them. By 1794 there were also mills at Arnold, Basford, Cuckney, Langwith, Mansfield, Pleasley and Worksop within the Sherwood region. However, it has been claimed that the first cotton mill at Cuckney was burned down in 1792 'by a careless boy'.[76]

The best known mill was possibly the mill at the head of Papplewick Dam, known as Linby, Castle or Top Mill, and built in an entertaining Gothic style. Its owner, Robinson, fought a legal battle against Byron over control of the water with dark allegations about deliberate flooding.

The coal trade was increasingly significant in the south-west of the district, but the related glass industry fared less well. Sir John Molyneaux was also constructing a drainage sough towards Hucknall Huthwaite in 1703, and financial support from the Duke of Newcastle was eventually forthcoming. It was completed in about 1774 with support from the Duke of Devonshire[77] and extended to five miles. Newcastle also had control of a mine at Brinsley with a Mr Savile.

Most landowners were content to lease mineral rights to local entrepreneurs who would take the risk and worry for them. Thus in 1726 John Fletcher took a 99-year lease from Sir Robert Sutton to work for coal in Greasley whilst in 1738 Ralph Edge, lord of the manor, let leases for coal in Strelley and Bilborough.[78]

Eighteenth-century improvements included the spread of schooling. Much was due to endowments such as that by John Bellamy of Edwinstowe who left some money in 1714[79] by which the children of 'poor, honest and religious parents' could be educated. The school only had room for eight pupils until it was rebuilt by Earl Manvers in 1824.

This era also saw the vast improvement of roads for the first time in over a thousand years. Those going from the North to the South had a choice between the Great North Road via Tuxford and the great highway from Nottingham through Sherwood to Worksop. Daniel Defoe, the novelist and traveller, much preferred the Sherwood route as 'it yields a hard and pleasant road for thirty miles together'. In 1787 a new turnpike road between Nottingham and Mansfield was completed on the current route, replacing the previous route via Papplewick. Other turnpikes followed, connecting Clowne to Budby and Mansfield to Worksop. An Act of 1806 authorised the improvement and turnpiking of roads connecting Mansfield, Southwell, Newark and Leadenham Hill in Lincolnshire. New bridges were added although the floods of 1795 removed a number of them, including that at Ollerton.

These improvements did not eradicate the hazards of crossing Sherwood. Throsby complained that 'you meet with a great variety of roads, branching here and there; handposts would be extremely useful to a stranger ... but rarely seen here'.[80] It could still be lonely and dangerous. One such time was in February 1771 when travellers were returning from Nottingham market in very cold, snowy weather. Ann Webster of Calverton left Nottingham at about 5pm on horseback with a neighbour. They stayed together until about a mile from her home where they separated. Two men, who had been sent out to meet Ann, went the wrong way. She never made it to her home; both woman and horse were found dead the next morning. At the same time Thomas Rhodes, who worked for William Chaworth of Annesley, and John Curtis were on the road to Mansfield with a team of horses when they met a footsoldier whose condition was rather desperate. They lent him a horse to get to safety, but their own horses then refused to move as they had lost their leader, with the result that both men died. On 13 January 1776 a man froze to death at Red Hill while returning to Papplewick and another woman was rescued from 'certain death' near the 'Hut' in Mansfield Forest and taken to Red Hill.

7

The Great Days of Land and Industry 1815-1901

The forests were brought under the control of the chief commissioners for woods and forests although the leading nobles could still expect the honours; the 4th Duke of Newcastle was appointed steward of Sherwood Forest in 1812. The Commission of Woods, Forests and Land Revenues replaced the surveyor general of forests in 1810; William Huskisson was the commissioner from 1814 to 1823 and Henry Pelham-Clinton, Earl of Lincoln, was commissioner from 1841 to 1846. Huskisson's enquiry in 1830 identified some abuses and eventually a New Inclosure Act was passed in 1850 to tidy matters up. At this time there was still some open land, so that travellers between Mansfield and Southwell 'pass for some miles through an open heath … a succession of undulating eminences, covered with short heath and shorter grass, and there some furze bushes, and occasionally a stunted oak'.[1]

The 'South Forest' at Edwinstowe was enclosed in 1818, out to King's Stand. Heathland between Creswell and Elmton in the north-west was not enclosed until 1850; most of it was then allotted to the owner of Barlborough Hall, who sold out to Portland and new farms such as Hazlemere were built. Wighay Common was not enclosed until 1855. Attempts to enclose Selston Common in 1877 resulted in riots and new fences were destroyed. A few open areas survived; Budby North and South forests were still unenclosed in 1853.

Enclosures and mechanisation created some victims and, in the 1830s, the setting fire to farm buildings and haystacks was widespread across the country under the name of 'Captain Swing'. Such incidents continued sporadically with an especially serious one in November 1845 when 14 haystacks were set on fire at Bestwood Park.

The gradual rise of agricultural prices in the first half of the century encouraged investment in farming in an era that became known as High Farming. In 1846 even 'poor forest land' at Edwinstowe was sold for £43 an acre when only £20 was expected.[2] Experiments with growing turnips manured by bones in the sandy soils near Clumber were initially successful in the 1820s, but by 1838 returns appeared to be declining.

In 1850 Clipstone was 'remarkable for its water meadows, the most gigantic improvement of its kind in England', financed by the Duke of Portland.[3] Four hundred acres of water meadow had been created in an arable farm of 2,000 acres using what had previously been a 'light sandy tract' of Sherwood. The waters were diverted to a higher level from where they could enrich the lower lands of the valley, which were used for Southdown sheep, in a scheme which cost £40,000;[4] the Duke of Portland hoped to create wealth from the sewage

43   *Map of Nottingham in the 1820s showing 'The Park', which was the former Castle deer park, and the rose growing area on Hunger Hill which reputedly inspired Britain's first 'rose show' in 1860. (Nottinghamshire County Council)*

of Mansfield. It was also claimed that estate improvements led to much of the old Clipstone royal 'palace' being knocked down in 1810. The boom did not last, though, and Portland reduced some of his rents by 29 per cent in 1850. Portland liked to be seen as a working farmer in a 'weather-beaten coat and huge leather shoes, extending above the knees.'[5]

44   *The clearance of forest allowed the growing of arable crops on soil that was to prove poor in the long term. Here the first tractor is being used at Black Hills Farm, Edwinstowe, c.1917-18. (Nottinghamshire County Council)*

By 1870 agricultural prices were falling. The Dukeries had much land that was of only limited or marginal value and were badly positioned to weather agricultural problems. By the 1880s families like the Newcastles were becoming sellers of land after centuries of acquiring it, but there were difficulties; the Duke of Leeds, who had an estate north-west of Worksop, could find no buyers.

Another unique type of 'agriculture' was rose-growing, especially on the clay or marl soils. In the 19th century the area north-east of Nottingham called Hunger Hill became especially noted for rose-growing which possibly began as a part-time activity of the Nottingham stockingers. By the early 1860s rose-growers began using glass frames. In April 1860, what was supposedly the first rose show in England was held in an inn at Hunger Hill.

Poaching remained a problem. Portland set aside some of his lands on the manors at Sutton in Ashfield, Mansfield Woodhouse, Clipstone and others for shooting; a 'committee of gentlemen' then formed an association in 1830, paying two gamekeepers and regulating

45   *At Clipstone a new watercourse was built to divert water at a higher level, from which it could irriagte the meadows below.*

the shooting. The landowners often combined forces against the poachers; in 1834 watchers employed by both Manvers and Portland were involved in a fight with armed men near Hanger Hill and three poachers were given prison sentences at Southwell. In November 1851 William Roberts, a Rufford keeper, was killed in a battle between four poachers

46   *Portland's famous water meadows can be seen in a pre-industrial landscape before the spread of coal-mining. (Nottinghamshire County Council).*

47   *The royal visit in 1881 was an occasion to celebrate the glories of Welbeck – largely forgotten for decades. The famous trees are shown and also how the grounds had been restored after the digging of the tunnels.*

and 10 keepers; the poachers included three framework knitters and a besom maker. The gamekeepers could also be the enemy of nature – an osprey with a five-foot wingspan was shot by a keeper at Clumber in 1825. The gentlemen's association was involved in a battle against poachers at Thieves Wood near Sutton in 1858. Ten men were convicted but convictions were reversed after a libel trial about doubtful testimony, although one of the men had nine previous convictions.

The Prince of Wales toured Clumber and Shireoaks in 1861; he also came by special train to Worksop to visit the Duke of Portland in November 1881 for four days of shooting. He was met by the Sherwood rangers and 54 of the Portland tenantry dressed up 'in hunting costume'. The prince enjoyed two days of shooting at Welbeck and more at Thoresby; this was hardly hunting, the prince favouring the mass slaughter by shot of slow moving, dull-witted birds. He visited areas such as Cuckney and Budby, enjoyed Welbeck's 'subterranean roadway', stayed in the Oxford wing, and delighted in the illumination of the riding school. This was lit with four chandeliers, each weighing a ton, and 2,000 gas jets. Another impressive feature was the library, divided into five chambers, and panelled.

Deer survived in parks, which were the subject of an important book published in 1892 by Joseph Whitaker of Rainworth Lodge. This book entitled, *A Descriptive List of the Deer Parks and Paddocks of England*, attempted a full survey of all the parks known to have existed. There were only 21 deer in the park at Rainworth, and Whitaker noted that Thoresby had the largest herd in the region with 630 deer and Welbeck, Rufford and Annesley only had between 200 and 400 deer.

48 *When this picture of Nottingham Park was taken in 1901 it was already becoming a mature estate, the fine houses shaded by trees.*

At its southern and western sides, the Forest was under threat from urban development and, in the case of Nottingham Park, this was a real end to its previous status. A few old trees survived: the Ravenshead, Pilgrim and Major Oaks were all known at this time and trees were still gaining names. The Major Oak is generally thought to have got its name from Major Rooke and may have also been known as the Queen's Oak and the Cockpen Tree, perhaps because its hollow trunk was used for breeding game cocks. Its fame was cemented by Tennyson, who enshrined it in *The Foresters* as the oak in which 12 people could shelter. The Simon Foster Oak, 'the finest oak in Birkland',[6] was named after an Edwinstowe man who exercised the rights of locals to gather bracken from the Forest and burn it – the ash could be sold for fertiliser. He also still used the right to pasture swine and reputedly sheltered under the tree that took his name until his death in about 1800. The Parliament Oak was still celebrated as the oldest tree in England with claims that it was 1,500 years old, and many

could still remember 'The Duke's Walking Stick', the tallest tree in Sherwood until it fell down. Others could recall Three Shire Oak, which stood at the junction of county boundaries in the west. Of unspoilt forest there was little. In 1853, Birkland, which belonged to Portland, was only 947 acres and Bilhagh, Manvers' property, covered only 540 acres.

The sale of the Byron family estates by the poet George Gordon, Lord Byron, was significant. The sale was condemned as 'an act alike morally and socially unjustifiable, unless under circumstances of the utmost urgent necessity'.[7] Newstead was sold for £94,500 in 1817.[8] In fact, similar circumstances were eventually to claim the other great estates and their aristocratic owners, few of whom survived unscathed far into the 20th centur.

George Gordon was the son of Captain John Byron and inherited Newstead and his title from his uncle. When the previous lord died in 1798, young Byron was brought south from Aberdeen and his mother took lodgings in Nottingham, as Newstead was rented out to Lord Grey de Ruthven. Byron got to know Newstead during his holidays from Harrow, also spending some of the time at Southwell where his mother lived. Lord Grey even allowed him the use of some rooms at the Abbey.[9] During this period Byron's first poems were printed by a firm from Newark. He began to live at Newstead in 1808, by which time 'he was far gone in everything dangerous and disreputable as a member of society'.[10]

At Newstead he fell in love with Mary Chaworth of Annesley Hall, but after he returned to Harrow she met Musters and Byron's happiness was lost. Years later, Washington Irving and Colonel Wildman made a pilgrimage to the spot where the legendary last parting of Byron and the affianced Mary Chaworth took place, celebrated in Byron's poem *Dream*:

> I saw two beings in the hues of youth
> Standing upon a hill, a gentle hill,
> Green, and of mild declivity, the last
> As 'twere the cape of a long ridge of such,
> Save that there was no sea to lave its base,
> But a most living landscape, and the wave
> Of woods and cornfields …

Irving was disappointed to find that the 'diadem of trees' that Byron referred to had gone. According to Rodgers, Musters cut the trees down as he did not like his wife being celebrated in the poems of such a disreputable character. Mary Chaworth insisted on keeping her name when marrying Musters, so the line became Chaworth Musters.

Byron lamented the poor state of repair of Newstead in verse:

> Through thy battlements, Newstead, the hollow winds whistle,
> Thou, the home of my fathers, art gone to decay;
> In thy once smiling gardens the hemlock and thistle
> Now choke up the roses that bloomed in the way.

Byron loved Newstead but could not afford it: 'I have now lived on the spot; I have fixed my heart upon it … but could I obtain in exchange for Newstead Abbey the first fortune in

49   *One of the famous 'named trees', the Simon the Foster tree, which grew in Sherwood over centuries. (Nottinghamshire County Council)*

50   *View of the romantic park at Newstead, where Byron briefly enjoyed some happy moments.*

the country, I would reject the proposition.'[11] Shortly after writing this he left England for two years. He visited only infrequently, but notoriously brought his half-sister Augusta there – they were said to be lovers. Byron attempted to sell Newstead from 1812 onwards. When it was 'sold' for £140,000 in 1813, the purchaser backed out and paid a forfeit of £25,000. Byron was left in a financial crisis despite the forfeit. He left Newstead in 1814, mainly living abroad from then on. Marriage to Arabella Milbanke in January 1815 started well, but after the birth of a daughter, named Augusta-Ada after Byron's half-sister, the couple separated. In 1817, he left England for the final time. Newstead was sold in 1818, then resold to Lt Col Wildman for £100,000 (or 90,000 guineas) who spent seven years repairing and rebuilding it. Byron died in Greece in 1824, but his body was returned to Nottingham where, according to Bailey, it was 'visited by many hundreds of people'[12] at the *Blackmoor's Head Inn*. The *Times* reported that 'vast numbers' watched the procession to Hucknall where Byrons 'poor black servant never took his eyes from the coffin, and bent his body that they should follow it to the last glimpse'.[13]

In 1860, Newstead came up for auction after Wildman's death. When it was visited by the American writer Washington Irving in the 1860s he found 'one of the finest specimens in existence of those quaint and romantic piles, half castle, half convent, which remain as ornaments of the olden times in England'.[14] Newstead passed to Mr Webb.

The nearby Annesley estate was held by the Chaworths. The Annesley family had achieved fame and fortune in Ireland, but their Nottinghamshire connections were mentioned in 1810 when the Countess of Annesley was tried for bigamy. Annesley was also visited by

Washington Irving who found the Hall a rambling pile, patched and pieced at various times'. Elderly Nanny Marsden opened the door to it's 'waste and empty halls'. She told Irving that Byron had been afraid to sleep there at first lest the ghosts of old Chaworths took vengeance on account of the family duel, but decided to use it's 'blue room' after being scared by a 'bogle' on the walk back to Newstead.

Newstead was not the only estate in trouble. The Hewet estate at Shireoaks had already seen its deer park converted into farmland and the house 'reduced to the condition of a farmhouse'.

In the Newcastle dynasty, the dominant figure of this era was the 4th Duke, Henry Pelham Fiennes Pelham-Clinton, who succeeded to the title as a minor in 1795. He was the son of Henry Fiennes Clinton, who had married the niece of the previous Duke of Newcastle. His social position was of great eminence, ranking only below the royal dukes as a member of the House of Lords. This social prestige was supported by great political influence; he had a controlling interest in the parliamentary boroughs of East Retford, Newark, Aldborough and Boroughbridge. His mother took initial charge of the finances and in 1802 began the development of the Park estate for housing, selling off plots of land at Standard Hill. Henry toured Europe during a brief peaceful interlude in 1802-3, but was trapped in France for four years when hostilities broke out again. He returned to England in 1806, showing little enthusiasm for foreign travel, and even less for radical politics from then on.

The traditionally stretched state of the Newcastle finances were buoyed by two decisions: a good marriage and the further development of the Park. Plans for the latter were well advanced by 1827 and building started in 1830. Nottingham Corporation did

51   *The Park at Nottingham had formally been the most southerly deer park of Sherwood, but by 1850 it was starting to be developed for housing. Land belonging to Newcastle, seen here, was progressively developed over the next 20 years to become the most fashionable residential area of Nottingham. (Nottinghamshire County Council)*

all they could to forestall the duke's attempts, although the benefits were felt by later generations. The duke sold Thurland Hall, which was demolished in 1829; but he retained the castle itself.

His position was helped by marriage to Georgiana Mundy of Shipley, Derbyshire, whereby in 1807 he gained a fortune of £190,000 and £12,000 a year. After 10 previous children, in 1822 the duchess gave birth to twins, Charles and Thomas, but died in childbirth aged only 33 at Clumber. After her death Newcastle became 'a manic depressive, prone in periods of euphoria to see himself as the saviour of his country and to take impetuous initiatives only subsequently to lapse into long periods of despondency and inaction'.[15]

With the capital, the duke consolidated his interests in Nottinghamshire. He acquired the Worksop Manor estate of 5,402 acres and Shireoaks of 3,783 acres[16] from the Duke of Norfolk in 1839 for £375,000[17] which, according to *The Times*, was because 'the entail was cut off'.[18] He felt this gave him 'the finest estate in England', although his obituary in *The Times* inferred that he made a number of 'not very fortunate purchases' of land and his estate was encumbered with a huge mortgage. Newcastle had no interest in living in the Worksop house, much of which was demolished in the 1840s, but it enabled him to increase the size of his landholdings. Stone from the house was used in rebuilding the church at Bothamsall, which he funded.[19] The estate included much of the town itself, out towards Welbeck as far as Sloswick, and Darfoulds and Harness Grove. In two years during the 1830s he spent £450,000 on Nottinghamshire land, most of it borrowed.

52   *The Newcastle mausoleum at Markham-Clinton during the interment of the 4th Duke in 1851.*

The smaller estate of Ranby Hall was bought by the Dowager Duchess of Newcastle in 1828; she used it as a home with her new husband, Lt Gen Sir Charles Crauford. The house was retained by the Pelham-Clinton family and in 1853 it was housing the unmarried daughters of the 4th Duke. Additional land around Ranby was bought by the 5th Duke. The house was used by the errant Countess of Lincoln, who referred to it as 'Hangby'.

53   *The Prince of Wales' arrival at Clumber in 1861.*

The Duke of Newcastle had the church at Markham Clinton built in 1832 with vaults underneath it for family interments, one of the first being his wife. There was also reinvestment in the house at Clumber, and Sir Charles Barry was commissioned to make improvements.

Newcastle was criticised for his political and religious opinions. He was disliked widely for his opposition to political reform and lost the Lord Lieutenant's post in 1839 because he opposed the appointment of nonconformist magistrates. He caught typhus in 1851 and is said to have almost suffered the Victorians' worst nightmare: being buried alive whilst in a coma. He died a few days later, however, and was buried at Markham Clinton. He left the Newcastle line in a poor financial state.

His will of August 1846 divided the family estates: all those bought from the Duke of Norfolk at Shireoaks and Worksop, plus Nottingham Park, were left to Lord Charles 'in tail male' or for life only; if no male children, they could revert to those of Thomas 'to the exclusion of any issue by his present wife'. The situation was made more complicated by the huge mortgages (£406,920) on these estates, so that some rights in them were sold off. The son of Lord Charles eventually brought a law suit over these properties, claiming the rights to them; this further drained the coffers with the result that the 7th Duke won the case in 1903, although the estates were held for life only.

The 5th Duke, Henry, was at least moderately successful in comparison. He was MP for Nottinghamshire in 1832-46 whilst Earl of Lincoln[20] and was also appointed Commissioner for Woods and Forests. Relations with his father had been strained since 1834; they fell out over Catholic emancipation and the Corn Laws issue. Henry was hounded out of his county seat by his father and took up a seat for Falkirk instead, which he held until 1851. His friend William Gladstone lost his place as MP for Newark and Lincoln firmly believed that he himself would be disinherited. He was appointed Secretary for Ireland in 1846 when he handled the famine relief effort. He made the mistake of taking the job of Secretary for War just before the outbreak of the Crimean War. Poor organisation was shown up famously by Florence Nightingale at Scutari. In January 1855 he sent 1,000 gallons of ale and 350 cases

54   *The famous lake at Clumber in 1861 with the miniature warship and boathouse.*

of preserved goods to the army; having left office, he spent two months in the Crimea itself. He regained the prestigious role of Lord Lieutenant in 1857 and this was an occasion for joyous celebration at Clumber, coinciding with his son, the Earl of Lincoln's 21st birthday. More than 500 of the county gentry attended a supper in January 1857, served at 12.30am with a 'grand boar's head' as the central dish. More than 300 horses had to be stabled there until gone 3am. The duke was lucky to survive the year for he set fire to his bedroom at Cavendish Square in December 1857. In 1858 he played a significant role as chairman of the Newcastle Commission on education. His management of the Colonial Office from 1852-4 and 1859-64 did not please Australian interests and Lord Stanley referred to him as 'a gentleman eminently fitted for private life'.[21]

In 1832 Henry, as Lord Lincoln, married Lady Susan Douglas-Hamilton, the granddaughter of William Beckford of Fonthill and daughter of the Duke of Hamilton; she was a dangerous combination of beauty and volatility. The first sign of scandal came in 1837, when a maid at Clumber handed Lord Lincoln a love letter written by his brother William to Lady Susan. Susan's reaction was hysterical, a tactic to avoid responsibility. In 1841 he described his wife's behaviour as 'a complete plan of moral assassination'.[22] He installed her and the children at Ranby and after a brief reconciliation she behaved indiscreetly in London before going to Gosport, where she was rumoured to have a lover. In August 1848 she left her husband and children for good and fell in love with Lord Horatio Walpole, later Earl of Orford, a notorious philanderer, with whom she eloped and had an illegitimate child. Although divorce was a costly and complex procedure involving an Act of Parliament, the Lincolns were divorced in 1850 after having five children.

The 5th Duke died suddenly in 1864, having appointed William Gladstone as one of the trustees of his estate. He was well-regarded, especially for providing decent houses at fair rents at Shireoaks. The duke's daughter bore her mother's name and, he feared, her temperament. She married the notorious Lord 'Dolly' Vane-Tempest, a man equally famous for drink and being supposedly 'mad', against her father's wishes. She was seduced by the Prince of Wales in 1867, bore him a daughter in 1871, and lived in comparative poverty after being discarded. Even greater scandal was to affect the family through their third son, Arthur, who had a brief career in the Royal Navy before becoming the MP for the 'family seat' of Newark in 1865. Lord Arthur was charged with the conspiracy to commit a felony, in this case sodomy, after being implicated with two men who dressed up as women and went by the names of 'Stella' and 'Fanny'. He died on 18 June 1870, the day before the trial was due to start, and many suspected suicide,[23] although there were later rumours he had fled to Canada.[24]

The 6th Duke was Henry. He was judged 'quite worthless' by Queen Victoria, and was so addicted to racing and gambling that he fled the country in 1860 with debts of £230,000,[25] becoming bankrupt again in 1869. One of the effects was that many Clumber staff lost their jobs. In 1861 he married Henrietta Hope, the heiress of Thomas Hope, which certainly delayed the Newcastles' financial ruin, although the bride's family never settled any of their wealth on her untrustworthy husband, who continued to gamble. 'It is thought that the young lady has been sold for a Ducal coronet,' Lady Londonderry commented. The Hopes had gained fabulous wealth as diamond dealers in Amsterdam; the Hope diamond of 44 carats had been bought by Miss Hope's grandfather for £18,000 and was later sold by her son for £120,000. This was allegedly a diamond acquired in India by a French explorer in about 1660, then stolen from the King of France during the revolution before resurfacing in London 20 years later. It was in possession of the Hopes by 1824 but caused a legal dispute between three brothers in 1839. Henrietta's son Henry inherited it in 1887. The Hopes had substantial estates around Dorking, which were left to Miss Hope's son Henry by his grandmother, but required court permission for any of them to be sold. The name of Hope was grafted onto all the other surnames. The duke separated from Henrietta in the early 1870s and he died in 1879.

55 *The 7th Duke showed his 'High Church' inclinations in his building projects which included a new church at Clumber Park.*

The 7th Duke, also Henry, inherited the estates and titles at the age of 15, but after a serious fall in childhood, which eventually led to his leg being amputated, he never really committed himself to public life. He was also very short, perhaps less than five feet. He stabilised the finances by selling some of the Worksop estate and also rebuilt the house after the fire of March 1879. This fire destroyed 18 rooms, a 'noble staircase' and 15 paintings that had only just arrived back from Burlington House. Some repairs to the house were made and a church was built in a 'High Church' style at Clumber in 1886-9. The duke also helped restore a 'Shrine of Our Lady' at Egmanton, gave land for the founding of Worksop College in 1887, and sold off his interests in a Newark brewery.

These were the last great days of Clumber. A miniature frigate, apparently weighing 60 tons, was installed on the lake; this was reputedly based on a model of a 'triumphal canoe' erected for the Prince of Wales during a tour of western Canada.[26] The remains of the frigate *Lincoln* can still be glimpsed beneath the Clumber waters.

By the 1880s estates based on farming were starting to struggle as food imports caused the fall of produce prices. In 1890, the Duke of Newcastle chose to sell off some of the Worksop Manor estate, which had only been acquired in 1838. The manor house and 1,644 acres sold slowly, with Nottingham brewer John Robinson taking the house for £30,000. Robinson was a brewer from Arnold who ran the Home Brewery in Daybrook, and his brother Samuel ran the Daybrook Laundry Company. Twenty farms, the estates of Manor Lodge and 735 acres of the Shireoaks Park estate were sold, raising £106,020. Robinson helps to illustrate the trend of the old aristocratic interests being replaced by new, and fairly transitory, industrial ones. Where Robinson in Worksop led, the Seely family and later the owners of the Raleigh followed.

56   *Though much reduced from its heyday in the 1600s, Worksop Manor was still substantial when Robinson took it over.*

57   *The Robinson brothers dominated Daybrook, one with a brewery and the other with Daybrook Laundry. (Nottinghamshire County Council)*

The Nuthall estate was bought by the Holden family. Captain Henry Holden became Chief Constable of Nottinghamshire. Colonel Robert Holden set aside a room of Nuthall Temple to distribute clothing, and occasionally food, to the poor.

The Rev. John Lumley-Savile, the 7th Earl of Scarbrough, was fortunate to succeed to the title in 1832, being only the fourth son of the 4th Earl, which perhaps explains his decision to seek a clerical career. He gained both Rufford and the estates at Sandbeck in Yorkshire, but was killed in a hunting accident at Markham Moor on 24 February 1835. He was succeeded by his son John Lumley-Savile, the 8th Earl, who had been born at Edwinstowe. He was maimed as a boy, supposedly through his father's violence. Before going to the Lords, Savile had been MP for Nottinghamshire and was also made Lord Lieutenant after the Duke of Newcastle was sacked for his famous 'offensive letter' to the Lord Chancellor in 1839. He was unconventional, and raised an illegitimate family by a woman 'of French origin'[27] known as 'Agnes Lumley', reputedly rescued from the Serpentine in London. He engaged Anthony Salvin to rebuild the Abbey at a cost of £13,000 from 1837-43, so that it had 111 rooms. He died in 1856.

The 8th Earl bequeathed Rufford and some Yorkshire estates to his second surviving son, Henry, who was a soldier. The Scarbrough title passed to Richard, Lord Savile of Tickhill Castle. Henry became a noted member of the racing fraternity and won the Derby with *Cremorne* in 1872 and the Ascot Cup in 1873. When Henry died, the estate passed to the fourth surviving son, Augustus, until his death in 1887, rather than to the next earl, Aldred.

The oldest surviving illegitimate son of John Lumley-Savile, the 8th Earl of Scarbrough, was John Savile Lumley. His career in the Foreign Office culminated in him being ambassador in Rome. He was interested in archaeology and some of his finds in Italy contributed to the

Savile Gallery in Nottingham Castle Museum in 1891. After the death of his half-brother Augustus in 1887 he gained Rufford, and following his retirement became 1st Baron Savile

of Rufford in 1889. He was very friendly with the Prince of Wales, who stayed at Rufford for the Doncaster races seven years in succession.[28] He improved Rufford, most notably in its art collections, and was a trustee of the National Gallery. He died at Rufford in 1896, without a wife or a child, and the estates passed to his nephew John Savile Lumley; his father, another of the illegitimate boys, was the Rev. Frederick Savile Lumley, rector of Bilsthorpe where Baron Savile was buried.

During the 19th century, Thoresby Hall gradually gained in status. At the start of the century the former Pierrepont interests were led by Charles Medows, the nephew of the 2nd and final Duke of Kingston. Having won most of the legal battles with the unfortunate Elizabeth Chudleigh, Medows changed his name to Pierrepont in 1788 and was engineered into the House of Commons at the behest of Newcastle where he became a supporter of Portland. This link was influential in his being created Viscount Newark in 1796 and 1st Earl Manvers in 1806. The Thoresby estate amounted to over 3,500 acres by 1853.[29]

58   Henry Savile, shown by Vanity Fair *in 1880, was most famous for his involvement in racing.*

The 1st Earl Manvers lived until nearly 80 and the title passed to his oldest surviving son, Charles, in 1816. Charles thus became 2nd Earl Manvers until his own death in 1860. The 1st Earl's daughter, Frances, married Admiral William Bentinck in a typical example of cross-Sherwood inter-marrying of the nobility.

59   *Scenes from Thoresby when the earl's oldest son, Lord Newark, reached the age of 21 in 1875.*

Thoresby was in a remote location and had no nearby church. The nearest settlement, Perlethorpe, was not a parish in its own right so Earl Manvers solved the problem by obtaining an Act of Parliament to establish it as a 'parochial chapelry' in 1836. The following year he endowed the living with £100 a year, and thus secured the right to appoint the vicar. It gained a fitting church in 1876 when Manvers brought in his architect, Salvin. The main access to the estate was via Ollerton Corner, where four lines of beech trees formed famous avenues. This access was later altered to Buck Gates after an exchange of land with the Duke of Portland.[30]

The old complaint about Thoresby's position continued; *White's* Directory thought it 'in an open but rather low situation'. The 3rd Earl Manvers engaged Anthony Salvin and William Burn to build a new Thoresby Hall in fabulous style and in a slightly higher position between 1864 and 1875; Manvers had perhaps seen the gloriously eccentric effort of Salvin's at Harlaxton, one of the great Victorian country houses, and perhaps wanted something similar. The old hall was demolished in 1873. This was the last period in which the Manvers family lived at Holme Pierrepont.

The Portlands largely succeeded in maintaining their estates at Welbeck. They had estates in London and a house at 11 St James's Square as well as Cavendish Square. A key moment for the Portlands and Sherwood was the transfer of remaining Crown lands in Sherwood to the Portlands in exchange for ecclesiastical rights in the parish of St Marylebone, London, which was served by four freehold private chapels and one leasehold. Sherwood transfers agreed in 1818 were not completed until 1828, and affected Cockglode. Portland then exchanged some lands with Earl Manvers, to provide a more consolidated Welbeck estate, although Portland retained the hay of Birkland.

60   *The resurgent splendour of Thoresby in its prime, photographed in 1901 after Salvin's rebuild.*

Lord William Henry Cavendish Bentinck (1774-1839), second son of the 3rd Duke, 'enjoyed a rakish life and consorted with dancers'.[31] He was governor of Madras in 1803 and later minister-plenipotentiary to the court of Sicily,[32] only to be recalled in disgrace in 1815. He returned to India as Governor-General from 1828 until 1835 and was more successful, Although he was unpopular for being an economiser, he tried to control extreme Hindu practices such as *sutte*, the self-immolation of widows on their husband's pyre. Back in

Britain he became a Glasgow MP, supplementing his income with appointments such as the 'clerkship of the pipe in the exchequer' which somehow yielded £1,131 a year.

His older brother the 4th Duke inherited the title in 1809, along with debts of £500,000; so he sold Bulstrode. He retained Harcourt House in Cavendish Square but sold some of the scattered estates. He was keenly interested in horseracing and his horse *Tiresias* won the St Leger in 1819. He married a rich woman, Henrietta Scott of Fife, with whom he had three daughters, and changed his name to Scott-Bentinck. Boosted by his wife's wealth, Portland acquired land and manorial rights in Cuckney and Langwith from Earl Bathurst in 1844, increasing his estate to 35,000 acres.[33] Portland maintained a proprietorial interest in 'his' villages; for example, Clipstone had no church so the drawing room of Park Farm was fitted out as a 'place of worship' in 1841, and the vicar of Edwinstowe was paid £50 a year for the inconvenience of providing a Sunday service there. Portland died aged 85 in 1854 at Welbeck, where he was justly celebrated by his tenants. His funeral was 'on the most limited, it may be said, meagre scale' in keeping with his

61   *Lord George Bentinck, portrayed at the time of his unexpected and dramatic death.*

wishes. Although he had asked to be buried in the churchyard at Bolsover, the family tomb was opened for the first time in 138 years and he was buried inside the church.

The 4th Duke's fifth child was 'Lord George', although his first name was also William. He was secretary to his uncle George Canning, then MP for Lyme Regis, for a period of about 20 years. He was the archetypal hunting MP, taking the 7am train out of London to go hunting at Andover, then returning to vote in the Chamber while still in his 'pink' coat.

Lord George was passionate about racing and was involved in betting, losing £30,000 betting on the St Leger in 1826. He shared a racing partnership with Charles Greville although the two fell out, possibly because Greville felt Bentinck's 'working' of the odds on his horses was close to dishonest, although Bentinck was generally a campaigner against corruption. He helped rebuild Goodwood and ran his own very large stable of horses, including the winner of the 1836 St Leger, *Elis*. He invented the practice of 'vanning' racehorses between courses to save wear and tear, but became most memorable for uncovering the scandal of *Running Rein* during the 1844 Derby when another horse, a year older, had been entered for the race for three-year-olds as part of a betting scam. Bentinck suspected a fraud from the outset and helped to bring it to court. With only a modest personal income, he relied on betting to finance the running of his stable: in 1845 he won £100,000, of which only £17,000 was actually prize money.

In April 1846 Lord George became leader of the Protectionist group in the Commons, a role for which he was wholly unprepared. It put him in direct opposition to Lord Lincoln, the Duke of Newcastle's son. In August 1846 he suddenly sold his whole racing establishment for only £10,000, when it was worth far more. One of his sales, *Surplice*, later won The Derby. For a short time he worked phenomenal hours in the political world.[34] He and Portland supported Benjamin Disraeli as a way of getting revenge on Peel over repeal of the Corn Laws. Disraeli was able to buy Hughenden, his country house, with loans from the Portland faction. Lord George's political leadership was largely a failure and he resigned in December 1847. In 1848 he witnessed both the triumph of horses that he had sold in the great races of the year and the collapse of his political career: 'He had nothing to console him, and nothing to sustain him except his pride,' wrote Disraeli.

He was only 45 years old when, on 21 September 1848, he suddenly dropped dead in Welbeck Park at Flood Meadow while on his way to dine with Earl Manvers at Thoresby. He was buried at St Marylebone, his death commemorated by ships on the Thames, and monuments were built in Mansfield Market Place, Cavendish Square and near to where he died.

The 5th Duke of Portland was John Cavendish Scott-Bentinck, born in 1800. When his brother died in 1824 he became Marquess of Titchfield and MP for Kings Lynn in keeping with family tradition. Due to ill health, he handed over his political career to his younger brother, George, and seems to have led a quiet life, except for the brief excitement of becoming the 5th Duke on the death of his father in 1854. He never married, having been rebuffed on several occasions. His greatest enthusiasm was for horses and the established church. A great rider in his youth, he had space for 100 horses in his stables and built a new riding school which was soon lit by gas and replaced that built in 1623. He became best known for the underground developments at Welbeck, which included a tunnel over

62   *Welbeck's Lion Gate.*

63 *Lord George Bentinck may be the Sherwood noble with the largest number of monuments – this is the one in the market place at Mansfield.*

1,000 yards long running from the house to the riding school. An even longer tunnel leading towards Worksop was intended for carriages and was used by the duke when he travelled to London in his special carriage. This carriage was curtained on all sides enabling him to travel to Worksop station and be loaded onto a train there without ever being seen. He left this way for London on 1 September 1878 and never returned.

Constructions included the 'ballroom', though other intended uses for it included a chapel and a picture gallery. His involvement with all this work was at a very practical level, the duke being happy to discuss projects with his labourers. He had a brief passion for roller-skating and built a rink for this purpose.

He did not neglect the house itself, adding modern plumbing and bathrooms: he installed a hydraulic 'shaft' to connect dining rooms and kitchens, and 'railway vans' ran along the passages. He only used a small suite of rooms himself, which were connected to the outside world by two letterboxes, and apparently ordered 'two quarts of beer and two of ale' every day, but never drank them. These were reflections of his eccentricity and isolation. So few used the rest of the house that by his death it was in a poor condition; most of the rooms lacked furniture and were painted pink.

His London home was Harcourt House at 19 Cavendish Square, in the garden of which he had a glass screen built to provide seclusion. A leasehold interest in this house had been won by the 3rd Duke through gambling. He possessed another house, 13 Hyde Park Gardens, which for 12 years was only looked after by a caretaker. The 5th Duke had an estimated income of £400,000 per year and land in eight counties. He still owned large areas of London including Great Titchfield Street, Great Portland Street and Portland Place and had two houses in Scotland and another in Northumberland. His 35,209 acres in Nottinghamshire earned him £50,000 per year but he owned 81,000 acres of Caithness. He died in 1879 and was buried at Kensal Green.

In 1879 the title passed to the 5th Duke's second cousin, William who arrived at Welbeck with his half-sister Ottoline and Ottoline's mother, his stepmother, who became Lady Bolsover in 1880. The house was in an unusual state and many of the family treasures had to be unpacked. Lady Ossington, who had married Mr Denison MP,[35] was left 13 Hyde Park Gardens and the Portland estates in London. Lucy, the widow of Lord Howard de

64   *The tunnels feature very heavily in these other views of Welbeck Abbey from 1881; the 'raising up' of part of the house can also be seen.*

Walden,[36] inherited the crucial Portland estates in London after the death of Lady Ossington, giving her an income of £180,000. The original Bentinck estates around Soho Square had been almost entirely sold by the 1880s. It is difficult not to see the death of the 5th Duke as the point from which the Portland decline set in as the estates were broken up.

The 6th Duke of Portland was also interested in horses and his own mare won the Portland Plate in 1881. In 1884, *St Simon* won the Gold Cup at Ascot; the cup was sold in 1950 by Welbeck Estate Company for £1,550. In 1885 his horses won 18 races. The duke also maintained Disraeli's memory by holding large meetings of the Primrose League at Welbeck with 2,000 meeting at the riding school in 1888. He used Welbeck occasionally but it was more generally the home of his stepmother, Lady Bolsover, until she died in 1893; he preferred 13 Grosvenor Square in London. He was appointed master of the Horse under Lord Salisbury's government in 1886 as well as chair of the Horse Breeding Trust. In 1888 he was one of two top owners in the country, winning £26,812 in 19 races; his horse *Ayrshire* won the 2000 Guineas and the Derby, while *Donavon* won 11 races and £16,487. The next year the duke won nearly £74,000 which was almost double any previous owner's record,

65 Vanity Fair *depicted the young 6th Duke of Portland as an elegant gentleman about town.*

with *Donavon* alone winning nearly £39,000 including the St Leger and the Derby and *Ayrshire* and *Semolina* winning another 14 races. This record stood until 1952. That year the duke married Winifred Dallas-Yorke, who was noted for her unusual ability (for someone of her class) to cook a meal. The duchess persuaded him to use much of the money to set up almshouses known as The Winnings. The following year must have seemed a failure for, although he came top again, he won only £25,000 despite *Memoir* winning the Oaks and St Leger.

At the end of the century the Portlands were less well off than they had been, although, according to *The Portland Peerage Romance*, the 6th Duke finished the century with 180,000 acres, an income of £160,000 a year, four country houses and another at Grosvenor Square in London.

The Duke of St Albans maintained his estate at Bestwood and a family home at Grosvenor Crescent in London. The 6th Duke, Aubrey, married Lady Louisa Manners but died in 1815. William, the 8th Duke, had 13 children by his second wife and died in 1825. In 1827 the 9th Duke, William Beauclerk, married actress Harriet Mellon, an alliance which was reputedly much disapproved of by George IV; a gentleman might keep an illegitimate actress, but certainly not actually marry one.[37] Harriet had inherited £900,000 from banker Thomas Coutts, but the Duke got none of it.

In 1862 the 10th Duke demolished the Plantagenet- era house and Samuel Teulon designed its replacement. In 1865 the new Bestwood house emerged in a Gothic style, interestingly combining Victorian redbrick with a baronial entrance hallway and a Tudor-style ceiling. It included a small chapel, which was replaced by Emmanuel church, also by Teulon, in 1869.

66   *The Winnings at Welbeck: almshouses built with the profits from horse-racing.*

The Prince and Princess of Wales visited Bestwood in 1878 and Prince Leopold stayed in 1881. Leopold's reason for the visit was to open University College, Nottingham. He also visited Newstead and took lunch at Welbeck. According to Nikolaus Pevsner, the architectural historian, the Prince of Wales was so struck with Bestwood that he employed Teulon to work on Sandringham. A lot of damage was caused, however, when the drawing room caught fire in April 1885, destroying 25 pictures including valuable works by Vandyke and Lely.

The duke played a modest role in political life, becoming a Liberal Unionist and a supporter of Joseph Chamberlain who was a visitor to Bestwood in 1888. He was actively interested in social reform and proposed a Bill for the reduction of railwaymen's working hours in 1891.

A new name in Sherwood was that of Seely. Charles Seely had been a Lincolnshire corn miller who invested in the Nottinghamshire coal industry and developed a career as a radical politician, during which he reputedly upset Queen Victoria by entertaining the Italian revolutionary, Garibaldi. Seely lived mostly on the Isle of Wight where he bought an estate. The development of the family's interest in mining necessitated a home in or near the coalfield. They acquired Sherwood Lodge, which Colonel Seely, who drew his title from the Robin Hood rifles, expanded considerably, adding a drawing room and library, before making substantial further land purchases including Haywood Oaks near Blidworth so that he had 3,000 acres in the county. He also bought Ramsdale, where a 'lofty hill' was considered as the site for a new house.

His son, Sir Charles (1833-1915), the 1st Baronet, lived on the Isle of Wight or at Sherwood Lodge, from where he managed the mines and developed a political career. He was elected for various Nottingham seats between 1869 and 1895. He was made a

67   *Bestwood Lodge was rebuilt in an interesting mix of styles, as seen in this 1878 illustration. Today as a hotel, it still looks very similar.*

baronet on 19 February 1896, became High Sheriff in 1890 and was first vice-chairman of Nottinghamshire County Council.

Often overlooked is Cockglode. After the death of Dr Aldrich in 1797, it became the home of Sir Robert Shore Milnes, whose wife was a member of the Bentinck family. He had been Governor of Martinique and then Quebec, was made a baronet in 1801 and died in 1837. The next tenant was Colonel Savile Henry Lumley, a younger son of the Earl of Scarbrough. He died in 1846 but his widow remained at the house until her own death in 1869. During this time it was described in *White's Directory* of 1853 as 'a beautiful mansion embowered in wood'. It then became the home of Cecil Foljambe, an MP from 1880 to 1892, although the main Foljambe family home was Osberton. In 1893 he was made Baron Hawkesbury of Ollerton, Sherwood Forest, in a revival of a title held by his grandfather the Earl of Liverpool. When appointed high steward of the royal household in 1906, he was also created Earl of Liverpool, but by then he had long left Cockglode and moved to Kirkham Abbey.

Politics
During the 19th century, the Dukeries gentry maintained the interest in politics developed by the Pelhams earlier, but no-one attained the eminence of the Duke of Portland, who had briefly been Prime Minister in 1783 and again in 1807.

The Newcastles had great influence during Nottinghamshire elections but they could not always get full control. This led to the bribing of voters, most famously in the East Retford elections of 1826 and 1830. These were so notorious that reformers presented a Bill to Parliament in 1830 to transfer its two seats to Birmingham. As a result, the freeholders of

Bassetlaw were combined with East Retford, with Lord Newark and Hon. Arthur Duncomb being the first MPs for the new seats. MPs were often seen as puppets, a losing candidate at Newark in 1829 complained that 'You send only my friend's body to Parliament – his mind, his understanding, is at Clumber'.[38] After the 1829 election, 36 tenant voters who did not back the duke's candidate were given notice to quit. This led to a bitter argument, it being felt that the duke only controlled Newark because he leased the lands from the Crown Commissioners of Woods and Forests, on which basis he exerted 'unbearable tyranny'.

The 4th Duke of Newcastle opposed Catholic emancipation and the reform of Parliament. After elections he evicted tenants who voted against his wishes, countering those who challenged him with, 'It is presumed then that I am not to do what I will with my own?' He refused to lease land in Nottingham to anyone not a member of the Church of England. Due to his obdurate stance, in the reform crisis of 1831, Nottingham Castle was attacked. The House of Lords rejected the Reform Bill, and a coachdriver announced in Nottingham on 10 October 1831 that London reformers were 'beating to arms'. An organised group attacked a mill at the Forest which belonged to a reform opponent, then Colwick Hall was looted. Attention turned to the castle, property of the most hated local opponent of reform, and the mob battered through its gates and set it on fire. Later in the evening, 'thousands thronged the Castle-yard, to gaze with mingled feelings on the dreadfully novel spectacle'.

Rioters were dispersed into the Park by soldiers, but then regrouped to attack textile mills. An attempt to attack Wollaton Park was stoutly fought off by a detachment of colliers, soldiers and yeomanry. Three men were executed for their role in the Nottingham riots.

Newcastle's London home in Portman Square suffered broken windows and even Clumber was fortified in case of attack.[39] Two hundred armed men and cannons guarded the house. Lord Lincoln moved his sisters to the house of a gamekeeper.[40] It did nothing to change Newcastle's opinions, however, and he was one of a handful of Lords who voted against the third reading of the Reform Bill in June 1832.

The riots were investigated by a commission and Newcastle was awarded £21,000 compensation. He attracted further criticism by complaining that this was not enough! The castle was left as a ruined shell brooding in the centre of Nottingham until the 6th Duke gave it over to Nottingham Corporation under a 500-year lease. It was re-opened as a gallery and museum in 1878 by the Prince and Princess of Wales. They arrived at Daybrook station where they were met by St Albans, who took them to stay in his home at Bestwood. The 'Midland Counties Art Museum' had been promoted by the late mayor of Nottingham, Mr Ward, and restored over two years with the help of Sir Henry Cole.

In his obituary, *The Times* wrote that the duke suffered from having had a 'narrow political education', neither attending Oxford nor sitting as an MP in the House of Commons, so that his politics reflected the 'bias of personal interest'. The Duke saw no reason to reform a system that gave him control over six House of Commons seats and resented having to surrender any of them in the name of reform. Two seats were held at each of Boroughbridge and Aldborough, with one seat each at East Retford and Newark. The result of reform was that he lost Boroughbridge entirely and Aldborough was partly disenfranchised.

Newcastle's era was that of High Toryism – 'when High Toryism was in the ascendant, no man's politics were so entirely in the right as those of the Duke of Newcastle' – which by the 1820s was fading. His visit to the King at Windsor in 1829 was seen in some quarters as an attempt to get power but it turned out to be 'a most mortifying failure'[41] and by 1830,

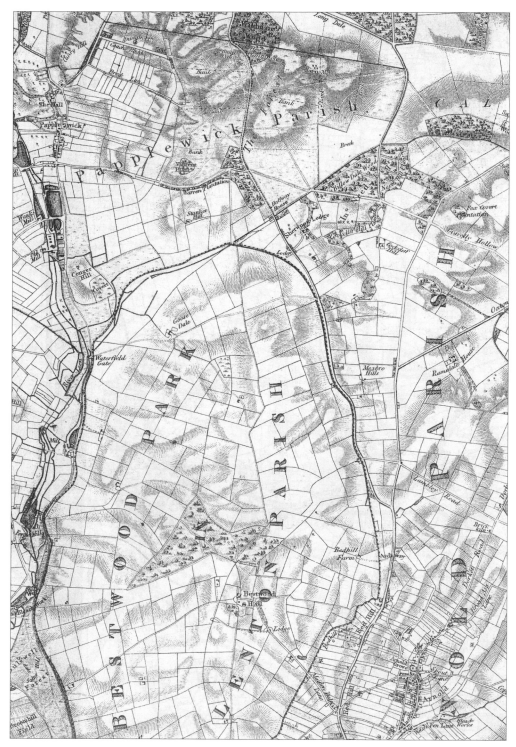

68   *Map of Arnold and Bestwood in the 1820s showing the huge extent of the Bestwood deer park which by this time had become enclosed fields. Note the way the North Road skirts the park before passing Sherwood Lodge – later the home of the Seely family – and entering unenclosed land in Papplewick. (Nottinghamshire County Council)*

69   *The opening of an art museum in the restored castle at Nottingham marked a great day for the Dukeries nobility but also a final abandonment of their capacity to maintain 'ducal palaces in a provincial town'.*

the duke was effectively a dog howling at the moon. His attempts to maintain an influence after 1832 were largely unsuccessful; he chose William Gladstone, a man on the rise, for MP of Newark between 1832 and 1846, but Gladstone went from being a fervent Tory to becoming the greatest Liberal politician of the century, and he resigned instead of continuing as Newcastle's poodle. Even his own son Henry, Earl of Lincoln, drifted towards liberalism after father and son were bitterly divided over the repeal of the Corn Laws in 1846. When he saw preferment, it was not always to pecuniary advantage; he persuaded George III to appoint him as a ranger of Sherwood Forest, a position which carried no pension. After the death of Portland in 1809 he became Lord Lieutenant and 'Custos Rotulorum', or Keeper of the Rolls, which was an expense, not an income, due to the cost of ceremonies. He lost this role to the Earl of Scarbrough in 1839, having incurred the wrath of the Lord Chancellor by refusing to appoint two men as justices on religious and political grounds. He seemed like a man from a bygone age when he died in 1851.

As in the Portland case of the acquisition of Sherwood lands from the Crown, the Newcastle family was touched by accusations of corruption. Lord Henry Lincoln, the 4th Duke's son, became Chief Commissioner of Woods and Forests from 1841 to 1846, and was then accused of advantageously acquiring the Hafod estate in Wales for his family. Lord Lincoln, who became the 5th Duke, enjoyed some success as a politician and over a 20-year period he became Chief Secretary for Ireland and the Secretary of State for War in 1854, but he was most successful as Colonial Secretary from 1859 to 1864.

Industry

Coal measures lay in huge quantities beneath the Sherwood estates, but in 1800 the depth was too great for mining to be commercially viable. It had spread to Teversall, however, where the mining interest had passed to the Carnarvons by marriage, and Portland Colliery at Selston, in the very west of Nottinghamshire, which opened in 1821. Mines were usually set up by small companies, leasing land from landowners such as the Byrons. Coalmining around Strelley and Bilborough was in decline by the 1820s. A huge number of operations developed in this area and there were still 66 collieries on the exposed coalfield in 1945.

Portland set about developing mines and the harbour at Troon on his Ayrshire estate. He also sold iron mining rights and had an ironworks at Cessnock. Others gained more from leasing land to supply Nottingham with water. The Nottingham Water Act of 1845 brought together several small companies at a time when rivers were being ruled out because of pollution. The first pumping station was built at Haydn Road, Basford, in 1857; it extracted about 2.5 million gallons a day. A pumping station opened at Bestwood in 1874 and this later supplied water to an additional reservoir at Papplewick in 1880. Mr Andrew Montagu, the owner of the Papplewick and Linby estates, struck a deal with a private company, but after Nottingham took over the lease there followed 11 years of legal dispute. In 1882, Nottingham Corporation decided to build a new pumping station at Papplewick and the engines started work late in 1884. In 1892 Nottingham began planning for another pumping station at Boughton, north of Ollerton. In 1898 a Bill was promoted to develop this scheme with a maximum depth of 350 feet and producing about 4.5 million gallons a day. When the engines were no longer required, it was decided to set up a trust to preserve Papplewick and sell the Boughton engine in order to provide funds.

West of Mansfield, collieries were helped by their proximity to the Cromford Canal's wharf at Pinxton and were soon connected to it by simple railways. The Mansfield & Pinxton Railway opened on 13 April 1819 when the first load of coal arrived at the company's 'wharf' in Mansfield. It was worked by a combination of horses and gravity until in 1847 it was taken over by the Midland Railway and considerably rebuilt. North opened his own private railway with the intention of using steam engines from Cinderhill to a wharf on the Wollaton Canal at Radford in 1844, reducing the price of coal in Nottingham by about a third.

The Butterley Company developed a mine at Selston which became Portland Colliery, opening in 1821 and soon producing record quantities. It was well positioned for Mansfield & Pinxton Railway, and won the contract to supply Mansfield gas works when that also opened in 1821.[42]

The growth of deep mining really started from Cinderhill, near Basford, in 1841-3 with what became Babbington Colliery. A key firm was North, Wakefield & Morley who opened Babbington, Newcastle, Broxtowe and Bulwell pits; North was influential enough to become Mayor of Nottingham and built substantial houses for his workers at Cinderhill.

Shafts were being sunk at Hucknall in 1851. Two shafts were sunk at Shireoaks as part of a strongly personal mission by Newcastle, and a coal seam of 3ft 10ins was found on 1 February 1859[43] at about 1,000 feet. The colliery was visited by the Prince of Wales in 1861, when he laid the foundation stone of the new church and the duke was awarded a medal in 1862 for 'perseverance in opening out a new district under difficult conditions'.

At Annesley, coal production started in 1865. It was the scene of some of the worst accidents of the period: seven men were overcome by carbon monoxide after an explosion of firedamp, partly caused by an outdated ventilation system which used a furnace rather than fans. Annesley had a starring role in the meeting of the British Association at Nottingham in 1866, when a paper about its geology was read. Sir Roderick Murchison, Director General of the Geological Survey, predicted that the coal deep under the sandstone north of Nottingham would be worked 'at some distant day'. This day arrived much more quickly than he had anticipated.

There were a number of mines in the concealed coalfield of the Leen Valley, such as those Newcastle sunk in 1853 and Bulwell Colliery, which was sunk in 1867-9. Some of these

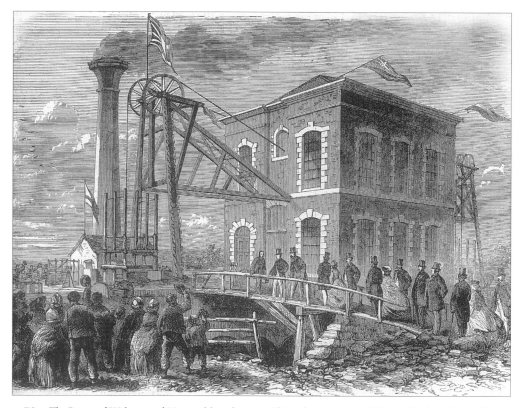

70   *The Prince of Wales visited Newcastle's coal mine at Shireaoks, a venture which brought the unhappy duke some public recognition and celebration.*

had direct importance for the families of Sherwood and the Dukeries including Annesley, Bestwood in 1871-2, Linby in 1873 and Newstead in 1875. The latter followed Col Webb's lease of the top hard coal under the Newstead estate to the Sheepbridge & Staveley Company, which formed the Newstead Colliery Company to exploit it.

Another group of deeper mines were sunk around Sutton in Ashfield at the same time, including New Hucknall in 1876-9 and Sutton in 1873. After 1875, this sudden rush to develop the concealed coalfield abated for some years.

By 1874 at least 12,000 were coal mining in Nottinghamshire, of whom two-thirds worked underground. New villages were built for them at places such as Annesley, Bestwood and Newstead, which had formerly been the preserve of estate and country workers. By the end of the century, nearly 27,000 were employed.

Portland had much to gain; he understood the importance of better transport to coal and became a subscriber to the Midland Counties Railway in 1832 which evolved into the Midland Railway. The most significant developments to benefit him were at Bolsover, set up by Emerson Bainbridge's Bolsover Company in 1889. By 1890 Portland was seeking to develop coal mining near Welbeck, with Creswell sunk in 1896-8, and in 1899 the Bolsover Company took out a lease on land east of Mansfield that became the Mansfield or Crown Farm colliery.

Another prominent Nottinghamshire family of coal owners were the Seelys. They bought the Babbington company's pits in 1872 and proved to be progressive employers,

71   *Map of Newstead and Sutton in Ashfield. The very obvious recent enclosures of much of Sherwood can be seen in the regular field patterns. Also notable is the early Mansfield & Pinxton Railway. (Nottinghamshire County Council)*

providing decent housing with gas and water, medical attention and a sick pay scheme. Colonel Seely ran the Babbington Coal Company and used it as a platform for his own political ambitions, advocating pensions for the widows of workmen killed in their labours.

Pleasley colliery opened in 1877 and interest in the concealed coalfield revived in the later 1880s, threatening Sherwood Forest from then on. The Butterley Company acquired land at Kirkby in 1887, where it developed a major new colliery with a brickworks. This generated its own electricity and became one of Britain's biggest mines. The company also made the revolutionary step of building miners' cottages with baths! Between 1890 and 1896, new mines were sunk at Kirkby Summit, Bentinck, Creswell and Warsop bringing mining well into the Forest. In 1890 a mine was being sunk on Portland's land at Whitwell. The New Hucknall company used its profits from the New Hucknall site to sink its own pit in Kirkby, which it christened Bentinck to reinforce associations with the Portlands, starting production in 1896. Just after the turn of the century there were sinkings at Gedling, Mansfield No.2 and Sherwood No.1.

The coal miners quickly formed associations, the first being at Kimberley by January 1844.[44] The Owners' Association moved to outlaw miners with any union membership, leading to strikes at Radford, Cinderhill, Selston and Kimberley in April 1844. The miners organised teams of 'beggars' who went out to collect funds from supporters in the Sherwood area and as far afield as Grantham, where they were threatened with arrest for vagrancy. One group was arrested in Sutton and incarcerated at Southwell, from where they returned to Mansfield through Sherwood with a musical accompaniment. After 1844, unionism in the area largely lapsed until 1863.

72   *Kirkby or 'Summit' Colliery closed in 1969. (Nottinghamshire County Council)*

After the formation of the Derbyshire & Nottinghamshire Miners' Association, the first strike took place at Cinderhill in 1865. Miners at Cinderhill, Babbington and Newcastle pits won an eight-hour day in 1866. This year also saw the start of a vitriolic lockout at Hucknall which lasted five or six months. In 1878 there was a strike at Bestwood due to a reduction in wages. Violence broke out, stones were thrown and a number of miners were arrested for intimidatory behaviour;12 were charged.

73   *Up to the early 20th century most mining in the shallow coal field was relatively primitive in its conditions; here what may well have been local timber is used to support the roof as coal was dug out in shallow seams.*

A new miners' organisation was founded in 1881. One of its first strikes was at Bestwood, which lasted three months and failed to force terms from the company. During the mid-1880s the Nottinghamshire Miners' Association seems to have been helped by coal owners such as Ellis and Colonel Seely.[45] Nonetheless, Bestwood was again on strike in early 1888. Pay increases resulted from the strike of March 1890; a large meeting of the men was held at Bulwell Forest on 15 March.

The increased wages were soon under threat when trading conditions declined in 1893 and on 12 August there was a big miners' meeting in Bulwell Forest. Eventually, however, most of the Leen Valley mines allowed the miners back at their old rates of pay since they were among the most profitable pits in the region, and could afford to pay better wages.

The hosiery trade was well established by 1800 and continued to grow around Mansfield and Sutton in Ashfield, where there were 1,702 hand frames at one time. Hucknall Torkard was also significant and there were 85 frames at Blidworth, 10 in Farnsfield and 382 in Calverton. The era of the hand frame, however, was already drawing to a close and times would have been hard for these relics of a domestic age.

The change from handcraft to mechanisation was violently resisted by Luddite groups, and in March 1811 frames were smashed in Bulwell, Lambley, Woodborough and Sutton in Ashfield, before anger spread to Mansfield. On 10 November an Arnold Luddite was shot dead while trying to break into a house in Bulwell. A cartload of frames were destroyed at Redhill; the Luddites apparently met at the Seven Mile Stone on the Mansfield road.[46] In 1814 Luddites killed William Kilby at New Basford. In 1818 there was a severe depression in trade which resulted in much suffering. Newcastle took an interest in the problem and recommended that unemployed workmen should emigrate to Cape Colony, and contributed £500 to a fund for this; 'Let me beg of you to bear up manfully, and make the best of even what you may consider an indifferent lot,' he told them.[47] Portland and Manvers then felt obliged to give a similar amount until about 300 families were able to emigrate. Nonetheless, villages on the fringes of Sherwood continued to be heavily involved in knitting, including 44 per cent of Lambley's people in 1851.[48]

The hosiery trade proved difficult to mechanise fully because it was hard to adapt the stocking frame to rotary motion. From the 1850s various approaches were available for using mechanical frames to knit fabric in tubular form and Cotton's Patent Frame of 1864 created the subsequent pattern of knitting parts of a garment in flat pieces before stitching them together. The result was the growth of factories, which mopped up the spare female workforce in mining areas. The textile trade grew erratically, however, and a large worsted mill built at Arnold in about 1792 was out of business by 1810, while village cotton mills at

74   *One of the last surviving stocking frames at work in about 1900; most were replaced by machinery.*

Linby and Papplewick had closed by about 1859 although Robinson, their owner, had built a new road between them. The demolition of more than forty houses followed as workers left.[49] One view is that they closed because landowner Andrew Montagu refused to renew their leases.[50] During the same era there were also cotton mills at Cuckney, which closed in 1844, Bulwell and Sutton in Ashfield. Old Forge Mills were owned by Portland.[51] The mill at Cuckney was converted into the village school by Portland. Langwith even had its own industrial hamlet called Cotton Mill Langwith with a mill, manager's house and rows of cottages on the River Poulter.

Mansfield was not only a centre for hosiery, but the spinning of cotton and wool also and by 1809 it had five cotton mills. In 1866 there were nine mills along the Meden and Maun rivers; William Hollins's mills at Pleasley Vale employed over eight hundred.[52] At least another 4,000 were employed in hosiery work within the Mansfield area. The making of tin boxes also started in the area in about 1870, again employing a female workforce.

Transport also improved. Some roads, such as Nottingham to Mansfield, had already been 'turnpiked'. In 1830 a Bill was laid before Parliament to expand the Mansfield turnpike to include a road linking Nottingham with the Mile Oak in Kirkby, and from there to Pinxton and South Normanton, with a branch off to the colliery near Pinxton Green. In the same session of Parliament, a Bill was laid for the construction of a toll bridge at Dunham, which was to have significant impact on road traffic across Sherwood. For a brief period Ollerton was a stop on the way for the London to Glasgow Royal Mail coach, which went via Newark and Worksop. The turnpikes were quickly threatened by railways and lost much of their traffic; a coalmine like Skegby, still using turnpikes in the 1840s, was very unusual.

Nottingham, Mansfield, Worksop and Newark were the main attractions to railway promoters. The Nottingham and Mansfield section of the Midland Counties Railway

75   *The mill (left) and millpond at Cuckney; the mill is still the village school.*

76 *Windmills were not a common sight in Sherwood as it was not a significant grain producer, but there were some around the fringes such as this one at Hucknall.*

opened on 19 September 1847. Running through Bulwell and Kirkby, this later gave much impetus to the local coal trade and at its northern end used the Mansfield & Pinxton Railway. Southwell and Mansfield were connected in 1871. The Great Northern opened its own local lines to access the coal, with a route through the Leen Valley in 1881. The Nottingham Suburban line was opened in 1889 but was swiftly undercut by trams and lost its passenger service due to wartime economies in 1916. Eventually a complex web of lines operated north of Nottingham with three separate routes from the city to Mansfield. Two factors ensured that the building of railway lines continued unusually late: the growth of the coalfield and the late arrival of the Great Central Railway in 1900 as a main line to London via Nottingham Victoria station.

The Lancashire, Derbyshire and East Coast Railway opened in 1896, but connected only Chesterfield and Lincoln via Edwinstowe. The special opening train ran from Liverpool Street to Chesterfield and Whitsun excursions were soon running from Liverpool Street, as well as from Kings Cross to Edwinstowe. It became known as the 'Dukeries Route' and attempted to promote Tuxford as 'Dukeries Junction'. The name was well-established by 1900. Newcastle was on its board until 1905.

THE MIDLAND HOTEL,

MANSFIELD.

(OPPOSITE THE RAILWAY STATION.)

— THIS —

First-class Family & Commercial Hotel

STANDING in its own grounds, is the most convenient, comfortable, and pleasantly situated Hotel in the Midland counties, for Tourists visiting the "DUKERIES," SHERWOOD FOREST, NEWSTEAD ABBEY, HARDWICK HALL, and other places of interest in the neighbourhood.

By special permission (of the noble owners), Keys and Passes of the private drives of the "DUKERIES" are kept at the Hotel.

CARRIAGES and CONVEYANCES of every description supplied on the most reasonable terms.

Loose Boxes and Lock-up Coach House.

HOTEL PORTER IN UNIFORM MEETS ALL TRAINS.

GEO. ALTON, Proprietor.

77   *This advert for the Midland Hotel in Mansfield is interesting for the way it promotes a Dukeries tourist trade through providing 'private passes' to the estates, encouraged by new railway connections.*

Railways encouraged visitors. A golf course was established at Lindrick by Sheffield businessmen in about 1890, who travelled by train and cut holes in the waiting room wall at Shireoaks station so that they could practise their putting. In 1957 their course staged the Ryder Cup! Travellers were also brought out by Ollerton Races. These were first run in 1838 and a two-mile course on Boughton Breck was set up on 2 May 1844.[53]

By 1841 Nottingham had 53,091 people and was by far the largest centre in the area, threatening Sherwood. The Borough Extension Act of 1877 increased its boundaries to include Bulwell, Sherwood itself, and parts of other former villages. Next came the towns which fringed the Forest: Newark with a population of 10,118, then increasingly industrial Mansfield with 9,665; Worksop had 6,129 people whilst Southwell, with 3,487, was well ahead of East Retford which had 2,340. Notable was the rise of Mansfield's industrial hinterland: Sutton in Ashfield with a population of 5,676 rated well in advance of many 'more important' towns. Sutton benefited from the trade in hosiery and tin boxes, and its population grew steadily. Kirkby grew at a faster rate between 1851 and 1901 than any local town except for Hucknall Torkard. Ollerton and Edwinstowe grew rapidly from 1801 to 1851, but then declined having a mere 986 and 690 people respectively in 1901.

The 19th century was an era of great church building, filling in gaps where hamlets had grown up within the boundaries of the huge medieval parishes of Sherwood. Shireoaks had no proper church until the rector of Harthill built a 'chapel of ease' there in 1809 which eased the life of the villagers since they did not have to travel to the actual parish church.

In 1800 only 66 Nottinghamshire parishes had their own school[54] but few were within Sherwood although Brunt's School at Mansfield had been established since 1706. In 1807 Manvers built a school at Budby; subsequently the countess paid for its upkeep and the clothing for 18 poor female pupils – which must have been virtually all the girls in the village.[55] Manvers helped with rebuilding Edwinstowe school in 1824 and funded a new infants' school in 1845. After 1810 the big church organisations began to build new schools. Shireoaks gained a National Society School in 1841 and Manvers built one for Kneesall in 1842. The National School in Ollerton, also founded in 1842, was funded by public subscription. Henry Knight, lord of the manor of Market Warsop, provided a school for that settlement with help from the rector. Sutton's National School, built in 1819, had to be replaced in 1845 and Blidworth's school opened in 1847.

Most unusual was the Clipstone school, built in 1842 to 1844. Portland ordered the building of Archway Lodge 'in the latest Gothic style', which had 'a noble carriage archway' in its centre, a house on each side, and a school room for poor girls over the top. The carriageway led to the Centre Tree, supposedly the middle tree in all of Sherwood. The lodge was a copy of the Priory gatehouse at Worksop, but was decorated with figures such as Robin Hood and Richard I, and was supposedly the first of a series of arches intended to link Welbeck to Nottingham. Another unusual Portland school was that set up at Cuckney as a National school in 1846, accommodating 200 children in the old mill; an infants' school was added in 1849.

Rainworth remained small, gaining its first wooden church in 1890 and its first pump for fresh water in 1895. Also slow moving was Clipstone which was described in 1853 as 'one of the poorest and most decayed villages in Bassetlaw'. The isolation of the area led to

The Dukeries Hotel, *Edwinstowe, part of the late 1800s/early 1900s tourist boom following the opening of the 'Dukeries route'.*

79   *Newark from the north in the mid-1800s. The train appears primitive even for that time!*

the construction of the Sherwood Forest sanatorium near Mansfield, which housed 24 TB patients and was opened by Portland in 1902. This was one of the few medical institutions established within the Forest although a small hospital and dispensary were set up in Wellow in 1842 from public donations. This was inspired by William Ward, a surgeon from Wellow, who felt that the hospital in Nottingham was too remote.

8

The Decline and Rebirth of the Dukeries

By the 1900s traditional hunting may have been in an almost terminal decline but shooting remained, attracting many visitors, such as the King and Queen of Spain to Welbeck in November 1907. The king went shooting with the duke 'in Sherwood Forest' and luncheon was served in a large marquee amidst the trees. The Queen of Spain went by motor car to visit the ruins at Bolsover whilst Mr Balfour played golf at Welbeck. The royal guests left on a special train from Worksop on 23 November. The Portlands were also prominent when the king and queen of their own country visited Nottingham on 24 June 1914; the Portlands met them at the station, where they were presented with a silver model of Lee's stocking frame.

In July 1923 the Prince of Wales paid his first visit to Welbeck where he met John Jones, aged 96, the oldest local resident, and Sgt Johnson VC from Worksop. His visit also included the opening of the Edwinstowe welfare centre. The king and queen came by train to Newark again on 9 July 1928. They drove through Sherwood to Worksop in order to open the Memorial Avenue. They were also to open Nottingham University and visit the Prince of Wales' farm at Lenton. Royal visits had now become functional and were no longer for entertainment purposes, although Edward VII stayed at Rufford for the Doncaster Races. Also, George V loved pheasant shooting, but Portland admitted to feeling 'ashamed' at the relentless slaughter enjoyed by the king at Welbeck.

The major estates continued to enjoy some income from shooting. When the Lound Hall estate was advertised for sale in 1943, it was reported that shooting and fishing rights yielded £367 per year. Into the 1960s Thoresby had 20,000 game birds on the estate, employed seven gamekeepers, and held shoots regularly. A more widely popular sport was fox hunting with the hounds of the Rufford Hunt. There was still hunting in Annesley Forest in 1923 as well as poaching to contend with. In January 1961 a policeman was shot at and wounded while trying to arrest poachers in Annesley Park. The estates continued to employ keepers, although the balance of the law shifted to the protection of wildlife as much as the discouragement of poachers, such as when two keepers from the Worksop Manor estate were fined for setting traps for birds of prey in 1999.

The Forest itself was certainly at a low point in 1900, but there was a gradual awakening in interest with a focus on its natural beauty, rather than its traditional potential for hunting. The Major Oak, being in a perilous condition, was protected by a fence after about 1908 and it also had a 'caretaker' of sorts by the late 1920s. In 1931 G. M. Ryan drew the attention

80 *The Grove and Rufford hunts meet at Rufford. (Nottinghamshire County Council)*

81 *The visit of King Edward VII and Queen Alexandra to Rufford in 1904. The apparent air of respectability covered a history of licentiousness that had brought sadness to one of the other Sherwood families. (Nottinghamshire County Council)*

of the Campaign for the Preservation of Rural England to the tree's needs, arguing that it required scientific intervention to survive. In 1964, lead sheeting was put up after vandals climbed the tree and tore branches off. In 1966 a 1000-year-old tree known as 'Robin Hood's Larder' was blown down on the Portland estate; this was the tree where Hood had reputedly stored his game. The Major Oak was also damaged by fire in August 1982 and a German machine was brought in to pump compressed air into the ground around it in 1985.

Attempts were being made to restore the ancient beauty of oak and birch woodland, but rabbits were an intractable foe of replanting and contributed to the poverty of the heathland landscape. It was still a common practice to graze cattle in the woodlands up until 1950.[1] The cattle, by grazing beneath the oak and birch trees, helped to maintain the 'open' woodland of Robin Hood mythology.

Commercial growing of conifers became well-established in the early 20th century. Late in the 1800s, trees like the Scots pine began to be grown, often in mixed plantations with beech. Prominent locations such as Ollerton Corner were planted this way between 1899 and 1909, with the help of steam ploughing. Up until the First World War planting was also intended to encourage pheasant shooting.

The First World War had an enormous impact. The Canadian Forestry Corps set up camp near Carburton. The Thoresby estate's income from timber in 1916 was four times higher than average before the war, and nearly four times higher again in 1918, representing a massive cull of the pine and mixed woodlands. The Clumber estate earned £69,000 for timber in 1917-8[2] – more than the £4 a week for renting Ranby Hall to the Royal Flying Corps.

After the war the government introduced a policy of encouraging native timber resources through a Forestry Commission. Planting was to be stimulated by subsidies. Though local landowners took up this course only slowly, they did so to the destruction of the traditional Forest, perhaps starting with Stilehollow Plantation on the Thoresby estate in 1918 which combined Scots pine and European larch. Much of the Rufford estate heathland was taken by the Commission on a 999-year lease and they took 2,000 acres of Clumber on a similar lease from 1938. The Commission was at least run by the gentry, with the 21st Lord Clinton its chairman from 1927-9.

There was another sharp increase in timber production in the early years of the Second World War. Earl Manvers was bitterly upset that many immature firs and larches were chopped down to provide pit props. Curiously, the same man was happy to offer the Timber Supply Department a number of 800-year-old-oak trees. During the Second World War, much of the timber on the Clumber estate was worked by Worksop firms.

The two world wars had other effects. In the First World War a training camp, called Clipstone Camp, was opened in 1915 near Forest Town. This camp could accommodate up to 30,000 men at a time. One of the first developments in the Second World War was the storage of ammunition at

82 *Lord Savile was a friend of Edward VII and was depicted in 1908 as every inch the hunting and shooting countryman.*

83   *'The Forest' remains an open area on the north side of Nottingham, best known for hosting the Goose Fair after it's transfer from central Nottingham in 1928, but perhaps less of a destination than it was in the past!*

various sites, including Clumber Park, handled from railway sidings near Ranby. In July 1940, complaints were made to the commander of Proteus Camp, near Ollerton crossroads that soldiers billeted in New Ollerton were ruining the lawns of the company houses. The military takeover of land began on 12 March 1942, affecting large areas. Ammunition was stored in Birklands, Bilhagh, near Ollerton Corner and in the Avenue Plantation. Budby South Forest became a tank training zone and the Proteus Camp was set up near Ollerton Corner. Trees at Ollerton Corner were cut down to make way for military use. The houses were extensively used, Rufford Abbey, for example, being in military occupation from 1939 to 1944.

The wartime use of the Forest continued to have an impact on Sherwood for a long time after: a fire in Clumber Park on 30 August 1946 reached ammunition dumps and set off explosions, causing great risk to soldiers and firemen. Exploding cartridges had similarly been a problem in a fire at Budby Common in 1929 and as late as May 1960 the War Department was putting up notices to warn people off Budby Common.[3] In 1952 the County Council agreed to a lease of parts of the Forest for a further 21 years of tank training, although the Major Oak was to be protected by fencing and with public access.

The Thoresby estate still used fences to manage deer movements in Thoresby Park and Bilhagh. In 1948, however, much of it was converted to arable land and the deer banished. Deer survived in some of the parks; in 1966 red and fallow deer could still be observed in Wollaton Park. Wild deer, though, had been important in the Sherwood ecology for grazing between the trees and maintaining the open spaces within the Forest.

Further tax concessions from 1946 encouraged the development of private woodlands and by 1949 the clearing of ancient oaks was gathering pace. Up until the 1960s, this was sometimes done by cutting out square sections so that they could be fired like a chimney.[4] By 1961 the Commission held 16,000 acres. Thoresby's Chestnut Avenue was only saved from destruction by its own staff on the direct intervention of Lady Manvers in the early 1950s. The Beech Avenue succumbed to a combination of neglect, old age and storm damage to be cleared away in 1976-8. Large portions of Birklands were cleared by the Forestry Commission in 1968 in order to establish yet more conifers, thus reducing a thousand years of Sherwood Forest to a mere remnant, although some parts were designated a Site of Special Scientific Interest in 1954. The Sherwood Forest Estate company began a new oak plantation and Americans could pay $25 to sponsor a tree. The new visitors' centre near Edwinstowe opened in 1976, with a visit from the Duke of Gloucester who also visited the Papplewick pumping station and Holme Pierrepont.

84   The 'Sherwood Foresters' were the most famous local regiment, although their main memorial stands at Crich in Derbyshire.

The combination of industrial pollution and a falling water table was reported as being a threat to the last native trees and the conifer plantations in 1971. A scientific study revealed that dust from the three smokeless fuel plants and lack of water meant that over 300 oaks were dying. At this time only 1,000 acres of dense woodland remained and only 200 acres of 'genuine forest'. At the same time £400 was spent repairing the Major Oak. In 1974

85   Part of the huge First World War camp at Clipstone. (Nottinghamshire County Council)

86   *The Major Oak remains a significant visitor attraction, though it is now protected carefully from human attention.*

the County Council published some major concerns about the future of the Forest; they wanted the area to be managed by one organisation with its own rangers, the reclamation of coal tips and the tactical withdrawal from the military camps.

Eventually conservation interests began to predominate and the tide of destruction was halted. The ecology is now better understood – for example, the effects of not grazing have been seen in the uncontrolled spread of birch. Generations had also harvested heather and bracken for fuel and bedding and grazing animals could not be re-established where there had been a number of years of growth without this human activity. Attempts have even been made to reintroduce sheep and cattle to graze the woodland. The Woodland Trust has attempted to preserve and restock deciduous woodland such as at Hannah Park near Worksop.

Until recently, farming continued to nibble away at Sherwood. Sugar beet factories opened at Newark in 1921 and in Nottingham in 1924; the farmers of the clays quickly took up the crop and acreage of sugar beet gradually took over from potatoes. Nonetheless, the marginal farmland of the sandstone area was badly placed to handle the difficult economic conditions of the 1930s and only the return of war provided any solace for hard-pressed Sherwood farmers. In 1930 Portland complained that 'nothing could save the industry from ruin except some form of safeguarding …' By 1936 it was being suggested that such poor soils should simply be allowed to go 'out of production'. Since 1945 increased pumping of water has helped solve one of the traditional Sherwood farming challenges. Nottinghamshire also benefited from government policy encouraging the farming of pigs, the production of which increased five times between 1947 and 1962, while the production of laying hens increased four times.[5]

Nottingham needed to spread northwards to engulf previously distinct settlements like Sherwood and Carrington. In 1920 an attempt to expand its boundaries had been rejected, so new corporation houses were built outside the city boundary. Parts of Sherwood village became council estates. Another attempt in 1932 incorporated Wollaton, Nuthall, Holme Pierrepont and parts of Gedling, Bestwood and Arnold. One of the most significant developments was the Bestwood Park council estate, where land was bought up in the 1950s and building completed in the early 1960s; it was built so quickly and without proper services that the doctor who served the area had to hold consultations in his parked car.[6]

The Families

The 6th Duke of Portland suffered over the infamous Druce legal cases in 1896-1908. It was alleged that the 5th Duke of Portland and T. C. Druce, the proprietor of the Baker Street Bazaar in London, were the same person and that the duke had faked the death in 1864 of his *alter ego*, burying an empty coffin. He then lived on simply as Portland before dying in 1879. After the 'burial' he lived until 1879, calling himself Mr Druce and Scott Portland, wore wigs and false eyebrows, suffered from a skin complaint that made him elusive and kept a beautiful woman called Elise. He also supposedly married Annie May Berkeley. All this was alleged by Mr Druce's daughter-in-law and recalled by Miss Mary Robinson, who said that she had grown up in Worksop in the 1860s and had become the Duke's mistress after a trip to Madame Tussaud's.

The case really began after the death of the 5th Duke in 1896 and was started by T.C. Druce's widowed daughter-in-law, Anna Maria, on behalf of her son. Herbert Druce resisted attempts to have his father's body exhumed and the courts ruled in his favour in

87 *Thoresby's Beech Avenue was famous for two hundred years until its destruction in the 1970s.*

88   *Sherwood itself is now just a drab suburb of Nottingham, but a hundred years ago it still contained pleasant corners with touches of the actual Forest, such as Edward's Lane shown here.*

1899. George Druce, an Australian miner, then put forward a case for having a prior claim to the estate above Mrs Druce's son as he was the grandson of the '5th Duke's' *first* marriage in 1816 – whereas it had been commonly supposed the 5th Duke had never married at all – and thereby held a claim on the peerage itself! In 1903 Mrs Druce was admitted to a mental home but the case continued because investors backed the claimants in the hope of winning a share of the fortune. In 1907 the Portland claimants brought a new action of perjury against Herbert Druce, the son of T. C. Druce, with Mary Robinson and 77-year-old Margaret Hamilton, who claimed to have been a close friend of the duke's, as key witnesses. Hamilton swore that T. C. Druce and the Duke of Portland had been the same person. The body of T. C. Druce was nonetheless exhumed from Highgate Cemetery in December 1907 and proved through reference to photographs to be the father that Herbert Druce had claimed. Of course, the fact that there was a body at all fatally weakened the claimants' cases. George Druce thus lost his attempt to be declared as the rightful duke.

Mary Robinson, who had been living in New Zealand when she read about the Druce claims in 1908, having moved there in 1875, proved to be a 'witness for hire'. Both she and Mary Hamilton were tried for perjury and on being found guilty, sentenced to prison. George Druce was not tried as he had not given evidence in court.

Also interesting was Lady Ottoline Cavendish-Bentinck, who moved to Welbeck in 1879 when her half-brother, William, succeeded to the title as 6th Duke. In 1902 she married Philip Morrell but enjoyed an 'open' marriage and affairs with Bertrand Russell, Augustus John, Dora Carrington and Roger Fry among others. She is usually regarded as the basis for Hermione Roddice in *Women in Love* and considered to be a possible Lady Chatterley. She died after being injected with an unproven drug by her doctor and was buried at Welbeck.

The 6th Duke himself was most interesting because of his wife, Winifred. She was the first president of the Society for the Protection of Birds, from 1891 to her death in

1954, and perhaps was the person who persuaded Queen Victoria to ban the wearing of 'osprey'[7] plumes by soldiers. She was active in the RSPCA and created a sanctuary for old pit ponies and seaside donkeys at Welbeck. She showed great care for local mining families, organising cookery and sewing classes. She founded the Harlow Wood orthopaedic unit on land given by her husband in 1928 and a memorial chapel was opened there after her death. The duchess continued to live at Welbeck until her death in 1954. *The Times* noted that 'she was an outstanding woman; and there are many to grieve over her passing'. The last really strong person associated with Welbeck, she left £87,000.

Meanwhile the Bentincks survived on the fringes of power. Victor Cavendish-Bentinck was a diplomat in Chile from 1933 and Lord Henry, the duke's half-brother, clung on as an independent Conservative after the First World War. In *Tory Democracy* (1918) he ranted against wartime profiteers, the vulgarisation of the Tory party and the granting of honours to the 'plutocracy'.[8] The family finances, however, were in sharp decline; they sold most of their Ayrshire estates – the remaining Scott inheritance – in 1920-2 and their estates in Northumberland were sold off in the late 1930s. The best investment appeared to be the Portland estate in central London, of which only small pieces were sold in 1914 and 1925, but these now belonged to the Howard de Walden line.

89   *Welbeck was immaculate in this picture taken at the turn of the century, but its eventual lease to the Army saved it from the fates of Rufford and Clumber.*

William Arthur became the 7th Duke from 1943. He was Chancellor of the new Nottingham University, which opened in 1948, and his various activities including being chairman of the NSPCC. He hosted a visit of the Duke of Edinburgh to Welbeck in 1956 but often used his house near Berriedale in Scotland. When he died in 1977, he left £4.3million. Welbeck was left to Lady Anne Cavendish-Bentinck and so the link with the ducal title was broken – its new owner lived in another hemisphere.

Ferdinand Cavendish-Bentinck became the 8th Duke in 1977 on account of his descent from the 4th Duke, the 7th Duke having only had daughters. He went to Africa in 1924 and lived in Kenya from 1934. A prominent campaigner for the interests of British settlers, he played a leading but unsuccessful role in Kenyan politics. Associated with some of the 'white mischief' of Kenyan high-living, he was divorced and remarried in 1950. He died in Nairobi in 1980.

The 9th Duke was Victor Cavendish-Bentinck who was born, perhaps fittingly, in Mansfield Street, London in 1897. He had a career in the foreign service which was scarred by a tempestuous relationship with his American wife. When he inherited the title in 1979 he inherited nothing with it and died without heirs in 1990. With him died the dukedom of Portland, which had survived from 1716 to 1990.

The title of earldom of Portland, however, has survived because it was created on different terms and passed to Henry Bentinck, a descendant from the 1st Earl's second marriage. He also had the right to be called Count of the Holy Roman Empire. After a career in the BBC and advertising, he died in 1997 when the title passed to his son Timothy, who had been born on a sheep station in Tasmania. The current Earl of Portland is mainly known as an actor in the role of David Archer in the BBC 4 radio series. One of the Bentincks' descendants, William Parente, still lives on the estate.

The 7th Duke of Newcastle, Henry, struggled to maintain an estate with staff costs of £9,000 per year in 1904.[9] He lived by selling portions of the estate but still had 35,000 acres on his death.

The 8th Duke of Newcastle was Henry Francis Pelham-Clinton-Hope. He added Hope to his name in 1887. In 1884 his grandmother, on the Hope side, died and he gained control of the Hope estate at Deepdene near Dorking for the period of his life only. He had to go to court to sell this property and others in Ireland. A life of gambling on horses and theatre productions caused three bankruptcies[10] and a shooting accident cost him a foot. He existed by gradually disposing of the Hope fortune; in 1898 he sold 83 pictures for £121,000 and another 20 in 1910. In 1917 he sold 30 tons of sculptures and vases, and nine tons of books for £134,918.

Lord Francis'[11] first marriage was to an American actress, Miss May Yohe, in 1894; she was supposedly of mixed Dutch and Red Indian parentage. The marriage was dissolved in 1902 when May ran off with the son of a former Mayor of New York. Miss Yohe was an enthusiastic subscriber to the legend, spread after 1909, that the Hope diamond brought a curse on its owners. She often claimed to have worn the Hope diamond, even on the stage, but also had a replica made and later generated a career out of the legend, writing a book and appearing in a film about it. Francis had got the court's permission to sell the diamond in 1901 for £29,000.[12] He then married an Australian, Olive Thompson, previously Mrs Owen, in 1904. The duke's second wife died suddenly in 1912, which was taken by devotees of the Curse as another sign. Their son Henry Edward became the 9th Duke while one of the daughters was briefly married to Kenneth Horne, the radio star.

The 9th Duke, Henry Edward, succeeded to the title in 1941 after the 8th Duke died at the Parsonage on the Clumber estate. He married an American, Eugenia 'Jean' Banks just after her divorce, but they divorced in 1940. As Lord Lincoln, he had inherited an interest in the Clumber estates in 1928 but closed the house and progressively sold the assets for up to £64,000. After a colourful wartime career, in 1946 the duke married again to Lady Diana Montagu-Stuart-Wortley, daughter of the Earl of Wharncliffe. Having given up Clumber, he retained a manor near Salisbury but by 1950 was living in southern Rhodesia on a tobacco farm. Even the manor, Boyton, which was bought with proceeds from the Clumber sales, was sold in 1961.

The Duke and Lady Diana separated in 1950. In 1958 Henry Pelham-Clinton-Hope was sued by a Turkish harbourmaster for adultery with his wife Sally Ann Wemyss Jemal in the Dorchester Hotel, London. The two had eloped from Kyrenia harbour in Newcastle's yacht. Following the scandal, the Duke married Sally Ann in Jamaica, but the marriage was not a success.

The 10th and final Duke was Edward Pelham-Clinton, great grandson of the 4th Duke. He enjoyed the title for only one month in 1988, then died leaving no heirs. The accumulated wealth of generations, first created by dynamic merchants in the 16th century, had been dissipated in gambling, expensive lifestyles and ruinous divorces which could not be sustained in an era of higher taxation.

Thoresby was run by the 4th Earl Manvers, Charles Pierrepont, from 1900 to 1926. The 4th Earl had been supported by an estate of 38,000 acres up to his death, though he had sold some before the Great War. Financial problems encouraged the sale of mineral rights and, by 1931, £60,000 had been gained from colliery rents. The 5th Earl spent a number of years in an asylum, leaving the control of Thoresby finances to a Master in Lunacy. Lands in villages such as Eakring and Kneesall were sold off piece by piece. He was succeeded by the 6th Earl, Gervas Pierrepont MC, from 1940-55. The house was sold to the National Coal Board (NCB) and then to a hotel company in 1989. The estate passed to his daughter Lady Rozelle Raynes, a noted author of nautical books, and eventually to H.P. Matheson.[13]

The line of the dukes of St Albans had produced little of any distinction. The 11th Duke, Charles, died unmarried in 1934; the title passed to his half-brother Osborne de Vere Beauclerk. He had served in the Boer War and as an aide-de-camp to General Haig in the First World War. He, too, died childless in 1989, so the title passed to his cousin Charles as the 13th Duke. Charles Beauclerk was a financier and chairman of the Grendon Trust, which was taken over in 1973. The circumstances of the takeover, Beauclerk's sale of shares, and the secret financial weakness of Grendon all led to Beauclerk being censured by the Takeover Panel and investigated by the Department of Trade in 1978. Reportedly, threats of being sued led to his move to France. The title is currently held by Murray Beauclerk whose son Charles, as Earl of Burford, achieved notoriety of a sort during the debate on the House of Lords Bill in 1999 when he proclaimed the Bill treason and leapt onto the Woolsack.

The Bowdens, owners of the Raleigh cycle business, moved into Bestwood Lodge. The founder of this 'dynasty' was Frank Bowden, who was American but came to Britain and acquired control of the Raleigh Cycle Company in 1891. He died of heart failure in 1921. His son, Sir Harold, and Lady Bowden took enthusiastically to the life of the country gentry at Bestwood, organising pheasant shoots on a regular basis and hosting a visit by King George and Queen Elizabeth of the Hellenes in 1926. Bestwood, however, was still seen as the 'home' of the Beauclerks and the duchess's funeral was held there in November 1926 followed by the duke's in 1934. Sir Harold was chairman of the British Olympic Association from 1931-5 and High Sheriff of Nottinghamshire in 1933. His role in the Olympics was a result of his personal interest in cycling as a sport. He retired as managing director of Raleigh Cycles in 1938 and lived until 1952.

The Bowdens had their own share of domestic disputes. In July 1931 there was a serious row over the food bills during a house party at Bestwood, following which Lady Bowden took off to Gleneagles. They got back together until February 1932 when Sir Harold walked out. Lady Bowden had accumulated debts of £25,000 at a time when her husband was experiencing a drop in his income and Lord and Lady Bowden were sued by dressmakers Ann Talbot Ltd for non-payment of £1,781. In February 1933 Lady Bowden brought a petition for judicial separation against her husband on the grounds of cruelty.

In early 1938, the 12th Duke of St Albans, crippled by death duties owed since 1934, decided to sell his Bestwood estate of 3,500 acres. Bestwood was actually taken over for military use during the Second World War and then became the Army's North Midlands District headquarters. The Ministry of Defence bought the Lodge in 1952 and it was used for the Army's Pay Corps until 1977. The headquarters of the Nottinghamshire Fire Service was also opened in its grounds while the actual Lodge is now a hotel.

The Seely family had become rich from Nottinghamshire coal, although they chose the Isle of Wight as their principal home. Sir Charles Seely was the 1st Baronet. His wealth from coal was used to buy land and build Sherwood Lodge; he left £1,052,070 when he died in 1915, which was the second largest fortune left that year. The family ran the Babbington Coal Company which joined with the Bestwood Company to form BA Collieries, who were planning to develop Calverton when war interrupted; in 1938 both Sir Hugh Seely and Frank Seely remained on the Board of BA. Frank was the second son of Sir Charles and like his two brothers also had a home on the Isle of Wight.

The 2nd Baronet, also Sir Charles Seely (1859-1926) was MP for Lincoln from 1895 to 1906 and for Mansfield from 1916 to 1918. The best known member of the family, however, was 'General Jack' Seely who also entered politics and became Secretary of State for War in 1912. He returned to his military career during the Great War and to politics again after it. This Seely, born in 1868 and made Baron Mottistone in 1933, became an outspoken advocate of appeasement and of Adolf Hitler between 1935 and 1939; it was 1941 before Seely recanted, but by that stage he was clearly seen as an apologist for the hated dictator. He died in 1947.

The 3rd Baronet, Sir Hugh Seely, was made Lord Sherwood after a political career.

Sherwood Lodge subsequently became headquarters for the National Coal Board in the area. The site was then taken over by Nottinghamshire Police, and the old house and church were demolished to make way for the new police headquarters in 1975.

The new threats for the aristocracy included land tax and death duties from 1894 and their gradual extension just before the Great War. The fall in profits from farming, and the consequent drop in land values, affected some of the Nottinghamshire gentry severely.

Worksop Manor was acquired by industrialist John Robinson in 1890. Robinson, who died in 1913, was noted for funding new churches in Worksop. His firm, Home Brewery in Daybrook, was taken over by Scottish & Newcastle in 1986 and closed in 1997. The building has been preserved as offices for Nottinghamshire County Council, whilst the family's laundry survives at Daybrook. His successor, also Sir John Robinson, was a successful breeder of horses; he lost his son in the Great War and built four almshouses for ex-servicemen as a memorial. Worksop Manor was sold again in 1929,[14] with its famous stud farm that bred the Derby winner *Papyrus*.

The Worksop lordship conferred the unusual duty of providing the right glove for the sovereign to grasp the sceptre with at the Coronation. In a tradition dating back to 1542 this duty had once been performed by the Earl of Shrewsbury; it had passed to the Newcastles through purchase, but had not been included in Edward VII's coronation due to illness. Newcastle played the role in 1911, also supporting the royal right arm. Newcastle continued to claim the right as lord of the manor, despite not having occupation of the manor itself. At the 1937 coronation, Lord Lincoln deputised for his father, wearing an RAF uniform as he was technically only a commoner. He was 'the only tenant in serjeantry to render in the Abbey itself the ancient service due for his lands ... by fitting on the King's right hand, which was to receive the royal sceptre, a glove richly embroidered with the Duke of Newcastle's arms'.[15]

Newcastle's Clumber estate ran at a loss, propped up by income from Newark and Nottingham property; the loss on Clumber and Worksop was £19,000 in 1907.[16] Between 1917 and 1921 Newcastle sold 10,500 acres. In 1916 he sold Ranby House and in 1919 he sold Ranby Hall. In 1927 he transferred virtually all the

90 *The Seely family were prominent in politics for several decades; here Major 'Jack' Seely limbers up for a speech in 1905. Later promoted to General and a post of Secretary of State for War, he came a noted supporter of Hitler in the 1930s.*

remaining property to the London & Fort George Land Company, of which he was a part owner, for £965,000, after which he was a mere tenant in his own house. The Land Company had been formed by Newcastle, the Earl of Rosse and some friends in 1913.

The house at Clumber was a costly liability. A large fire damaged the domestic quarters in 1912. The 7th Duke spent his time at Windsor, Berkeley House or Hay Hill. At the very end of 1928 the new 8th Duke announced that he would close up Clumber, a decision 'which has caused regret throughout the whole of the north Midlands'.[17] Even when he visited the estate, he chose to stay at Barnby Moor. Clumber was largely unused through much of the 1930s and mostly demolished in 1938; plans to build a smaller home for the family never came to fruition. The London & Fort George Land Company sold off some portions; the Lound Hall estate was offered for sale during the Second World War when it disposed of 5,750 acres across 10 parishes, including 44 farms. Next came the sale of the Park estate in Nottingham in 1939, where 160 acres had been developed with houses held on long leases; this was sold in 1939 to the University of Oxford, flush with cash from Lord Nuffield's legacy.

The 8th Duke offered to loan Clumber's art collection to Nottingham Castle, and the pictures were being installed by September 1929. Huge numbers of manuscript volumes were given to the British Museum and nearly £25,000 was raised by Lord Lincoln when he sold some 130 of the pictures at Christie's in 1937. A few weeks later he sold some of the 4th Duke's library at Sotheby's for £38,000, including several items previously loaned to the British Museum.[18] Then in October Christie's moved into Clumber itself for seven days of selling, which included ten bronze model cannons from the famous lake frigate sold for £51. Panelling from the Clumber Oak Room was bought by the County Council for its new County Hall.

Not everything was sold off as the duke had planned to give some of the Surrey lands gained via the Hope marriage to the local people. This included Glory Woods, Dorking, in 1929; however, the duke discovered that Surrey County Council planned to build a bypass through the area and delayed the presentation ceremony until alternative plans had been made. In 1934 he complained that the council had played a 'dirty trick' on him by changing the plans again. He had more success in selling Box Hill to Leopold Salomons and Miss Warburg at 'preferential rates' for the National Trust. The duke moved to the Hope house at Harrowlands near Dorking.

91   *The last great days of Clumber, viewed from across the lake with the church rising above the trees.*

In 1942 the duke told the London & Fort George Land Company that he had no further use of the Clumber and Worksop estates. A plan to sell much of the area around the house to Worksop College came to nothing. In 1944 the National Trust launched an appeal for £45,000 to buy the estate, the largest appeal by the Trust for 20 years because 'no property in the midlands could have a more powerful appeal on grounds of natural beauty or romantic associations than this part of Sherwood Forest'.[19] Given the destruction of the house, the replacement of oaks by pines, and the general devastation of wartime use, this seems a rather hyperbolic account. The whole of Clumber Park was sold to the Trust in 1946; 3,900 acres were bought for £45,000.

Public access depended on the clearance of ammunition. The first section to open was the south bank of the lake but it was not until 1952 that the war office had finished clearing the north side, the house area, and the lime tree avenue.

In 1949 the London & Fort George Land Company sold 1,191 acres of the Worksop Manor estate for £47,989 – land that earned only £2,600 a year from rentals. The company retained the lordship and because of this there was an unseemly dispute over the coronation of Elizabeth II; the lordship was vested in the London & Fort St George Land Company, part-owned by the Newcastles, but did this still give the duke the ancient right to present the glove at the coronation? Even Worksop itself tried to claim the right. The Court of Claims ruled in 1953 that a company could not present the glove and the honour was transferred to the Worshipful Company of Glovers, who made the glove anyway. They kindly agreed to put it in a casket with the Worksop coat of arms on it.

The Portland estates went through similar turmoil. In 1927 the interests of the Portland estates were formed into the Welbeck Estate Company. In January 1941 the Duke of Portland sold 10,000 acres, having sold 4,700 acres of his land in Scotland and Northumberland 18 months earlier. This was lamented by the *Daily Express* as 'the passing of an age', in words reminiscent of the comments on the sale of the Newstead estate 130 years earlier. Portland blamed the sale on the loss of income after mining royalties were taken away by the Coal Mines Act.[20] The house was taken over by the Army as an educational centre in 1946 and in 1952 opened as a military school for 450 boys aged 15 to seventeen. At the time of the school opening, the dowager duchess was still living in part of the house and Reynolds' painting 'The Angel in Contemplation' was still hanging in the ballroom, having been bequeathed to the 3rd Duke by Reynolds himself. Assets were gradually sold off, and various old and medieval books in 1953 and 1954 raised nearly £12,000. The Army's lease on the house ended in 2005 and its college moved to new premises in Leicestershire. The Welbeck estate remains the undeveloped tourist gem of Sherwood.

The Savile family were also retrenching and their estates in Yorkshire were sold in 1932. In April 1938, Alderman Sir Albert[21] Ball, a former Lord Mayor of Nottingham, and father of the First World War air ace of the same name, signed a contract to buy much of the Rufford estate from Lord Savile, who was still a minor. The estate included 18,600 acres and several villages. Parts of the estate were said to be 'ripe for building development' although Ball was unable to find a tenant for the house. This sale attracted much attention as it was the fifth of the great Nottinghamshire estates to be sold, although Wollaton and Newstead had both been acquired by Nottingham Corporation. In May, Ball decided to resell the estate and broke it up into 400 lots including six shops, 128 cottages and over 1,000 acres of 'oak woodland'. The contents of the house were auctioned off over 10 days in autumn 1938 and included two 16th- century Sherwood rangers' tunics.[22] By August 1939, Ball had managed to sell about 14,000 of the 18,500 acres for £250,000. The Savile family reserved access to their burial ground 'in the wilderness'.

The house was sold to Henry Talbot de Vere Clifton, but was almost immediately taken over for military use and left in a ruinous state. The derelict house was bought by the County Council in 1952, after a public campaign to save it and attempts by Clifton to have it redeveloped. Much of it was in dangerous condition, however, and had to be demolished in 1956-7. In 1969 the County Council decided to convert parts of Rufford into a country park, and a park ranger service was set up. A five-year improvement programme began on the grounds, including a £55,000 restoration of the lake, and the planting of 10,000 trees.

The Chaworth-Musters family were still living at Annesley. They were much discussed in 1939 when a scheme to move the disused Annesley All Saints church to Mansfield was proposed. In 1977 there was a further row when plans to demolish the church, which by then had been redundant for 100 years, were announced. Colonel Chaworth-Musters was High Sheriff for a time and also a leading Conservative, briefly achieving some notoriety in 1965 when accused of breaching Parliamentary privilege by instigating press coverage of the Ashfield Labour MP's visit to North Vietnam. In 1973 there was brief consideration of Annesley Hall becoming the national coaching centre for the Football Association[23] after the family moved to Felley Priory.

The Thoresby estate covered over 15,000 hectares in 1900 but by the end of the century had been reduced to only 5,000, of which 1,000 hectares remained commercially managed woodland. When the estate was surveyed in 1914, it included about 530 hectares of old oak and birch woodland – the traditional Sherwood Forest landscape. Young birch were still being planted for their 'silvery barks and graceful foliage'. In the years leading up to the First World War, the estate tried to be commercial; sales of timber brought in about £1,300 a year and game shooting almost half as much.[24] These amounts were tiny in comparison with the revenue from coal rights gathered in from the 1920s. To pay death duties Holme Pierrepont and over 5,000 acres were sold in 1941. Manvers tried to raise more money by selling his Laxton estate in 1950, which included the famous 'open field' farming system based on a three-field rotation of wheat, 'bean' and fallow. The estate included six farms and about 1,800 acres of which a quarter was still farmed in a medieval style. The resultant outcry led to its sale to the Ministry of Agriculture in 1951, but in 1979 it was again threatened when the Thatcher government ordered the ministry to sell all its land; this time it was sold to the Crown estate for £1m, bringing a technically 'royal' interest back into the area.

Another scheme to defray expenses was to divide the main house and rent part of it out as two flats.[25] In April 1957 the house was opened to the public for the first time but in December 1979 it was announced that it was to be bought by the National Coal Board who proposed mining underneath it. It stood deserted from 1980, and in 1983 it was described as 'now gradually crumbling as a coal seam is mined under its foundations'. This might have been the end, but by this time Victorian architecture was fashionable again and Thoresby attracted great interest, with the Prince of Wales visiting in 1984. The best proposal to rescue it from disaster was conversion to a luxury hotel which has, in a way, recaptured the atmosphere of how it would have been in the days of country house parties for Doncaster Races. The house and its contents were sold in 1989 to the Warner Group. As a hotel it is successful because it follows the principles of 'ostentation and active entertainment' upon

92   *The demolition work at Rufford included the whole block on the left and much of the central range shown here, beneath which were the monastic structures.*

which the house was originally built. It has also been seen as more beneficial to the local economy than the hermetically sealed Center Parcs, despite the latter's head office having been opened on the old colliery site in Ollerton.[26]

One of the first losses was that of Nuthall Temple in 1929, although it was not a total loss at the time. It was auctioned in 1929 and the contents and fittings then removed. What was left was blown up to make way for the M1 30 years later in 1966.

In 1925 Nottingham Corporation purchased Wollaton Hall and its park for £200,000. In 1930 Sir Julian Cahn bought Newstead and presented it to Nottingham Corporation in 1931. These were the first serious steps in making a public heritage of the houses. Julian Cahn (1882-1944), was the son of Albert Cahn, the founder of the Nottingham Furnishing Company. By 1943 when he retired and sold out to Great Universal Stores, he controlled a chain of between 300 and 400 stores. Cahn also arranged for Sir Reginald Blomfield to design the Miners' Rest Home in Hucknall.

The only significant new country house of the 20th century was built at Lound Hall, near Bevercotes, in the 1920s, replacing an earlier farm. At the time it was in an idyllic location among the birch woods and alongside the River Maun, but by the late 1950s coal had encroached and it was taken over by the National Coal Board. Standing on the Newcastle estate on land purchased by Sir Gilbert Holles, 3rd Earl of Clare in the 17th century, in the early 1920s it was the home of George Cradock, a wire rope maker and director of British Ropes Ltd. The estate was put on the market in 1943, offering 5,747 acres 'lying in a ring fence', including 971 acres of woodland, as well as 44 farms and the 'modern residence' of

Lound Hall which at the time was 'let on a full repairing lease'. The tenant since the mid-1930s was Harold Peake, an old Etonian and Guardsman who was a director of coal companies. Peake bought the estate and lived there until reselling it in 1953, getting £83,000 for 2,399 acres of it. Peake joined the Auxiliary Air Force in 1936 and had become its first director by 1938-9, director of Air Force Welfare and director of RAF Public Relations, and was promoted to Air Commodore also setting up an RAF Film Production Unit. After the war he enjoyed a successful industrial career, eventually becoming chairman of both Lloyds' Bank and Rolls Royce.

The site was taken over by the National Coal Board when Bevercotes was developed. It had a brief and abortive history as a mining museum; this was stifled by the 1984 mining strike and the relics transferred to a mining museum near Stoke. The mining museum was set up by Alan Griffin and a Mr Storer, who were NCB employees but began the task through personal interest.

Mining spread only slowly into Sherwood Forest because the coal was deeper beneath the surface further to the east. Joseph Rodgers, writing in 1908, said that the coal mines would cause the end of Sherwood because 'the smoke and sulphur emanating from these works are fatal to the oak'.

Gedling opened in 1902 and the sinking of two shafts at Rufford Colliery, Rainworth, began in 1911. By January 1912 *The Times* was able to speak of coal 'invading' Sherwood Forest;[27] Welbeck Colliery was sunk in 1913-15 by the New Hucknall company which also ran Bentinck colliery. The Bolsover Company negotiated a lease of 6,000 acres for coal rights on Portland's Clipstone estate with a possible shaft at Balker Farm and another mine was being created at 'Rufford'.[28] Mansfield Colliery had reached coal in 1905 and was already producing a million tons a year by 1912. Portland was a beneficiary of the spread of coal: in 1911 the Bolsover Company was producing two million tons a year, largely from his land, and Mansfield was also leased from him. Coal was reached at Rufford in 1913 but the war delayed progress elsewhere so that the Bolsover Company did not reach coal at Clipstone until 8 April 1922, at 640 yards underground, and at Thoresby until 1928. Thoresby became one of the best of the Sherwood area collieries, producing more than a million tons a year.[29]

Worksop became a mining town and was surrounded by pits at Firbeck, Steetly, Shireoaks and Manton. The latter was fully operational by 1907 and employed 3,000 by 1927, to the benefit of Newcastle from whom mineral rights were leased.

Earl Manvers auctioned mineral rights beneath his estates in February 1920. This was a major climbdown, because Manvers had been a leading opponent of coal mining in the Dukeries only six years earlier. He even resisted an offer to work the Thoresby minerals from the new pit at Ollerton, on Savile's land, expressing a desire to preserve the forest and the large unenclosed areas.[30] Thoresby was begun in 1925, really bringing the coal industry into Sherwood Forest because its site was so close to the Major Oak itself. Old oak trees had to be felled to make space for it. Earl Manvers' land agent was still trying to prevent the colliery being named 'Thoresby'[31] in 1924 – 'colliery near Cockglode' was suggested instead. The pit was powered by electricity brought in from other sites of the Bolsover Company. In 1923 the Bolsover Company bought Edwinstowe Hall; it was fitted out as a 'weekend home'

93   *Miners at Rufford Colliery, Rainworth, working on sinking the shaft in 1911-13. (Nottinghamshire County Council)*

In November 1924 the *Nottingham Journal* complained that the two schemes were 'largely identical' and in March 1925 plans for the LMS line were abandoned. In December 1925 a joint companies Bill was duly presented and given Royal Assent in July 1926. The line was to run from north of Nottingham to Papplewick, Linby, Bestwood, Calverton, Oxton, Farnsfield and Rufford to a junction at Ollerton, with a line running on via Walesby, Haughton and Babworth to East Retford.

One of the worst mining accidents was at Rufford on 7 February 1913, when 14 men were killed. Overwinding caused a water barrel to fall down the shaft, demolishing scaffolding. At Bilsthorpe in 1927, 14 were killed during sinking operations. Another serious disaster was at Bentinck, near Kirkby Woodhouse in 1915, when 10 died. One of the most unusual accidents occurred at Bestwood in February 1929; two men were killed and four injured by a fall of ice down the shaft which cut open a cage 450 yards down. There was a constant flow of water down the sides and the miners had tried lighting fires to stop it from freezing. A remarkable rescue occurred at Thoresby in 1951 when two men were brought out after being trapped for 27 hours by a roof fall; they had survived by holding their helmets over their faces and breathing through the holes.

In 1934 the Papplewick pumping station was affected by plans to sink a new shaft for Babbington colliery. The solution was for Nottingham Corporation to buy the coal under its waterworks sites, which it did in 1938; £3,800 was paid to the Linby and Babbington colliery companies, the Montagu estate and Sir Hugh Seely. By 1967 the Papplewick and Boughton pumping engines were at the end of their working lives and the Corporation considered converting the pumps to electricity; this was met by a request from the Minister of Public Buildings & Works that Papplewick, at least, should be scheduled as an industrial monument.

East of Mansfield, Forest Town was developed as a 'model village'. The greatest days in Forest Town's history must have been the visit of the king and queen in 1914, who made an unexpected call on the home of miner Mr Mottishaw. Welbeck colliery was served by nearly 880 new houses built between 1912 and 1926 on the outskirts of Mansfield – not too near Welbeck Abbey. The Bestwood Coal & Iron Company was building 200 new houses in 1924. New Clipstone had 648 new houses in the 1920s and Blidworth 821. Rainworth, which had had barely a dozen houses in 1900, mushroomed: its first school was opened in 1914 and another in 1924. By 1945, the eight collieries in the district were employing about 12,000 men.

In 1923 it was predicted that the population of the area would grow by 80,000.[35] New mining settlements were influenced by Sir Arthur Markham's first 'colliery village' near Brodsworth in Yorkshire. In August 1926, *The Times* referred to new Sherwood villages as being 'pleasant in their variety of architectural design' and fully fitted with sports grounds and churches. Eight thousand new homes were planned for New Ollerton by the Butterley company, to be lit with electricity from the colliery power plant elsewhere on the company's system so that there would be no smoke in Sherwood. Homes were supplied with hot water and heated by exhaust steam from the colliery. It was an isolated place with no other employment, so the company speculatively built a factory to employ women even after being unable to convince a hosiery company to build one on advantageous conditions. They

96   *Map of the coal mines of Sherwood and its fringes, showing the large number of small mines in the west and the fewer, but bigger mines of the eastern concealed coalfield. (Andrew Nicholson)*

managed to rent the factory to a hosiery company in 1937 and aimed to provide 600 jobs for women, thereby helping to attract mining families to move and remain there, but only 250 were working there in 1939.[36] The clothing trade has continued in Ollerton to the present day, until recently under the name of Etam, and now Clipper. The coal company deliberately recruited younger men and a baby boom resulted; by 1941 there were 4,130 people living in 858 tenanted houses.[37]

An extra 1,000 houses were planned at Edwinstowe. The new roads were all graded by name. If you got promoted, you might have to move from Third Avenue to First Avenue, where the clerical officials lived. Development did not always run smoothly and there was a fierce row between the County Council who wanted to open a new school in Ollerton, and the Rural District Council who had failed to provide sewerage and a road surface in 1927. There were also new churches; the Butterley Company wanted a large, Catholic 'cathedral of the Dukeries' at New Ollerton whilst other new churches were built at Bilsthorpe, Clipstone and Langold. The Stanton Company built a pub at Bilsthorpe and called it *The Stanton Arms*.

New schools were being provided at Hodsock, Langold, Edwinstowe, Ollerton and Bilsthorpe as well as a new technical high school in Mansfield. Edwinstowe grew from 963 people in 1921 to 2,818 10 years later, Ollerton from 676 to 3,912, Blidworth from 2,033 to 5,316 and Bilsthorpe from 134 to 1,972.

Despite the new villages, life in the Dukeries coalfield was not a roaring success. This was partly due to the nature of the work for, although the pits offered regular employment, the depth meant that it was warm work. Miners and their families also disliked 'the rawness and isolation of these mining villages planted in a hitherto rural area'.[38] Antipathy could be mutual: the *Newark Advertiser* referred to 'an influx of folk alien alike in thought and tradition, in outlook and purpose to the natives and rural folk amongst whom they have set themselves down'.[39] The new villages never grew as much as expected with only two thirds of

97   *Forest Town was one of the earliest, and least inspiring, of the new mining villages. (Nottinghamshire County Council)*

the planned houses at New Ollerton being completed and at Bilsthorpe the Stanton company built only 400 of the anticipated 1,560 houses. New houses at Edwinstowe amounted to half those intended. The new housing at Blidworth was placed in the hands of the Industrial Housing Association, who wanted a 'garden suburb' akin to Letchworth; houses had hot water circulated from a central point which also provided for the pithead showers.

The growth of New Ollerton was overseen by an unusual witness, future poet C. Day-Lewis whose father was vicar of Ollerton. He would have seen that the shops opened in New Ollerton quickly finished off Ollerton's claim to be a commercial centre. One of the neighbours in Ollerton was John Baker, Lord Savile's agent, who lived in the old Markham residence of Ollerton Hall for 40 years; in 1924 he moved out to be replaced by Montagu Wright, the Butterley Company's manager, who lived there until 1947. Edwinstowe Hall was bought by the Bolsover Company in 1923 but its mining agent lived at Edwinstowe House.

Labour disputes occurred frequently. In 1910 a strike at Clifton Colliery lasted over seven months and another at Annesley affected 1,300 men. Even wartime did not result in constant work, as when the 47 boy pony drivers at Bestwood brought the colliery to a standstill in June 1916 because they objected to working on Friday afternoons. The strike of 1919 saw pit flooding problems at Manton and Shireoaks. In 1921 there was a national lock-out for four months, but it was a failure for the men.

The 'Great Strike' was caused largely by the owners' proposals to cut wages. It began on 4 May 1926, affecting immense numbers in Nottinghamshire since the Bolsover Company alone employed 16,000. Key Nottinghamshire figures, such as Frank Varley and George Spencer, favoured compromise. The new Sherwood pits were lukewarm in their support for the cause and Blidworth, Clipstone and Ollerton continued to work.[40] Ollerton was only idle for a month.[41] Blidworth was the last to come out and among the first where men returned

98   *New Ollerton was built with substantial houses and wide streets, but, as with all new towns, the initial impact was harsh and soulless. (Nottinghamshire County Council)*

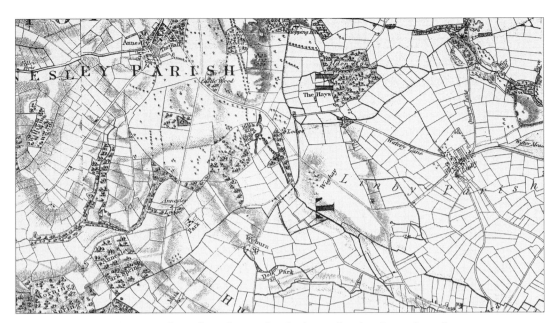

99   *Map of Annesley with parts of Linby. (Nottinghamshire County Council)*

to work. Miners began to drift hungrily back. By early August, 700 men were working underground in Nottinghamshire. On 19 August 1926, 100 miners met the employers 'secretly' at Edwinstowe Hall to discuss terms. By early October, nearly 33,000 men were at work and Nottinghamshire leader, George Spencer, was seen as a traitor by other miners' leaders. Spencer, faced with a meeting with coal owners at Hill Top on 5 October, had placed greatest emphasis on getting the jobs of his remaining strikers back. He was ejected from the miners' conference as 'a blackleg of the worst order' by the crushing margin of 759 votes to four.[42] Spencer, however, had widespread support in the Dukeries collieries and eventually there was a split in representation for the Nottinghamshire miners that was not partially healed for a decade. Many parallels have been drawn between these events and those of nearly sixty years later.

The setback of the General Strike was short-lived. By January 1927 coal had been reached at Blidworth and Ollerton whilst good progress was being made at Bilsthorpe and Thoresby.

The nationalisation of coal royalties in 1938 was a first step to the full national takeover of the industry in 1947. This halted the landowners' steady income from mineral rights and contributed to the abandonment of several of the estates, but they were not entirely losers on the deal for they gained in compensation – Portland recieved £1,976,775.[43] Edwinstowe developed in importance as the NCB's East Midlands headquarters.

Calverton pit was started by the Bestwood Company, whose Bestwood mine had spread so far to the east that access to and from the surface was becoming a serious problem. A new shaft was being sunk at Calverton when war intervened, so for a time this was only used to move miners up and down whilst coal continued to leave via Bestwood. This was most beneficial to the miners who had moved into housing in Calverton, which was later completed as an independent colliery with its own branch railway; coal was first produced from its shaft in 1952.

The most unusual of the Nottinghamshire coal strikes occurred in the middle of the Second World War. Efforts to recruit sufficient men to go underground had failed, and the authorities began compelling surface workers to go down the shafts. At Newstead a surface worker, Sidney Page, was imprisoned for refusing to work underground and all the men went out on strike on 13 September 1943. Very quickly, all the Leen Valley pits came out in sympathy. Page agreed to a compromise deal that allowed him to resume surface work once the war had finished and the Home Secretary himself authorised Page's release from prison. Following this, conscription for underground work began with the 'Bevin Boy' scheme of December 1943.

There was also a training scheme for those opting to work in the mines and a central training school was based at Cresswell, from which the first intake 'graduated' in February 1944. There was even a coalface for training purposes at Gedling colliery. The miners' role in the war was marked by a visit of Lord Montgomery of El Alamein in 1947; he spoke at Edwinstowe and visited Thoresby and Mansfield collieries.

Bevercotes was the last colliery to be opened in the Sherwood area. It was designed to be the first 'fully automated' colliery and was connected to the Trent power stations by its own railway line from Ollerton which opened in 1960. Coal production began in 1961 and the miners were housed in new housing at New Ollerton, Tuxford and Ordsall. Bevercotes had production problems and there were several periods when work was suspended, such as between 1961-4.

100 *Bestwood Colliery aerial view - this colliery became a key part of the "BA" mining group run by the Seely family. (Nottinghamshire County Council)*

The new communities in and around Sherwood were exceptionally vulnerable to the eventual decline of the coal industry. The first indication of trouble ahead was the closure of Bulwell colliery in 1945. Occasional colliery closures included Bestwood in 1967, Firbeck in 1968 and Kirkby Summit in 1969. Bestwood, which had once employed over 2,000 men, closed without any formal ceremony and 610 men simply transferred to other pits. The opening of the Trent power stations, however, especially West Burton (1969), Cottam (1969), Staythorpe (1950/62) and High Marnham (1962), provided a reason for the Sherwood pits at least to be optimistic. The first power station at Staythorpe near Newark was under construction in 1948 with a second authorised in 1951. The mechanisation of loading and unloading coal trains on the 'merry go round' system was developed in the mid-1960s and first introduced at West Burton, then at Cottam.

Poignantly, Alan Griffin wrote about the concealed coalfield mines in 1971: 'At the time of writing all the collieries of the newer concealed coalfield still have many years of life in them and their levels of output continue to rise.'[44] Within 15 years, the industrialisation of Sherwood went into a cataclysmic reverse. Nottinghamshire was affected by the national coal strike of 1972 when the meals-on-wheels van was picketed on the basis that it came from the NCB headquarters at Edwinstowe, shop windows were broken in Clipstone for selling pre-packed coal and some policemen were injured in scuffles at Calverton.

On 6 March 1984 the National Coal Board announced 20,000 job losses and members of the National Union of Mineworkers (NUM) went on strike. At this time the Union was based at Berry Hill, Mansfield. The strikers, however, were strong in Yorkshire and weak in Nottinghamshire, where many miners continued working. By 13 March pickets from Yorkshire were active at the pits around Sherwood, helping to close Bevercotes, Whitwell and Cresswell. The next day 8,000 extra police were sent to Nottinghamshire and many were housed in the old Sherwood army camps. On 15 March a Yorkshire 'flying picket', David Jones, was crushed to death at Ollerton. Police began heading off flying pickets before they got near the pits and some described Nottinghamshire as effectively isolated behind a police blockade by 19 March.

Several Nottinghamshire miners actively opposed the strike, including Chris Butcher, a Bevercotes miner who lived at Ollerton and who went under the code name of 'Silver Birch', and Roy Lynk, a branch secretary from Sutton colliery. The Nottinghamshire Working Miners' Committee had taken shape by May 1984. In November the Nottinghamshire miners won a right to work case at the High Court and mass-picketing at Shireoaks and elsewhere was outlawed in February 1985.

The NUM split, creating a breakaway Union of Democratic Mineworkers. On 3 March 1985 the NUM conference voted narrowly for a return to work and the strike was over. Costs of policing the dispute in the county came to £50 million.[45] The destruction of the coal industry, though, was only just beginning. Roy Lynk assured his members that 'there are no Nottinghamshire collieries in the review procedure' and that all were safe, whereas Arthur Scargill had claimed that half would close. In this, if nothing else, Scargill was right.

The retrenchment of the coal industry followed quickly. Important names such as Blidworth and Shireoaks were quickly culled, Mansfield Crown Farm Colliery closed in 1988, Rufford Colliery and Bevercotes ceased production in 1993. By January 2000, only Clipstone, Harworth, Thoresby and Welbeck remained open; they employed a total of 1,174 staff which was barely the equivalent of one large mine in the 1940s. Clipstone closed in 2003.

The industry left a legacy of subsidence and coal tips, causing a variety of problems. In September 1957 a swimming pool in Arnold suffered serious problems when a 50-foot crack opened up and swallowed 12,000 gallons of water. At the same time plaster fell from the library ceiling and a drapery shop in Nottingham Road began to collapse. This was the culmination of problems that had seen parts of the town sink by over two feet in three years. All was due to the workings of Bestwood Colliery, which passed right under Arnold.

In May 1973 a £133,000 scheme was announced to landscape 171 acres of colliery waste at five sites including Skegby, Kirkby and Bestwood. At Kirkby 54 acres of railway sidings were to be returned to farm and woodland. More recently, Rotary Wood has been planted on the site of a Thoresby tip and the tips at Bevercotes have been landscaped and planted. The headstocks at Clipstone are now a listed building and remain a remarkable sight.

The structures in the Carboniferous rocks created oil deposits at a number of places around Eakring.[46] Waxy green oil seepages in local coalmines had been used for greasing wagon axles.[47] Oil was discovered at Kelham in 1908 when drilling for coal and in 1920-3 an attempt was made to produce it economically. Subsequent test drillings revealed the Kelham Hills oilfield two miles further north and pumping a quarter mile south of Eakring

began in 1939. During the Second World War viable oil deposits were of great significance and in 1941 there were successful discoveries at Dukes Wood, near Kirklington, and Kelham Hills. Early in 1943, a group of expert oil engineers from the USA were brought across to Britain on the *Queen Elizabeth*. At first they were installed in the old Byron house, Burgage Manor, in Southwell, but they eventually took over much of Kelham Hall from its tenants, the Society of the Sacred Mission. Another strike was made at Caunton in 1943. During the course of the War, Nottinghamshire contributed 403,345 tons of oil with a main despatch siding at Eakring.

Further discoveries were made at Egmanton in 1955 and Bothamsall in 1958. For a few years the indigenous oil

101   *Clipstone colliery closed in 2003 but the famous twin headstocks are protected from demoilition. (Nottinghamshire County Council)*

production benefited from preferential rates of duty but, after this ended in 1964, the Nottinghamshire oil field contracted to just Egmanton and Bothamsall.

The hosiery trade remained strong around Mansfield – which was also noted for the production of tin boxes before the Great War. In February 1940 it was reported that all available hosiery workers were engaged in making uniforms, whilst lace workers were helping with nets for camouflage and minesweeping. In the mid-1960s hosiery was still a very significant employer in Nottingham, the towns of the Erewash Valley, and around

Mansfield. Mansfield, Sutton and Kirkby probably had over 8,000 hosiery workers between them with other smaller centres at outlying locations such as Ollerton. The lace industry, however, never moved far from Nottingham and the Erewash Valley.

The value of Sherwood as a supplier of water to Nottingham has continued, reaching further afield. After the Second World War new boreholes were opened at Lambley, Halam and Markham Clinton reaching up to 23 miles from the city. The boreholes at Markham Clinton reach down 740 feet through the clay to the sandstone. In 1965, the sandstones were supplying 23 million gallons a day to Nottingham.

The opening of the 'Dukeries route' railway line at the end of the 19th century provided some impetus to tourism, but the spread of motor transport after the First World War provided the crucial step. Tourism grew so rapidly that by 1922 'trippers' were becoming a nuisance and Nottinghamshire County Council passed a bye-law ordering visitors not to 'blow a horn, use a noisy instrument or sing loudly'. Lord Manvers complained that, 'they begin early in the morning and by the middle of the day many of them are worse for drink and in a disgraceful condition … the practice of throwing coppers in the road for the children to scramble after is a real danger'.[48] Tourism also introduced the threat of fire. In 1929, 500 acres of forest at Budby Common were damaged by a fire that made the Ollerton to Worksop road impassable. There was the added problem of hundreds of small explosions as blank cartridges left from the First World War ignited with the heat.

102   *The main sights of the Dukeries crowded into one postcard.*

After the destruction of a large part of Birklands by the Forestry Commission in 1968, remaining portions were leased to Nottinghamshire County Council by the Thoresby estate in 1969. The Major Oak was part of this, but many other spectacular trees of equal worth had already been lost, and some only recently. The public now had better access to what remained of 'unspoilt' oak woodland as the Council took over former Ministry of Defence lands in Birklands and by 1978 had a country park of 448 acres. The visitor centre was opened in May 1976 but had to be rebuilt after fire in 1980, by which time it was helping to bring a million visitors a year to the Major Oak.[49] In 2002 Sherwood was designated a National Nature Reserve, principally because it had over 1,000 ancient oaks.

The Sherwood Forest Center Parcs site opened in July 1987 at a cost of £50 million, and occupied 400 acres previously forested with conifers. The company subsequently moved its head office onto the new Sherwood Energy Village site, which replaced the colliery at Ollerton and provided 380 jobs.

103   *Ollerton Hall, originally a home for the Markham family and latterly for mining managers, has endured years of dereliction but when this picture was taken in 2007 was being prepared for renovation.*

Tourism also brought demand for better roads, although the greatest pressure was always for roads linking Nottingham to the North. The route from Nottingham to Bawtry was reconstructed in 1925 to replace the Mansfield route. Access to Sherwood was also improved by enhancements to the route across Gunthorpe Bridge, which had only been built in 1873; the new road connected the Fosse Way to Ollerton by way of a new bridge in 1929 and, incidentally, enabled some traffic on the north-south axis to bypass Nottingham. By 1928 there were protests that a road improvement scheme at Budby Corner threatened unique 'Swiss chalet' style houses. A significant later improvement was the opening of the M1, on the western edge of Sherwood, in 1966. Nonetheless, it arrived at a price with the final demolition of Nuthall Temple, which is one of the area's greatest losses.

As roads developed, railways contracted. The very rural route from Mansfield to Southwell lost its passenger service as early as 1929, although the section south of Southwell survived until 1959. The contrasting 'Nottingham Suburban' line had been a victim of wartime economies in 1916, including Sherwood station. The 'Dukeries route' lost its passenger service between Chesterfield and Shirebrook in 1951, and all the way to Lincoln in 1955.

The tourist economy has been encouraged throughout this period by the growth of the 'Robin Hood industry'. For Robin Hood, the 19th century had been the era of the pantomime and the romantic adventure story whilst the 20th century saw film and TV adaptations, each of which renewed interest in an enduringly popular legend.

Sources and Bibliography

Archard, Charles, *The Portland Peerage Romance* (1907)

Bailey, Thomas, *Annals of Nottinghamshire* (1853)

Butler, L.I., *Linby and Papplewick Notebook* (1953)

Brand, K., *The Park Estate, Nottingham* (1984)

Cannadine, David, *The Decline & Fall of the British Aristocracy* (1990)

Chambers, J.D., *Nottinghamshire in the Eighteenth Century* (1932)

Dixon-Kennedy, M., *The Robin Hood Handbook* (2006)

Edwards, K.C., *Nottingham and its Region* (1966)

Fletcher, John, *Ornament of Sherwood Forest* (2005)

Gervat, Claire, *Elizabeth, The Scandalous Life of the Duchess of Kingston* (2003)

Grant, R., *The Royal Forests of England* (1991)

Griffin, A.R., *Mining in the East Midlands* (1971)

Jacks, Leonard, *The Great Houses of Nottinghamshire and the County Families* (1881)

Kaye, David, *A History of Nottinghamshire* (1987)

Kelch, Roy, *Newcastle: Duke without Money* (1974)

Kottler, D., Lavers, C. and Watkins, C., 'The Transformation of Sherwood Forest in the Twentieth Century: The Role of Private Estate Forestry', *Rural History* (2005)

Munsell, F.D., *The Unfortunate Duke* (1985)

Rodgers, Joseph, *The Scenery of Sherwood Forest* (1908)

Schazmann, P.E., *The Bentincks* (1976)

Swinnerton, H.H., *Nottinghamshire* (1910)

The Illustrated London News

The Times

Thompson, E.P., *Whigs and Hunters* (1975)

Thoroton, Robert, Throsby, John (ed.), *The Antiquities of Nottinghamshire* (1790-6)

Transactions of the Thoroton Society, various dates

Turberville, A.S., *History of Welbeck* (1938)

Victoria County History: *Nottinghamshire*

Waller, R.J., *The Dukeries Transformed* (1983)

Weir, C., *Nottinghamshire Heritage* (1991)

Wood, A.C., *Nottinghamshire in the Civil War* (1937)

Woodward, G.H. and G.S., *The Secret of Sherwood Forest* (1973)

I am very grateful to the libraries at Retford, Newark, Nottingham, Lincoln and Holborn for providing me with resources and a comfortable place to work. I would also like to thank those who have helped with the pictures including Sarah Speight and Andy Nicholson, who has done a fantastic service to Nottinghamshire history through his work in making many resources available online.

Notes

1 Landscape and Early History; pps.1-4

1. K.C. Edwards, *Nottingham & Its Region* (1966), p.5.
2. Edwards, p.192.
3. *Transactions of the Thoroton Society* (2002), pps.41-6.
4. C. Weir, *Nottinghamshire Heritage* (1991), p.36.
5. *Nottinghamshire & Derbyshire Notes & Queries* (1894).
6. David Kaye, *A History of Nottinghamshire* (1987), p.26.
7. David Hay, *The Making of South Yorkshire* (1979).
8. H.H. Swinnerton, *Nottinghamshire* (1910), WS.
9. Kaye, p.28.
10. J. Cox, 'The Forest of Sherwood', in E.L. Guilford (ed.), *Memorials of Old Nottinghamshire* (1912), p.107.

2 Barons and Monks; pps.5-11

1. Kaye, p.44, gives 1067.
2. Edwards, p.236.
3. R. White, *Worksop, the Dukeries and Sherwood Forest* (1875).
4. J. Cox, 'Newstead Priory & The Religious Houses of Nottinghamshire' in E. L. Guilford (ed.), *Memorials of Old Nottinghamshire* (1912).
5. Thomas Bailey, *Annals of Nottinghamshire* (1853), p.23. Bailey makes de Busli the leading Norman landowner with 86 'townships', followed by d' Eincourt with 34 and Fitz-Hubert with 10.
6. Kaye, p.39.
7. White, op cit, p29.
8. Bailey, p.32.
9. *The Times*, 5 September 1938.
10. Edwards, p.210.
11. Joseph Rodgers, *The Scenery of Sherwood Forest* (1908), p.386.
12. Also attributed variously to Thomas of Cuckney.
13. Though Bailey (p.65) says Thomas.
14. Rogers, p.263.
15. *White's Directory* (1853).
16. J. Cox, op cit, p.60.
17. Weir, p.33.
18. Sometimes referred to as Ralph Britto, eg Kaye p.55, who gives a date of 1156.
19. Bailey, p.174.
20. Bailey, p.309. For this reason the Annesley title became associated with the Irish peerage.
21. Alternatively 'Lexington' or 'Laxton'.
22. Rogers, p.65.
23. *DNB* refers to the family as 'Lexinton' throughout its entry on Stephen Lexinton.
24. C. Brown, *History of Nottinghamshire* (1896).
25. Kaye, p.51.
26. Kaye, p.70.
27. Kaye, p.55.
28. Edwards, p.236.

3 Sherwood Forest in the Middle Ages; pps.12-19

1. Simon Schama, *Landscape and Memory*

(1995), p.143.
2. Kaye, p.38, says 1130; *Transactions of the Thoroton Society*, 2001, pps.101-9 says first reference 1177.
3. Bailey, p.310.
4. Schama, p.145.
5. Bailey, p.101.
6. Wm Nelson, *The Laws Concerning Game* (1753).
7. Weir, p.14.
8. J. Cox, op cit.
9. David Crook, *Maud de Caux and the custody of the forests of Nottinghamshire and Derbyshire, Henry III Fine Rolls Project* (2006).
10. *Transactions of the Thoroton Society* (2002), pps. 67-9.
11. Bailey, p.64.
12. J. Cox, p.112.
13. Assize of the Forest, 1184, clause 12.
14. J. Cox, 'The Forest of Sherwood' in E.L. Guilford, *Memorials of Old Nottinghamshire* (1912), p.107.
15. K. Brand, *The Park Estate, Nottingham*, Nottingham. Later reduced to only 130 acres.
16. Edwards, p.212.
17. L.I. Butler, *Linby & Papplewick Notebook* (1953), WS.
18. Weir, p.12.
19. Weir, p.41.
20. *Transactions of the Thoroton Society* (2004).
21. T. Cook, 'Bestwood Park' in *Nottinghamshire Historian* (1974).
22. *Journal of the Thoroton Society* (2004) p.109.
23. *White's Directory* (1853).
24. Rodgers, p.418.
25. P.E. Jones in *Transactions of the Thoroton Society* (2003), pps.105-7.
26. *The Times*, 1 May 1937, refers to the discovery of a map from 1376 showing the location of King's Trist.
27. *Journal of the Thoroton Society* (2004), p.109.
28. *Charter of the Forest*, clause 6.
29. Edwards, p.212.
30. Bailey, p.175.
31. Kaye, p.40.
32. Weir, p.38.
33. R. Thoroton & J. Throsby, *The Antiquities of Nottinghamshire*, vol II (1796), p. 257.
34. J. Cox, 'Newstead Priory and the Religious Houses of Notts' in E. L. Guilford (ed.), *Memorials of Old Nottinghamshire* (1912).
35. *Transactions of the Thoroton Society* (2002), pps.73-8.
36. *Transactions of the Thoroton Society* (2002), pps.73-8, says the Rufford monks had another at Kirton by 1250, which must have been very close to their one at Boughton; also Sir William de Sutton's one at Eakring (*c.*1240) was close to the Gant one mentioned.
37. Thoroton & Throsby, vol II, p.279.

38. *Transactions of the Thoroton Society* (2002) pps.71-2.
39. Joseph Rogers, *Sherwood Forest* (1908), p.19.

4 Dissolution and New Dynasties; pps.20-33

1. Chambers, p.155.
2. L.I. Butler, *Linby & Papplewick Notebook* (1953), WS.
3. Quoted from 'Carlyle's Historical Sketches' by Rodgers, p.277.
4. *Nottinghamshire & Derbyshire Notes & Queries* (1894), p.90.
5. 1623 according to K.Brand, *The Park Estate Nottingham* (1984); 1622 according to *Transactions of the Thoroton Society* (2002), p.81.
6. In 1517 six houses were falling down.
7. Temporary arable areas that were returned to 'forest' after a few years – this type of farming suited the poor soils of Sherwood.
8. Their title was Shrewsbury and the family name Talbot.
9. *DNB*, George Talbot, 6th Earl of Shrewsbury.
10. Weir, p.58.
11. Some sources, eg Brown's *History of Nottinghamshire*, say the Duke of Norfolk acquired it from Henry VIII but *Transactions of the Thoroton Society* (2002) says it was sold by the Crown in the 17th century.
12. J.D. Chambers, *Nottinghamshire in the Eighteenth Century* (1932), p.4.
13. *DNB*, Sir John Harington (1560-1612).
14. *DNB*, Savile family.
15. It should be noted that several generations of Byron bore the name of John.
16. *The Times*, 9 January 1860.
17. *Nottinghamshire & Derbyshire Notes & Queries* (1893), p.195.
18. A.R. Griffin, *Mining in the East Midlands* (1971).
19. Weir, p.38.
20. Osborne gained the patronage of a wealthy benefactor by rescuing his infant daughter from the Thames – and later married her.
21. *Transactions of the Thoroton Society* (2003).
22. 'Barley' is given by *DNB*, but Rogers gives 'Barlow'.
23. Archard says he bought it from three obscure men. He also claims that Bess of Hardwick's designs for the new house were dated 1604.
24. *DNB*, William Cavendish.
25. Transactions of the Thoroton Society, 2003.
26. J.D.Chambers, p.6.
27. A.B. Beaver, *Aldermen of the City of London*, London, 1913.
28. *DNB*: Sir William Holles.
29. *DNB*: Sir William Holles. This was John Babington of Rampton who had acquired the estate through marrying a

Stanhope of Rampton. The Babington family were often referred to as 'of Dethick' in Derbyshire but had included a sheriff of Notts and had owned land in the county for several centuries; Henry Babington married Frances Markham, daughter of Sir John, and their son was involved in the 'Babington Plot' to free Mary Queen of Scots. He had been a page in Shrewsbury's service.
30. *Transactions of the Thoroton Society of Nottinghamshire* (1930).
31. Bailey, vol 1, p.412. Not the only example of Bailey's censorious moral tone, but perhaps exaggerated in that the family cannot have been utterly destitute when they still held lands. According to the *DNB* the wastrel son was actually the oldest, Thomas, who inherited lands in Lincolnshire and Norfolk and supposedly died in prison.
32. Subsequently Lound Hall.
33. Rodgers, p.238.
34. Rodgers, p.276, estimated that the incident occured in 1597 but he was born in 1598 (DNB).
35. Chambers, p.22-3.
36. Chambers, p.6.
37. *DNB*, Denzil Holles.
38. Rogers, p.153.
39. C. Brown, *A History of Nottinghamshire* (1896).
40. Robert White, *Worksop, The Dukery & Sherwood Forest* (1875).
41. Kaye, p.50.
42. Blaskerville, cited in *Linby and Papplewick Notebook*, WS.

5 War and Restoration; 34-45

1. W.E. Doubleday, Nottinghamshire Villages – Holme Pierrepont, Notts history WS.
2. Bailey, p.968.
3. A.C. Wood, *Nottinghamshire in the Civil War* (1937), p.15.
4. Wood, p.34.
5. Wood, p.122.
6. Wood, p.50.
7. Wood, p.43.
8. Rogers, quoting an edition of the *DNB*.
9. Rogers, p.359.
10. Wood, p.63.
11. Wood, p.94.
12. Wood, p.98.
13. Wood, p.112.
14. Wood, p.159.
15. *Nottinghamshire Historian* (1974).
16. Wood, p.164.
17. Kaye, p.68.
18. *Nottinghamshire Historian* (1974).
19. E.P. Thompson, *Whigs and Hunters* (1976), p.176.
20. Weir, p.38.
21. Rogers, p.154.
22. Although the current owner, Robert Brackenbury, claims descent from the 3rd Earl Manvers.

23. Rodgers, quoting Howitt's *Rural Life*.
24. Chambers, p.162.
25. Rodgers, p.327.
26. J. Cox, p.117.
27. John Evelyn, *Silva or Sylva*, part 16.
28. *The Times*, 26 July 1890.
29. Rodgers, p.287.
30. Chambers, p.157.
31. Gervase Holles the historian was connected with the Grimsby branch of the family and brought up as an orphan at Haughton.
32. *DNB*, John Holles, Duke of Newcastle upon Tyne.
33. Rodgers, p.291.
34. *The Times*, 27 February 1923, says that 'he acquired Welbeck in 1695' but the view of *DNB* is that it came to him through his wife's inheritance.
35. Rodgers, p.291.
36. *DNB*, John Holles. The *DNB* is so impressed with this facet of his career that it mentions it twice in six lines.
37. *DNB*, Sir George Savile, with reference to Bishop Burnet's *History*.
38. *DNB*, Sir George Savile.
39. *DNB*, Henry Savile.
40. P.E. Schazmann, *The Bentincks* (1976), pps. 83-102.

6 The Rise of the Landed Estate 1700-1815; pps.47-73
1. Horace Walpole is credited with the first use of the 'Dukery', later becoming 'Dukeries'.
2. Rogers, p.86.
3. J. Cox, p.117.
4. Rodgers, p.295.
5. Though the name came later.
6. Rodgers.
7. E.P. Thompson, p.41.
8. *Transactions of the Thoroton Society* (2002), p.103.
9. Some sources place the meeting at Retford.
10. Bailey, pps.1088-9.
11. Referred to in an article in *The Times*, 17 February 1938, which erroneously stated the meeting to have been at Retford.
12. K. Brand, p.4.
13. Edwards, p.166.
14. Thoroton and Throsby, vol.11, p.279.
15. Weir, p.31.
16. E.P. Thompson, p.39.
17. Throsby, vol.III, p.407.
18. One historian has claimed that an apparent lack of popular protest against this as evidence that the ordinary people were grateful to be protected against the deer. However, for the next hundred years common rights were ruthlessly suppressed by all-consuming landowners.
19. Bailey, p.1093.
20. Rodgers, p.326.
21. *Transactions of the Thoroton Society* (2002), pps.103-8.
22. Bailey, vol.2, p.51.
23. Bailey, p.1096.
24. Kottler, Watkins and Lavers, 'The Transformation of Sherwood Forest in the Twentieth Century: The Role of Private Estate Forestry', *Rural History* (2005), p.95.
25. Bailey, vol.2, p.144.
26. *DNB*, Sir George Savile.
27. Rodgers, p.359.
28. Bailey, vol.2, p140 says through second son of his sister, wife of Earl of Scarbrough.
29. R. Kelch, *Newcastle: A Duke without Money* (1974), p.28.
30. The house was 66-67 Lincoln's Inn Fields.
31. Kelch, p.30.

32. Claims vary, but earlier Nottinghamshire historians claimed 'half a million' while the *DNB* gives £20,000. The latter was an annual income, and the former is perhaps a capital sum.
33. Street names include Holles, Harley, Henrietta, Welbeck, Bentinck streets and Portland Place. Harley Street and Oxford Street are clear, but Wigmore Street is derived from the Harley family possessions in Herefordshire.
34. Kelch, p.36.
35. This was the title awarded to William Cavendish in 1665 though it had subsequently lapsed.
36. We may assume that Haughton was no longer suitable or had become uninhabitable.
37. Kelch, p.vii.
38. Kelch, p.7.
39. Bailey, vol 2, p22.
40. He made a significant contribution to the University's architecture by employing Stephen Wright, who also worked for him at Clumber.
41. Horace Walpole, 'Memoirs of the Reign of King George II' quoted in Kelch, p.190.
42. Kelch, P.122.
43. *DNB*: Henry Fiennes Pelham-Clinton.
44. Munsell, *The Unfortunate Duke* (1985), p.5.
45. Schazmann, p. 126.
46. *DNB*, Edward Harley, 2nd Earl of Oxford.
47. Rodgers, p.297.
48. Rodgers, vol.2, p.234.
49. Sources vary as to dates in March or April.
50. Gervat, *Elizabeth, The Scandalous Life of the Duchess of Kingston* (2003), p.54.
51. F. Fraser, 'If You Seek His Monument' in C. White (ed.), *The Nelson Companion* (1995), p.130-1.
52. Gervat, P.93.
53. *DNB*, Henry Pelham-Clinton.
54. *DNB*, Topham Beauclerk; he would not be the only member of the Dukeries aristocracy to deserve this epithet.
55. To take inevitable comparisons even further, she grew up being known as 'Lady Di'.
56. Rodgers, p.388.
57. Thoroton and Throsby, vol.III, p.406.
58. Weir, p.60.
59. *The Times*, 2 June 1790.
60. Rogers, p.149.
61. Throsby, vol.III, p.344.
62. Various dates for the fire have been given, including 20 and 26 October.
63. *Linby and Papplewick Notebook* citing Mrs Delaney in 1756.
64. There is still a house at Edwinstowe named Villa Real. It was said to have been taken down and rebuilt on higher ground and that it was the home of William, who died in 1759 (Rodgers).
65. *DNB*, Catherine Mellish and also William Mellish – it is rare for both halves of a couple to have separate entries in the *DNB*.
66. Bailey, p1187. Mellish was first elected in 1741 but 'Kitty' died in 1747 – at the election that year Mellish was returned unopposed so it would seem that, sadly, the story is not true!
67. Rodgers, vol.2, p.145-6: it should be recalled that Rodgers had a strong dislike of rapacious landowners.
68. Weir, p.41.
69. Thoroton, vol.II, p. 157.
70. Rodgers, p.327.
71. Rodgers vol.2, p.146-7 cites 9 Geo. III c.16.
72. Rodgers, vol.2, p.168.

73. *Nottinghamshire & Derbyshire Notes & Queries* (1894).
74. Chambers, p.81.
75. *Linby and Papplewick Notebook* confirmed in other sources.
76. Bailey, vol.2, p.142.
77. Griffin, p.5.
78. Griffin, p.23.
79. *White's Directory* gives 1719.
80. Thoroton and Throsby, vol.II, p.163.

7 The Great Days of Land and Industry 1815-1901; 74-112
1. *The Times*, 29 August 1850.
2. *The Times*, 30 March 1846.
3. Archard, *The Portland Peerage Romance*, reports that he was called 'Farmer Duke'.
4. Reported as £80,000 in Archard.
5. Archard.
6. Rodgers, p.85.
7. Bailey, vol.1, p.409.
8. *The Times*, 19 April 1924.
9. Rodgers, p.391.
10. Bailey, vol.2, p324.
11. Letter written in March 1809.
12. Bailey, vol.2, p.332.
13. *The Times*, 19 July 1824.
14. *The Times*, 27 January 1866.
15. J. Wolffe, *The Protestant Crusade in Britain* (1991), cited in *DNB*, Henry Pelham-Clinton.
16. Figures from the Pelham Clinton v Duke of Norfolk law case, resolved in 1903.
17. Bailey, vol.2, p.427 though *DNB* gives £370,000.
18. *The Times*, 26 July 1890.
19. Bailey, vol.2, p.440.
20. This title was held by the heirs to the Newcastle dukedom.
21. *The Times*, 15 April 1856.
22. Munsell, p.39.
23. R. Norton (ed.), *My Dear Boy* (1997).
24. J. Fletcher, *Ornament of Sherwood Forest*, p.177.
25. Munsell, p.273.
26. *The Times*, 9 October 1865.
27. *DNB*, John Savile.
28. *The Times*, 5 May 1938.
29. *White's Directory*, 1853.
30. Rodgers, p.345.
31. *DNB*, Lord William Cavendish-Bentinck.
32. Schazmann, pps.190-214 provides much detail of his career around the world.
33. *DNB*.
34. Schazmann, p.211, claims generally an 18-hour day.
35. Denison rose to become Speaker of the Commons and Viscount Ossington. Lady Ossington built the famous 'coffee palace' opposite the castle in Newark.
36. She took the married name of Ellis – her husband, the 6th Baron, had died in 1868.
37. Although, in the case of the Beauclerks, this was merely in keeping with family tradition.
38. *The Times*, 9 March 1829.
39. *The Times*, 11 January 1851.
40. Munsell, p12.
41. *The Times*, 16 March 1829.
42. Griffin, p.28.
43. *The Times*, 26 July 1890.
44. Griffin, p.71.
45. Griffin, p.130.
46. Rodgers, vol 2, p.240.
47. *The Times*, 3 August 1819.
48. Weir, p.107.
49. L.I. Butler, *Linby and Papplewick Notebook*, WS.

50. *Linby and Papplewick Notebook*, WS.
51. *The Times*, 15 December 1838.
52. Edwards, p.474.
53. *White's Directory* (1853).
54. Kaye, p.78.
55. *White's Directory* (1853).

8 The Decline and Rebirth of the Dukeries; pps.113-143
1. Kottler, Watkins and Lavers, p.99.
2. J. Fletcher, *Ornament of Sherwood Forest* (2005), p. 155
3. *The Times*, 2 June 1960.
4. Kottler, Watkins and Lavers, p.104.
5. Edwards, p.267.
6. *The Times*, 6 October 1966.
7. In fact they came from breeding egrets, not ospreys.
8. D. Cannadine, *The Decline & Fall of the British Aristocracy* (1990).
9. Fletcher, p.110.
10. Fletcher, p.73.
11. As most of the males were given the first name Henry, they were usually known by their second name.
12. John Fletcher in *Ornament of Sherwood Forest* comments on the difficulty of saying exactly what was paid for the diamond – the figure given here is the lowest published estimate. The diamond itself caused fitting carnage in the lives of subsequent owners who were variously assassinated, killed and drowned.
13. Kottler, Watkins and Lavers, p.108.
14. *The Times*, 27 July 1929.
15. *The Times*, 13 May 1937.
16. Fletcher, p.115.
17. *The Times*, 1 January 1929.
18. The main item was the Lamoignan Book of Hours for £13,500.
19. *The Times*, 27 October 1944.
20. R. J. Waller, *The Dukeries Transformed* (1983), p.154.
21. Waller p.154 says Albert.
22. *The Times*, 5 September 1938.
23. *The Times*, 3 May 1973.
24. Kottler, Watkins and Lavers, p.100.
25. *The Times*, 10 November 1950.
26. Research report on Tyntesfield, Bristol, which can be found at the following web reference: http://web.changenet.sk/aa/file7b2b95567ef29173cb6d44cc904e9140/Appendix2Research%20Report%20-%20Tyntesfield%20-%20UK.doc.
27. Presumably Welbeck Colliery.
28. *The Times*, 24 January 1912.
29. Griffin, p.166.
30. Waller, p.67.
31. Kottler, Watkins and Lavers, p.102.
32. Waller, p.13.
33. Which *The Times* mistakenly called 'Coxglade'.
34. *The Times*, 4 February 1925.
35. Waller, p.57.
36. Waller, p.92.
37. Waller, p.41.
38. Waller, p.49.
39. *Newark Advertiser*, 5 October 1927.
40. Waller, p.240.
41. Weir, p.119.
42. Griffin, p.246.
43. Cannadine, p.125.
44. Griffin, p.177.
45. *The Times*, 15 January 1985.
46. K.C. Edwards, *Nottingham and its Region*, p.39.
47. Woodward and Woodward, *The Secret of Sherwood Forest* (1973), p.15.
48. *The Times*, 27 April 1922.
49. *The Times*, 25 September 1980.

Index

Aberdeen, 65, 81
Aegis Trust, 130
Aethelfrith, King of Northumbria, 3
Afforestation, 12, 14, 16
Agister, 13
Aldrich, George, 69
Alfred, King, 4
Anne, Queen, 47, 48, 52
Annesley: 8, 16, 28, 39, 51, 56, 65, 69, 79, 81-2, 102, 103, 113, 128, 137; Park, Ireland, 8
Annesley: Sir Frances, 33; Sir John, 8; Ralph de, 8
Arnold, 17, 20, 69, 72, 107, 119, 141
Assarts, 15
Assize of the Forest, 14, 15
Athelstan, King, 4
Averham, 10, 39

Babbington colliery, 106, 125
Babington, John, 31
Babworth, 133, 135
Baker, John, 137
Ball, Sir Albert, 127-8
Banqueting Dale, 47
Barlborough, 74
Barnby Moor, 125
Barry, Sir Charles, 85
Basford, 16, 69, 72, 102, 106
Bassetlaw, 4
Bawtry, 2, 143
Beauclerk: Aubrey, 5th Duke of St Albans, 64; Aubrey, 6th Duke of St Albans (1765-1816), 96; Charles, 11th Duke of St Albans (1870-1934), 123; Charles, 13th Duke of St Albans (1915-88), 123; George, 3rd Duke of St Albans, 64; George, 4th Duke of St Albans, 64; Henry, 1st Duke of St Albans, 44; Murray, 14th Duke of St Albans (1939-), 123; Osborne, 12th Duke of St Albans (1874-1964), 123-4; Lord Sidney (Topham), 64; Vere, 64; William, 8th Duke of St Albans (1766-1825), 96; William, 9th Duke of St Albans (1801-49), 96; William, 10th Duke of St Albans (1840-98), 96-7, 99
Beaumont, Huntingdon, 26
Beauvale, 8, 11, 24
Beckford, William, 86
Bellamy, John, 73
Belle Eau, 2
Bentinck: Hans William, 1st Earl of Portland (1649-1709), 26, 45, 62; Henry, 1st Duke of Portland (1682-1726), 45, 60; Margaret Cavendish née Harley, Duchess of Portland (1715-85), 60, 61, 71; Timothy, 12th Earl of Portland (1953-), 123; Admiral William, 90; William, 2nd Duke of Portland (1709-62), 60, 71

Bentinck colliery, 105, 130, 135
Berengarius, 7
Berry Hill, 132, 140
Bestwood, 11, 15, 16, 18, 20-1, 25, 36, 38-9, 44-5, 64, 74, 96-7, 102-3, 119, 124, 135; colliery, 103, 106, 135, 137, 140, 141
Bevercotes, 9, 129; colliery, 130, 139-40
Bevercotes, William de, 9
Bilborough, 4, 18, 26, 69, 73, 101
Bilby, 3
Bilhagh, 14, 15, 22, 51, 70, 81, 118
Bilsthorpe, 2, 25, 90, 116, 132-3, 136-7
Birklands, 1, 14-15, 22, 51, 70, 81, 91, 118, 142
Black Act, 48
Blackwell, Sir Thomas, 34
Blakiston, Sir William, 37
Blidworth, 3, 13, 14, 16-17, 20, 69-71, 106, 111, 132, 135-8, 140
Blomfield, Sir Reginald, 129
Blyth, 4, 5, 9, 23, 37, 39, 40
Bolsover, 1, 6, 23, 28, 37, 40, 55, 66, 69, 92, 103, 113
Bothamsall, 5, 13, 41, 84, 141
Boughton, 10, 18, 70, 102, 110, 133
Bowbearer, 21, 47
Bowden: Frank, 123; Sir Harold, 123-4
Breadsall, 16
Brecks (temporary clearances), 23, 51, 70
Bristowe, John, 58
British Museum, 60, 126
British Ropes, 129
Broxtowe, 2, 4, 24, 102
Brunts, Robert, 38
Buck Gates, 90
Budby, 15, 73, 79, 110, 116, 118, 142
Bulcote, 12
Bulstrode, 45, 60, 62, 67, 92
Bulwell, 17, 22-3, 26, 65, 102, 106, 109, 140
Burlington House, 61, 87
Burn, William, 90
Burton, Abbot, 7, 8
Busli: Ralph de, 5; Roger de, 5, 10, 12, 13
Byron: Colonel Gilbert, 38; George Gordon, 6th Lord (1788-1824), 65, 81, 82; Hugh de, 7; Sir John (d.1625), 23, 26; Sir John, 1st Lord Rochdale (1599-1652), 27, 34, 38; John (Admiral) (1723-86), 65; John or 'Mad Jack' (1756-91), 65, 81; Sir John, 11, 13; Ralph de, 5; Richard, 2nd Lord Rochdale (1605-79), 34, 37, 38-9; William (m.1660), 26; William, 4th Lord Rochdale, 45, 47; William, 5th Lord Rochdale, 64-5, 81

Cahn, Sir Julian (1882-1944), 129
Calverton, 14, 16, 33, 39, 69, 73, 106, 135, 138-40
Canning, George, 62
Cantelupe, Nicholas, 8
Capel, Lord Arthur, 38

Carburton, 7, 15, 23, 33, 115
Carr, John, 61, 66
Carrington, 119
Cattle, farming of, 15, 20, 70, 115
Caunton, 10, 133, 141
Caux: Maud de, 13, 18; Robert de and family, 10, 13
Cavendish: Charles (son of Bess) (-1617), 26-8; Sir Charles (1620-43), 28, 36; Elizabeth, Countess of Lennox, 25; Frances, née Pierrepont, Duchess of Newcastle, 41; Henry, 2nd Duke of Newcastle upon Tyne (1630-91), 29, 40-2; Henry, Lord Mansfield, 39; Margaret, Duchess of Newcastle, 41; Margaret, née Lucas, 29; Sir William (1508-57), 27, 28; William, 1st Marquess and Duke of Newcastle upon Tyne (1592-1676), 28-9, 34-41; William (1610), 22; William, 1st Earl of Devonshire 28; William, 4th Duke of Devonshire, 60; William, 5th Duke of Devonshire, 73
Cavendish-Bentinck: Anne, 122; Dorothy, née Cavendish, Duchess of Portland, 60; Ferdinand, 8th Duke of Portland (1889-1980), 122-3; Lord Henry (1863-1931), 118, 121; Victor, 9th Duke of Portland (1897-1990), 122-3; (Scott-Bentinck), William, 4th Duke of Portland (1768-1854), 74, 77, 92, 101, 104, 107; William, 6th Duke of Portland (1857-1943), 78, 96, 104, 112-3, 119-21, 128, 130; William Arthur, 7th Duke of Portland (1893-1977), 122, 139; William Henry, 3rd Duke of Portland (1738-1809), 48, 53, 61-2, 66, 69, 70, 94, 98, 101, 128; Lord William Henry (1774-1839), 71, 92; Winifred, 120-21
Cavendish-Scott-Bentinck: (William) George (1802-48), 92-3; William, 5th Duke of Portland (1800-79), 79, 93-4, 120-1
Cavendish Square, 55, 60, 86, 90-1, 93-4
Center Parcs, 129, 142
Centre Tree, 111
Chamberlain, Joseph, 96
Charcoal, 17, 22, 40
Charles: I, King, 22-3, 28, 34-5, 37-8; II, King, 39, 40, 44-5, 64; Prince of Wales, 128
Charter of the Forest, 16
Chatsworth, 28, 32, 40
Chaworth: George, 8; Lord John (d.1644), 27, 34; Mary, 81; Lord Patrick(1635-93), 39; William, 64-5, 73
Chaworth-Musters: Col John (1890-1970), 128; Sir John, 33, 81
Chief Justice, of the Forest, 13
Chudleigh, Elizabeth, 62-3, 90
Cinderhill, 102, 106
Clare Market, 32, 42, 54

Claremont, 57-9
Clifton: Sir Gervase, 34; Henry, 128
Clinton: Catherine née Pelham, 59; Henry, 7th
    Earl of Lincoln, 59; Lord Charles, 115
Clipstone, 4, 12, 15-8, 20-1, 24-5, 33, 40, 74-5,
    77, 92, 111, 115, 130, 135-6, 138, 141
Clowne, 73
Clumber, 5, 43, 51-3, 55, 58-9, 65-6, 69, 71, 74,
    78, 84-5, 98-9, 115-6, 123, 125-6; church,
    88; spaniel, 60
Cnut (Canute), King, 12, 16
Coal, industry, 11, 71, 73, 101-3, 130-2, 132-40
Cockglode, 15, 69, 91, 98, 130, 132, 133-4
Colchester, 29, 38
Cole, Sir Henry, 101
Colwick, 18, 26, 33, 40, 99
Commissioners for woods and forests, 74, 85,
    99, 101
Cooper: John, 38; Sir Roger, 37-8
Cossall, 11
Cottam, 25, 140
Coventry, William, 43
Cradock, George, 129
Cratley, 6
Crauford, Lt Gen Charles, 85
Cresswell, 1, 74, 139-40; colliery, 103
Cromwell (Notts.), 2
Cromwell: Oliver, 36; Thomas, 23
Crown Farm (Mansfield) colliery, 103, 130,
    139-140
Cuckney, 4, 5, 7, 9, 11, 19, 33, 35, 72, 79, 92,
    108, 111

David, King of Scotland, 5
Daybrook, 88, 99, 124
Day-Lewis, Cecil, 137
De Walden, Lucy, 94, 122
Deepdene, 124, 127
Deer, stags etc., 12, 13, 15-18, 20, 22, 39, 40, 42,
    47, 48, 50-3, 70, 79, 83, 116
Deforestation, 13, 15, 16, 18, 22
Deighton, Robert, 26
Digby, Sir John, 34-5
Disraeli, Benjamin, 93, 96
Dogs, hunting with, 16-17
Dover Beck, 72
Drayton, West, 41
Druce, legal case, 119-21
Dukeries Junction, 109
Duke's Walking Stick, 48, 81
Dumble (landscape feature), 1
Dunham, 42, 108

Eakring, 18, 70, 123, 141
Edge, Ralph, 73
Edmund, King, 4
Edward: I, King, 8, 14, 16; II, King, 7-8, 16; IV,
    King, 11, 27, 65; the Confessor, King, 4; VI,
    King, 27; VII, King, 79, 86, 90, 96, 99, 102,
    113, 125; VIII, King, 113
Edwin, King of Northumbria, 3, 4
Edwinstowe, 1, 9, 14-17, 24, 35, 39-40, 52, 68,
    73-4, 79, 89, 92, 109-10, 117, 130, 132, 136-40
Egmanton, 5, 70, 88, 141
Eleanor, Queen, 5
Elizabeth: I, Queen, 20, 22, 25, 28, 33; II,
    Queen, 128

Elkesley, 133
Elmton, 74
Enclosures, 13, 15, 17-18, 20, 22, 40, 52-3, 67,
    69, 71, 74
Erewash, River, 1
Evelyn, John, 40
Everingham, de, family of, 13
Eyre, Justice in, 10, 14, 16-17, 20, 48, 51, 62

Farnsfield, 2, 38, 106, 133
Faucumberge, Henry de, 9
Felley, 8, 15, 23, 39, 128
Fitz-Hubert, Ralph, 5
Fitzstephen, Ralph, 13
Flammaugh: Richard de, 7; Thomas de, 7
Folewood (Fulwood), 50, 57
Foljambe, 54, 69; Cecil, Baron Hawkesbury and
    Earl of Liverpool, 98
Forest: courts, 13-14; foot, 17; laws, 12, 14;
    Town, 115, 135
Forest, New, 12
Forestry Commission, 142
Fosse Way, 2
Foster, Simon, Oak, 79
Fox, George, 24
Frescheville, Colonel John, 37
Fulwood, 14
Furnival, Gerard de, 6, 18

Gainsborough, 36
Gant, Gilbert de, Earl of Lincoln, 5-6, 18
Gatefird, 69
Gedling, 16, 35, 105, 119, 130, 133, 139
George: I, King, 57, 65; II, King, 58; III, King,
    59, 68, 71, 101; IV, King, 96; V, King, 135
Gladstone, William, MP, 85-6, 101
Gordon, Arabella, née Milbanke, 82
Greasley, 8, 24, 73
Great North Road, 73
Greendale Oak, 40, 47
Grendon Trust, 123
Greville, Charles, 92
Grey: de Ruthven, Lord, 81; Lord John, 16
Griffin, Alan, 130, 140
Grove, Jonathan, 38
Gwynne, Nell, 44-5, 64

Hacker, Colonel Francis, 39
Hanger Hill, 77
Hannah Park, 118
Harcourt House, 92, 94
Hardwick, Elizabeth of, 23, 25, 27
Harington, Sir John, 25
Harlaxton, 90
Harley: Edward, 2nd Earl of Oxford (1689-
    1741), 47, 53, 55, 60; Henrietta, née
    Cavendish-Holles, 42, 54-5, 60, 66
Harlow Wood, 122
Harrowlands, 126
Hatfield, 3, 48; Chase, 4
Haughton, 11, 20, 31, 37, 42-3, 53, 55-6, 135
Hay, Thomas de la, 15
Hays see enclosures
Haywood Oaks, 97
Helwys, Thomas, 24
Henderson, Sir John, 35
Henrietta Maria, Queen, 28, 36
Henry: I, King, 12, 15; II, King, 7, 8, 12-15; III,

King, 10, 13, 14, 16; VII, King, 11, 20; VIII,
    King, 20, 25
Hervey, Augustus, Earl of Bristol, 62
Hewet, Dr John, 38; Rev. John, 65; Thomas, 33;
    Thomas (1656-1726), 65; Sir William, 33
Highams, Thomas, 71
Hill, John, 35
Hockerton, 4
Hodsock, 4
Holden: Henry, 89; Robert, 89
Holles: Denzil, 32, 34, 39, 42; Gervase, 34, 41;
    Gilbert, 3rd Earl of Clare (1633-89), 39, 41,
    129; Grace, née Pierrepont, 41; Sir John, 1st
    Earl of Clare (1564-1637), 22, 31-2; John,
    2nd Earl of Clare (1595-1666), 32, 34-5, 38-
    9, 41; John, 4th Earl of Clare, 1st Duke of
    Newcastle upon Tyne (2nd creation) (1662-
    1711), 39, 41-3, 51-2, 54, 65, 73; Margaret,
    née Cavendish, Duchess of Newcastle, 41-3,
    54; Sir William (1471-1542), 29-31;
    William, (1642), 34
Holme Pierrepont, 10-1, 23, 32, 40, 42, 63, 90,
    117, 119, 128
Home Brewery, 88, 124
Hooton, Elizabeth, 24
Hope diamond, 87, 122
Howard: Bernard Edward, Duke of Norfolk,
    84; Edward, 9th Duke of Norfolk, 67; Mary,
    Duchess of Norfolk, 68; Thomas, 8th Duke
    of Norfolk, 67
Hucknall, 82, 103, 106, 129; Huthwaite, 73;
    Torkard, 110
Hunger Hill, 76
Hunting, 12, 13, 15-6, 18, 22, 40, 42, 48, 50,
    77-8, 113
Huskisson, William, 70, 74
Hutchinson, John, 34, 36-9

Idle, River, 3
Industry: cotton, 108; iron, 33; tin boxes, 110
Inkersall, 6
Irving, Washington, 82

James: I, King, 20, 22, 28, 32; II, King, 43-4
John, King, 9, 10-1, 13, 15-6
Jonson, Ben, 22

Kelham, 38, 71, 141
Kelly, Sophia, Countess of Annesley, 82
Kersall, 7
Kew, 60
Killamarsh, 33
Kimberley, 105
King's Mill, 2
King's Stand, 16, 74
Kingshaugh, 15, 18
Kirkby in Ashfield, 3, 18, 69, 105, 109, 135,
    139, 141
Kirkby Summit colliery, 105, 140
Kirklington, 141
Kiveton Park, 26
Kneesall, 5, 18, 110, 123
Knight: Henry, 110; Isaac, 48
Knitting industry (hosiery), 33, 72, 106-8, 136, 141

Lacock, Philip, 38
Lacy: Reginald de, 9; Roger de, 5; Sir John de,
    Earl of Lincoln, 5

Lambley, 15-6, 69, 106-7, 142
Langold, 48
Langton Arbour, 15-6
Langwith, 7, 26, 72, 92, 108; Nether, 15
Laxton, 5, 10, 13, 18, 25, 70, 128, 130
Lee, William, 33, 72
Leeds, Duke of, 76
Leek, Thomas, 15
Leen, River, 2, 50, 68, 72
Leigh, Augusta, née Byron, 65, 82
Lenton, 7, 15, 24, 69, 113
Lespegend, 12
Levinz, William, 53
Lexington: John de, 9; John of, 13; Richard of,
    10, 13; Robert of, 10
Linby, 3, 11, 14-15, 17, 20, 27, 39, 72, 102, 108,
    135; colliery, 104
Lincoln, 11; Earl of (Stoke), 11
Lindley, Thomas, 38
Lindrick, 110
Lisle, Brian de, 13
London & Fort St George Land Co., 125, 126-7
Lound, 41, 113, 126, 129-30
Lovetot: Matilda de, 6; Richard de, 5; William de, 5
Lowther, Sir James, 61
Luddism, 106
Lumley: Richard, 4th Earl of Scarbrough (d.
    1782), 54, 89; Richard, 9th Earl of
    Scarbrough (1813-84), 89
Lumley-Savile: Augustus (d.1887), 89; George,
    3rd Baron Savile (1919-), 129; Henry
    (d.1881), 89; Rev. John, 7th Earl of
    Scarbrough (1761-1835), 54, 89; John, 8th
    Earl of Scarbrough (1788-1856), 89, 101;
    John, 1st Baron Savile (1818-96), 89-90;
    Richard, 6th Earl of Scarbrough (1757-
    1832), 54
Lyndhurst Wood, 71
Lynk, Roy, 140

Magna Carta, 13, 16
Major Oak, 2, 47, 79, 113, 115, 117-8, 132, 142
Manchester, Earl of, 37
Mansfield, 1-2, 5, 9, 15, 18, 24, 36, 38-9, 53, 70,
    72-3, 75, 93, 103, 105, 106, 108-9, 112, 128,
    136, 141; Woodhouse, 2, 12, 24, 34, 76
Manton, 130, 138
Manvers: Annora de, 10; Lady Marie-Lousie,
    118
Maplebeck, 10
Markham: Arthur, MP, 70-1; Sir Arthur, 135;
    Clinton, 85, 142; East, 10; Gervase, 31-2; Sir
    Griffin, 25; Henry, 11; Sir John (d.1559), 25;
    Sir John (Stoke), 10-11; Moor, 89; Sir
    Robert, 10-11; Thomas (1560s), 20, 25;
    Thomas (1642), 34, 36; West, 10, 35;
    William de, 9
Marylebone, 67
Matilda, Queen, 5, 9, 11
Maun, River, 3, 129
Meden, River, 72
Medows, Philip, 63
Mellish, William, 68
Memorial Avenue, 113
Militia Act, 71
Miller of Mansfield, 15
Mills, water, 11, 108
Milnes, Sir Robert, 98

Miners, unions and associations, 105-6, 137, 139-41
Molyneaux, Sir John, 73
Montagu: Andrew, 102; Frederick, 68; Mary
    Wortley, 62
Montrose, Earl of, 37
Monyash, William, 11
Morrell, Lady Ottoline, née Cavendish-
    Bentinck, 120,
Muskham: North, 9; South, 18, 37-8
Musters, John, 39, 51

National Coal Board, 128, 129, 130, 139-40
National Trust, 127
Neville, Hugh de, 13
New Hucknall colliery, 104, 105
Newark, 1, 6, 11, 16, 18, 22, 35-40, 44, 59, 71,
    73, 81, 83, 87, 99, 108, 110, 113, 118, 126
Newcastle: colliery, 102, 106; House, 54, 57-8
Newstead, 7-9, 15, 17, 24, 27, 40, 69, 81-3, 104,
    127; colliery, 104, 139
No Man's Wood, 71
Norfolk, Duke of (1530s), 24
Normanton, South, 108
Normanton-by-Clumber, 4
North Road (Nottingham-Blyth), 7, 18, 73
Norton by Cuckney, 7, 19, 26, 33
Nottingham, 4-6, 11, 16, 19, 27, 34, 36-7, 58,
    61, 73, 76, 81, 130, 141; boundaries of, 110,
    120; Castle, 5, 9, 13, 15, 17, 22, 28, 36-8, 41-
    2, 55, 57, 59, 84, 90, 99, 127; Park, 15, 18,
    20, 22, 28, 40, 42, 50, 59, 79, 83, 84, 85, 126;
    University, 97, 113, 122, 123, 126
Nunes, John, 9
Nuthall, 35, 65, 89, 119, 129, 142

Oak, 16-7, 20, 40, 47, 79, 118-9, 130, 142
Oatlands Park, 59, 66
Oil, 132, 141
Ollerton, 4, 11, 25, 35, 36, 54, 73, 90, 108, 110,
    113, 115-6, 118, 129, 132, 135, 136-40, 143
Ordsall, 139
Osberton, 24, 26, 65, 98
Osborne, Edward, 26
Osprey, 78
Ossington, Lady, 94
Ouseland, 14
Owthorpe, 39
Oxford Street, 55

Paegend, 12
Page, Sidney, 139
Paine, James, 68
Palmer, Laurence, 35
Papplewick, 5, 8, 20, 27, 33, 68, 72-3, 102, 108,
    117, 135,
Parente, William, 122
Parliament Oak, 16, 47, 79
Paulinus, Saint, 3
Peake, Harold, 130
Pelham: Catherine, née Manners, 58; Grace,
    née Holles, 43, 54; Henry (1694-1754), 42-
    3, 58; Sir Thomas, 43, 54, 62; Thomas, 2nd
    Earl of Chichester, 61
Pelham-Clinton: Arthur (1840-70), 86-7;
    Charles (1813-94), 84, 85; Edward, 10th
    Duke of Newcastle (1920-88), 123;
    Georgiana, née Mundy, Duchess of
    Newcastle, 84; Henrietta, née Hope, 87;

Henry, 9th Earl of Lincoln and 2nd Duke of
    Newcastle under Lyne (1720-94), 59, 63,
    65-6, 71; Henry, Earl of Lincoln, 43;
    Henry, 4th Duke of Newcastle under Lyne
    (1785-1851), 60, 68, 74, 83-4, 89, 98-101,
    107, 126; Henry, 5th Duke of Newcastle
    (1811-64), 84-6, 93, 101-2; Henry, 6th
    Duke of Newcastle, 13th Earl of Lincoln
    (1834-79), 74, 87, 99; Henry, 7th Duke of
    Newcastle (1864-1928), 85, 88, 109, 122,
    125-6, 130; Susan, née Douglas-Hamilton,
    Countess of Lincoln, 85, 86; Thomas, 3rd
    Duke of Newcastle under Lyne (1752-95),
    59 Thomas (1813-82), 84-5
Pelham-Clinton-Hope: Francis, 8th Duke of
    Newcastle (1866-1941), 87, 119, 122, 125-
    7; Henry Edward, 9th Duke of Newcastle
    (1907-88), 122-3, 127
Pelham-Holles: Henrietta née Godolphin, 57;
    Thomas, 1st Duke of Newcastle upon Tyne
    and 1st Duke Newcastle under Lyne
    (1693-1768), 42-3, 50-1, 54, 56, 58-9
Perlethorpe, 4, 39, 90
Peverel, William de, 7, 12
Pierrepont: Charles (Medows), 1st Earl
    Manvers (1737-1816), 63, 67, 70-1, 90, 110;
    Charles, 2nd Earl Manvers (1778-1860), 73,
    78, 90, 93, 107, 110; Charles, Viscount
    Newark (1805-50), 98; Charles, 4th Earl
    Manvers (1854-1926), 123, 130-2, 133;
    Evelyn, 5th Earl and 1st Duke of Kingston
    (1665-1726), 45, 51, 62, 67; Evelyn, 2nd
    Duke of Kingston (1711-73), 51, 62-3, 90;
    Evelyn, Viscount Newark (1775-1801), 71;
    Evelyn, 5th Earl Manvers (1888-1940), 123,
    132; Frances, née Cavendish (c.1637-95), 28,
    33, 35, 38; George (1541), 26; Gervas, 6th Earl
    Manvers (1881-1955), 115, 123, 128; Henry
    de, 10-11; Henry, 2nd Earl of Kingston upon
    Hull (1606-80), 33-5, 38; Sir Henry, 28, 32;
    Robert, 1st Earl of Kingston upon Hull
    (1584-1643), 32-3, 34-6; Robert (c.1635-
    69), 62; Robert, 3rd Earl of Kingston (1660-
    82), 33; Sydney, 3rd Earl Manvers (1825-
    1900), 90; Sir William de (1600), 23;
    William (1607-78), 33, 35, 38-9; William
    de, 10; William, 4th Earl of Kingston (1662-
    90), 40
Pigs, in the forest, 12, 79
Pilgrim Oak, 79
Pinxton, 102, 108
Pleasley, 72, 105, 108
Plumpton, Sir Ralph, 12
Poaching, 14, 18, 39, 48, 77-8, 113
Poe, Richard, 20
Political life, elections, 71, 83, 85, 93, 98-101
Portland Colliery, 101-2
Portland or Barberini Vase, 60
Power stations, 139
Poyntz, Colonel Sydenham, 37
Proteus Camp, 116

Radford, 69, 102, 105
Raedwald, King of East Angles, 3
Railway: Great Central, 109, 133; Great
    Northern, 109; Lancashire, Derbyshire &
    East Coast, 109; Mansfield & Pinxton, 2,
    102, 109; Midland Counties, 103, 108

Railways, 26, 133, 135, 142-3
Rainworth, 3, 15, 79, 111, 130, 135
Raleigh bicycles, 88, 123
Sir Walter Raleigh, 25, 32
Ranby, 3-4, 85, 86, 116, 125
Ranger, 13, 15, 21, 78, 101, 129
Ravenshead, 79
Raynes, Lady Rozelle née Pierrepont, 123
Red Hill, 73, 106
Reeve, John, 15
Regarders, 16
Regehere, 3
Repton, Humphry, 66-7
Retford, East, 42, 62, 69, 71, 83, 98-9, 101, 110, 135
Richard: I, King, 6, 16; III, King, 11, 18
Roberts, William, 77
Robinson: John, 88, 124-5; Sir John, 126
Rodgers, Joseph, 71, 130
Rooke, Major H., 2, 79
Roos: Anne, 25; John de, 9; Lord (1660), 33; William de, 9
Rotherham, 6
Rufford, 5-7, 15-6, 18, 22-3, 25, 36, 38, 40, 43-4, 48, 51, 53, 70, 79, 89-90, 115, 116, 118, 127-9, 132; colliery, 130, 132, 135, 140
Rumwood, 14
Rupert, Prince, 28, 37
Rutland, Earl of (1622), 22; Henry, Earl of (1549), 20
Ryton, River, 3

Saint Loe, Lord, 28
Saint Marylebone, 55, 70, 91, 93
Salt, trade in, 11, 13
Salterford Lane, 11
Salvin, Anthony, 89-90
Sandstone, 1, 19
Savile: Sir George (1549-1622), 25; Sir George, 2nd Bt. (1583-1614), 26; George, 1st Marquess Halifax (1633-95), 38, 43, 44; Sir George 7th Bt. (1678-1743), 53, 54; Sir George, 8th Bt. (1726-84), 53-4, 69, 72; Gertrude née Pierrepont, 33, 43; Sir Henry (1517-69), 25; Sir Henry (1642-87), 44; Sir John, Bt., 53; Lady Mary née Pratt, 53; Lady Mary, nee Talbot, 25; Sir William (1600), 23; Sir William, 3rd Bt. (c.1612-44), 27, 34-6; William, 2nd Marquess of Halifax (1665-1700), 26, 44, 53
Savile Lumley, John, 2nd Baron Savile (1853-1931), 90, 132, 137
Schools, 73, 110, 135
Scott, Henrietta, 92
Scratta Wood, 2
Sedley: Charles, 64; William, 65
Seely: Charles, MP (1803-87), 97; Colonel Sir Charles, 1st Bt. (1833-1915), 97, 105, 106, 124; Sir Charles, 2nd Bt. (1859-1926), 124; Sir Hugh, 3rd Bt. and 1st Baron Sherwood (1898-1970), 124, 135; General John, 1st Baron Mottistone (1868-1947), 124
Selston, 74, 101-2, 105
Seven Mile House, 20
Shambles Oak, 47

Sheep farming, 7, 11, 17, 20, 23, 53, 70, 74
Shelburne, Earl of, 53
Shelford, 8, 31, 37; Priory, 24
Sherwood, 3, 4; Crown lands in, 70-1, 74, 90, 101, 129; Lodge, 97, 124, 126; (settlement), 119
Sherwood Forest: boundaries of, 16, 21, 39, 47; farming in, 15, 17, 20, 23, 39, 48, 51, 69, 70, 74, 118-20; forestry in, 16, 20, 39-40, 52, 115, 118-9, 128, 143; legal system, 13-14, 16, 18, 20, 39, 48-9, 51, 74; roads in, 18, 73, 108, 143; tourism in, 118, 129-30, 132, 142
Shire Oak, 40, 79
Shireoaks, 33, 38, 65, 69, 79, 83-6, 88, 102, 110, 130, 138, 140
Sitwell, George, 33
Skegby, 3, 24, 38, 69, 102, 141
Sloswick, 84
Smythson, Robert, 23, 28
Soho, 45, 60-1, 94
Southwell, 2, 15, 19, 38, 73, 77, 81, 105, 109-10
Spencer: Diana, 64; George, 138
St Paul's Cathedral, 40
Stanhope: Anne, 32; Edward, 20; Sir John, 16; Sir John (1599), 28; Colonel Michael (d.1648), 38; Colonel Philip (-1645), 37; Philip, 1st Earl of Chesterfield (1584-1656), 34, 37-8; Philip, 5th Earl of Chesterfield (1755-1815), 69
Stephen, King, 5, 9, 11
Stewart, Robert, Lord Castlereagh, 62
Stoke, Battle of, 10-11, 20, 38
Strelley, 23, 26, 73, 101
Stuart: Arabella, 25; Charles, Earl of Lennox, 25; Prince Henry, 32
Surveyor general of woods etc, 20, 51, 65
Sutton in Ashfield, 14, 69, 76-8, 103-6, 110-1, 140, 140
Sutton: Henry de, 11; Robert, 73; Robert de, 10; Robert, 1st Lord Lexington, 34, 38-9; Stephen de, 11; Thomas Manners, 1st Baron Manners (1756-1842), 71

Talbot: Charles, 12th Earl and 1st Duke of Shrewsbury (1660-1718), 45; Edward, 8th Earl of Shrewsbury (1561-1617), 22, 25; George, 4th Earl of Shrewsbury (1468-1538), 24; George, 6th Earl of Shrewsbury (1528-90), 20, 25, 28; Gilbert, 7th Earl of Shrewsbury (1552-1616), 26-8
Talman, William, 40
Teulon, Samuel, 96
Teversall, 101
Theobalds, 45
Thoresby, 3, 33, 39-42, 51, 62, 67, 79, 90, 113, 115, 116, 123, 128-9, 132, 142; colliery, 130, 132, 135, 138-9, 141
Thorneywood Chase, 16, 20, 39, 51, 53, 69
Thornhagh, Colonel Francis, 37
Thornhill Hall, 25, 43-4
Thoroton, Robert, 51, 70
Throsby, John, 51, 66, 73
Thurgarton, 4, 8, 37
Thurland Hall, 22-3, 32, 59, 61, 84
Tickhill, 5, 37, 89
Topham, Richard, 64

Trent, River, 1-3, 18
Trespass, offence of, 12
Trussebutts, Sir William, 17
Tuxford, 2, 9, 18, 37, 73, 139

Upton, 37

Vanbrugh, Sir John, 57
Vane-Tempest, Lady Susan née Pelham-Clinton, 86
Varley, Frank, 138
Venison see deer
Verderers, 8, 13-14, 20, 40, 51, 70
Vert, forest law of, 12, 16-17
Vesci, John de, 6
Villareal, 68-9
Villiers, George, Duke of Buckingham, 22, 28, 41, 43

Wales, 33
Walesby, 3, 24-5, 70, 135
Wallingwells, 24
Walpole: Horace, 59; Horatio, Earl of Orford, 86
Warner Group, 128
Warsop: colliery, 105; Market, 3, 9, 25, 37, 51, 110
Water supplies, 102, 119, 135, 141
Webb, William 82, 103
Welbeck, 7, 15, 18, 19, 22-4, 26-8, 35-7, 40, 42, 47, 51, 55, 60-1, 66, 69, 79, 84, 92-3, 96, 103-4, 113, 121, 123, 127; colliery, 130, 132, 135, 141; Estate Company, 128
Wellow, 6, 9, 25, 70, 112
Wentworth, Sir Thomas, Earl of Strafford, 25
Whalley, Richard, 26
Whitaker, Joseph, 79
Whitwell, 105, 140
Wildman, Lt Col, 82
Wilkins, William, 67
William: I, King, 5, 7, 13; II, King, 13; III, King, 42, 44-5, 65
Williamson, Sir Thomas, 41
Willoughby, 38; Philip, 17; Sir Richard de, 18; William, 39
Wimpole, 55, 60
Winnings, The, 96
Wiverton, 8, 33
Wollaton, 11, 18, 20, 26, 51, 99, 119, 120, 127, 129
Woodborough, 16, 38, 106, 133
Woodward, 13
Wool, trade, 11
Worksop, 2, 4-6, 8-9, 11, 15, 18, 69, 72, 94, 79, 108, 113, 127-8, 130; College, 88, 127; Manor, 18, 20, 22-3, 25, 28, 33, 40, 47, 67-8, 84-5, 87-8, 113, 124-5, 127; Priory, 5-6, 17, 24, 33, 111
Wren, Sir Christopher, 40
Wright, Stephen, 65
Wulfsi, 4

Yohe, May, 122
York, 3, 19, 34
Yoxall, James, 70

Edwinstowe and Clipstone mapped in the 1820s. King John's Palace can be identified and another 'King's Stand' north-west of Rufford. Hops are still being grown around Rufford and Cockglode nestles in a plantation, as yet unthreatened by the arrival of mining. (Nottinghamshire County Council)